VICTORY

IN THE

FALKLANDS

VICTORY

IN THE

FALKLANDS

by

Nick van der Bijl BEM

Pen & Sword
MILITARY

First published in Great Britain in 2007 by
Pen & Sword Military
an imprint of
Pen & Sword Books Ltd
47 Church Street
Barnsley
South Yorkshire
S70 2AS

ISBN 978 1 84415 494 4

A CIP catalogue record for this book is
available from the British Library

Typeset in Sabon by
Phoenix Typesetting, Auldgirth, Dumfriesshire

Printed and bound in England by
Biddles Ltd, King's Lynn

Pen & Sword Books Ltd incorporates the Imprints of Pen & Sword
Aviation, Pen & Sword Maritime, Pen & Sword Military, Wharncliffe
Local History, Pen & Sword Select, Pen & Sword Military Classics and Leo
Cooper.

For a complete list of Pen & Sword titles please contact
PEN & SWORD BOOKS LIMITED
47 Church Street, Barnsley, South Yorkshire, S70 2AS, England
E-mail: enquiries@pen-and-sword.co.uk
Website: www.pen-and-sword.co.uk

This book is dedicated to the men and women who were part
of and supported the Falklands Task Force,
and to their families.

Contents

List of Maps and Diagrams

Foreword

In 1982, two countries went to war over a group of isolated islands of little strategic value in the South Atlantic. One country had played a significant role in the economic development of the other and both had a keen interest in rugby union, polo and football. Neither had a major disagreement until 1982 when both went to war over nationalism. One side sailed nearly 8,000 miles from the early European summer, across the equator to the early Antarctic winter and, accompanied by triumph and tragedy, drove their enemy into a situation whereby surrender was the only option, before asking, in that matchless sense of military humour, 'Where's the transport home?' The welcome by the people of Great Britain was almost Victorian and will not be forgotten. The welcome to the abandoned men of the losing side was frosty. The war, in the early southern hemisphere winter, was probably unique in that there were no atrocities, the rules of warfare were followed and there has been no lasting dispute between the protagonists, apart from the occasional diplomatic foray to divert attention from domestic affairs.

A large number of informative and analytical books have been written about those four months of hostility, and this one is another. The book began its life as part of the Pen & Sword *Battleground* series but has since strayed into an account of the contest between the two armies. Although warfare has changed since 1982 from conventional front lines to asymmetric operation, in which there are no front lines, I have included quotes from a variety of sources to illustrate that the activity, incidents and emotions experienced by the combatants were no different before the Falklands or since. I have included contemporary maps and diagrams to add flavour to the text, together with as many photographs as possible that have not been seen before.

As always, I must thank several people. Over the years, I have collected all sorts of memorabilia, not a small percentage either deposited on my desk or sent through the mail, often anonymously, with the comment: 'Thought you might like this.' To these colleagues and donors, I am grateful for their consideration; some are Argentine. As always, there are enough stories, accounts and views to fill several volumes, however I hope that those who have provided me with information will understand that space is limited. I must thank Major Chris Baxter RM, who has allowed me to use several photographs from the 1st Raiding Squadron, Royal Marines archives. He commanded this unit of small boat coxswains during the campaign. To Bobby Gainher, who undertook the editing entirely by e-mail, which was a new experience for me. To John Noble, who undertook the complexities of the indexing. To Brigadier Henry Wilson of Pen & Sword Books Ltd, for his support and encouragement. To the staff of Pen & Sword Books, and others involved in the production of this book. And finally to the authors and publishers of the works from which I have quoted in order to provide a balanced account of the Falklands War.

Most importantly, to my wife, Penny, who spent many lonely hours while I worked at this project and then was kind enough to proofread the text. She is one of the often forgotten army of family and friends who uncomplainingly experienced the highs and lows of the spring and summer of 1982, and whose role is rarely mentioned. Penny has been incredibly supportive of this and other projects.

Nick van der Bijl
Somerset

Glossary

AFV	Armoured Fighting Vehicle
ARA	Armada Republica Argentina
ASW	Anti-Submarine Warfare
BAS	British Antarctic Survey
BMA	Brigade Maintenance Area
Camp	The Falklands territory outside Stanley
CB	Citizens' Band (radio network)
CLIFFI	Commander Land Forces Falkland Islands
CO	Commanding Officer
COMAW	Commander Amphibious Warfare
CTF	Combined Task Force
CTG	Combined Task Group
CVR(T)	Combat Vehicle Recce (Tracked) – refers to a family of British tracked light-armoured vehicles
DCM	Distinguished Conduct Medal
DSC	Distinguished Service Cross
FCO	Foreign and Commonwealth Office
GHQ	General Headquarters
GPMG	General Purpose Machine Gun (British, 7.62mm)
HF	High Frequency (communication channel band)
HQ	Headquarters
'Kelpers'	Literally, seaweed collectors
LADE	Lineas Aereas del Estado. The Argentine state airline.
LARC-5	Lighter Amphibious Resupply and Cargo Series 5. US amphibious wheeled vehicle.
LAW	Light Anti-Tank Weapon (66mm)

LCT	Landing Craft Tank
LCU	Landing Craft Utility
LCVP	Landing Craft Vehicle and Personnel
LFFI	Land Forces Falkland Islands
LPD	Landing Platform Dock
LSL	Landing Ship Logistic
LVTP-7	Landing Vehicle Tracked Personnel Series 7. US tracked amphibious assault armoured personnel carrier.
MAG	Miteailleuse d'Appui Général, literally GPMG. Belgian 7.62mm GPMG support machine gun.
MEZ	Maritime Exclusion Zone
NAS	Naval Air Squadron
NCO	Non-Commissioned Officer
NGFO	Naval Gunfire Support Officer
OC	Officer Commanding
OCRM	Officer Commanding Royal Marines
OP	Observation Post
QRF	Quick Reaction Force
RAMC	Royal Army Medical Corps
RAPC	Royal Army Pay Corps
RCT	Royal Corps of Transit
REME	Royal Electrical and Mechanical Engineers
SAMA (1982)	South Atlantic Medal Association (1982) – veterans' association
SAS	Special Air Service
SBS	Special Boat Squadron
'Tab'	Tactical approach to battle. Although primarily associated with the Parachute Regiment, the word was also used by other infantry units.
Tactical HQ	Tactical Headquarters – a small battle HQ
TEZ	Total Exclusion Zone
UKLF	United Kingdom Land Forces
UN	United Nations
VHF	Very High Frequency (communications channel band)
66mm	66mm Light Anti-Tank Weapon

Chapter One

The Historical Perspective

Roughly 6,700 miles from Great Britain and 350 miles from South America lies the Falkland Islands archipelago of two main islands and over 200 smaller ones, mostly treeless, with a total area of about 4,700 square miles. There are good anchorages and the windswept terrain is generally hilly moorland with an abundance of wildlife.

The British first took an interest in the islands in 1592 when they were sighted by the Elizabethan explorer John Davis as his ship was driven off course in a storm. A century later, the privateer John Strong landed and named them after Anthony Carey, 5th Viscount Falkland, First Lord of the Admiralty. In February 1764, Louis Antoine de Bougainville, largely inspired by the loss of Canada to the British, founded the settlement of Port Louis in Berkeley Sound with immigrants from St Malo and named the islands 'Les Iles Malouines'. The British reacted by despatching Commodore John Byron, grandfather of the poet, and he raised the Union flag at Port Egmont on West Falkland on 12 January 1765. In January the following year, Captain John McBride landed a 100-strong garrison and gave the French six months to leave.

In April 1767, the French sold Port Louis to Spain, who christened the islands 'Las Malvinas'. For the next two years, the British and Spanish existed in isolation until Captain Anthony Hunt encountered a Spanish warship. In June 1770, five ships from the Spanish province of Buenos Aires threatened Port Egmont and while Hunt was negotiating terms, 1,600 troops landed and forced the twenty-three Royal Marines to surrender. The British were outraged. Prime Minister Lord North considered war and Foreign Secretary Lord Weymouth resigned. In 1982, another Hunt and party of Royal Marines were forced to surrender and another minister resigned. When Louis XV of France told Charles III of Spain that he would not support war with Great Britain, North agreed to Spain's sovereignty over Las Malvinas, but omitted this clause from their copy of the declaration. In 1771, Spain returned Port Egmont to the British. Three years later, when the British abandoned the Falklands, Lieutenant S.W. Clayton RN, the garrison commander, hammered a lead plaque, carved by HMS *Endurance*'s shipwright, on the fort door:

Be it known to all nations, that Falkland Island, with this Fort, Stonehouse, Wharf, Harbour, Bays and Creeks thereunto belonging, are the Sole Right of His Most Sacred Majesty George III, King of England, France and Ireland, Defender of the Faith etc. In witness whereof this plate is set up, and his Britannic Majesty's colours left flying as a mark of possession.

Significantly, the statement referred only to 'Falkland Island', i.e to West Falkland, so does Britain have a valid claim? Great Britain recognized Spain's claim to East Falkland and Port Louis remained unmolested until abandoned in 1806.

The islands remained in Spanish hands until 1816 when the United Provinces of the Rio de la Plata claimed Spanish colonies in the region, including the Falklands. Four years later, Port Louis was reoccupied and in 1828, colonists from the newly created Argentina under Louis Vernet claimed the islands. On 2 January 1833, a British flotilla, commanded by Captain John Onslow, forced the garrison to surrender and deported Governor Pinedo. Argentina's claim was that the islands had been inherited from Spain after Britain had abandoned them, however she was a minnow compared to the growing imperialism of Great Britain.

When two administrators left by Captain Onslow were murdered in January 1834, a naval party from HMS *Tyne* rebuilt Port Egmont fort. Nine years later, Lieutenant Richard Moody RE arrived with a Royal Engineer detachment and, on being appointed Governor, moved to Port Stanley where he established the Legislative Council and is commemorated by the barracks. In 1849, pensioned Royal Marines provided the garrison until 1858 when Royal Marines, accompanied by their families, took over as the Falkland Islands Garrison Company for the next twenty years, while Port Stanley established itself as a coaling port. The Falkland Island Company was founded in 1852 by the debt-ridden Argentine, Samuel Lafone, who purchased the soggy mass of Lafonia to develop his Royal Falkland Land, Cattle, Seal and Whale Fishery Company and cleared his debts by introducing sheep. With sheep came shepherds from Scotland, Wales and the West Country, including from the hamlet of Goose Green in Somerset, all of whom lived in Company-owned settlements in the 'camp', the interior outside Stanley. The islands were largely unaffected by the two world wars, other than when they provided shelter for the Royal Navy after the Battles of the Falklands in 1914 and River Plate in 1939. Great Britain left economic development to the Falkland Island Company.

Meanwhile, Argentina grumbled. The dispute was discussed at the UN Security Council in 1964 in which she argued that Las Malvinas must be returned, not only for legal reasons, but also to end a regional relic of colonialism. Britain replied that the islanders would not be tranferred against their will. When, in September, an Argentine pilot landed on Stanley Racecourse and planted an Argentine flag, the British sent the ice patrol ship HMS

2

Protector to land her Royal Marine detachment. This detachment was replaced by Naval Party 8901 (NP 8901), whose strategic role was to:

> Enable the seat of government to be continued in the event of hostilities. Provide alternate covert communication to and from UK. Impede incursions which might affect government and endanger the community. Maintain a cohesive presence in the event that government be discontinued, i.e. resistance.

In 1965, the UN invited Argentina and Great Britain to negotiate under Resolution 2065, in which the Falkland Islands is listed as a colony and members are reminded that under Resolution 1514, the UN undertakes to 'bring to an end everywhere colonialism in all its form', and, in the case of the Falklands, only 'in the interests of the population'. By now, the islanders had developed into stubborn pro-British colonialists. In 1966, the nationalist Condor Gang hijacked a Dakota, the first in aviation history, and landed on Stanley Racecourse with the intention of capturing the islands. Their imprisonment in Argentina enhanced the view that Britain had little interest in the islands. By the 1970s, Argentina was a nation besieged by middle-class revolutionary groups. President Jorge Videla suppressed them in the vicious Dirty War, which not only broke the back of his opponents but led to Argentina becoming a political pariah. The economy collapsed. In 1976, when Argentina occupied South Thule, the British response was muted, but when she threatened the Falklands, Prime Minister James Callaghan sent a small naval task force to the region. The roles of NP 8901 were expanded to buying a three-week bargaining window at the UN, the time needed to assemble a task force. In 1980, President Roberto Viola undertook to return Argentina to democracy and the hand of international reconciliation was extended to Argentine/US military exercises. On 8 December 1981, Viola handed over power to General Leopoldo Galtieri, son of a poor Italian immigrant, cavalry officer and Army Commander. Backed by Admiral Jorge Anaya, Commander-in-Chief of the Navy and school friend, and Brigadier General Lami Dozo, head of the Air Force, he formed a junta. However, the economy was dire and the Papal resolution over the Beagle Channel dispute with Chile seemed likely to go against Argentina. The Junta needed a diversion.

Irresistible to Anaya was the recovery of Las Malvinas. He had first mooted the idea in 1960 and then in the mid-1970s, with Admiral Emilio Massear, the Navy commander, he refined the scheme to remove the islanders to Uruguay and resettle the islands. The Air Force were lukewarm. To Galtieri, the proposition was tantalizing, especially as January 1983 was the 150th anniversary of the deportation of Governor Pinedo. The Junta also believed Argentina's new relationship with the US to be an advantage. When Great Britain announced that (a) the Antarctic Patrol Ship HMS *Endurance* was to be decommissioned and not replaced, (b) that the British Antarctic Survey (BAS) base at South Georgia would be closed, (c) that Prime Minister

Margaret Thatcher had denied the Falkland Islanders full British citizenship, and (d) that Nicholas Ridley, Under-Secretary of State at the Foreign Office, seemed sympathetic to a lend-lease agreement with Argentina, the Junta interpreted that Britain had lost interest in the islands and therefore could be pushed into transfer negotiations. On 15 December 1981, Admiral Anaya flew to the main Argentine Navy base at Puerto Belgrano and instructed the newly installed Chief of Naval Operations, Vice Admiral Juan Lombardo, to update plans to liberate the Falkland Islands. On 5 January 1982, the Junta prepared a contingency plan for 'the employment of military power' should diplomacy fail under National Strategy Directive 1/82:

> The Military Committee, faced with the repeated lack of progress in the negotiations with Great Britain to obtain recognition of our soveriengty over the Malvinas, Georgia and South Sandwich island; convinced that the prolongation of this situation affects national honour, the full exercise of sovereignty and the exploration of resources; has resolved to analyse the possibility of the use of military power to obtain the political objective. This resolution must be kept in strict secrecy and should be circulated only to heads of the respective military directives.

Preliminary plans were to be ready by mid-March, with implementation ready by 15 May. Occupation was to be bloodless. Very few in Argentina, a country whose international experience was largely confined to South America and who had not fought a major war for 120 years, knew they were about to declare war on Great Britain, whose international career extended over several centuries and who had the long habit of losing battles but winning wars.

Chapter Two

Crisis in the South Atlantic

The Argentine Navy saw an opportunity to expand its regional ambitions during negotiations between the Argentine scrap metal merchant, Constantino Davidoff, and Christian Salveson of Leith, South Georgia, to dismantle the derelict whaling buildings on South Georgia. This developed into Project Alpha.

> The idea was to mingle military personel with Davidoff's workforce so that they would be part of a 'legal' landing party on South Georgia. Later they would be joined by a group of Marines who would set up a permanent military base of some 14 men from April – after Endurance was scheduled to depart the South Atlantic. By the time the British realised what had happened, it would be too late for them to respond. Thereafter the Argentine presence would be assisted by broadcasts of weather and navigational reports. (Freedman, *Official History*, Vol 1)

The icebreaker *Almirante Irizar* (Captain Cesar Trombetta, Commander, Antarctic Squadron) was contracted on 20 December 1981 to support Davidoff, and arrived off Leith after a four-day passage in which Trombetta maintained radio silence. He then flouted international convention by not reporting to the Magistrate and British Antarctic Survey (BAS) Base Commander. On 4 January 1982, Argentina rejected Britain's protest of the violation of its sovereignty. That 'Las Malvinas es Argentina' had been chalked on a wall was reported to Governor Rex Hunt in Stanley, as were observations by BAS scientists on 21 January that the Panamanian-registered yacht *Caiman*, which had tied up at Leith, had three powerful radios of types not normally associated with business trips. It was skippered by an Argentine, Adrian Machessi, who claimed to be an employee of the bank funding Davidoff's contract.

> A broadcast was picked up from the 'Caiman' to Buenos Airies in which the Master provided details of the BAS base and its administration, and

advised the quick confirmation of the contract. (Freedman, *Official History*, Vol 1)

However, the Foreign and Commonwealth Office (FCO) were inclined not to provoke matters which could have an unforseeable outcome. Meanwhile, scrap prices were falling and there were good commercial reasons for Davidoff to begin work.

By early January, Vice Admiral Lombardo, Major General Osvaldo Garcia, Commander V Corps, which covered the Atlantic Littoral, including the Falklands and its Dependencies, and Brigadier General Siegfriedo Plessl of the Air Force, had formed a working party to plan Operation Rosario. They envisaged military operations beginning about September 1982, after the southern hemisphere winter, and to allow the annual February conscription to be more fully trained. Rear Admiral Carlos Busser, who commanded the Marine Corps and was a keen 'Malvinist', was instructed to plan the seizure of the Falklands and South Georgia on the same day. In a classic example of effective operational security, details remained with those only who needed to know.

On 29 January, Commander Alfredo Weinstabl, who commanded the 2nd Marine Infantry Battalion at Puerto Belgrano Naval Base, was summoned from leave to see Busser. Weinstabl:

'Mission: To recover the Falkland Islands and to restore it in perpetuity to the sovereignty of the Nation'.

Admiral Busser explained to me that because of the poor progress in the negotiations over the Falklands, plans had to be drawn up for an operation to retake the islands by means of an amphibious operation in which, if it should happen, the No. 2 Marine Battalion, my Battalion, would be the nucleus of the landing Force. (*Operacion Rosario*)

Three days later, Weinstabl confirmed that his Battalion should be ready by 15 April and next day he briefed his Operations Officer, Captain Nestor Carballido. At HQ Marine Corps, they analysed the latest topographical, social and military intelligence and by the end of the month Weinstabl had agreed courses of action with Naval Air and Maritime staffs. On 1 March, after his Battalion returned from leave, Weinstabl briefed his second-in-command, Lieutenant Commander Guillermo Santillan, that with the Battalion only half amphibious trained after an exercise with the US Marine Corps in 1981, he was to develop amphibious training.

Meanwhile, HMS *Endurance* (Captain Nick Barker), which had slipped out of Chatham on her last voyage in October 1981, was preparing to return home. Barker, an experienced polar seaman with, to the annoyance of the FCO, a good rapport with the Argentine Navy, had reported tension amongst Argentine officers. Captain Russo, the Puerto Belgrano Naval Base Deputy Base Commander, told him, 'There is to be a war against the Malvinas. I don't know when, but I think quite soon.' Chilean naval officers also told Barker that they suspected that Argentina was planning something, all of which he passed to London. Diplomacy continued but by March the Argentine Foreign Minister, Costa Mendez, had become so impatient that he declared, 'Argentina reserves the right to put an end to this process and freely elect whatever path may serve her interests.'

On 7 March, Lieutenant Veal RN, a member of a Joint Services expedition on South Georgia, watched an Argentine Air Force C-130 Hercules actually on a photo reconnaissance mission cross the island. Several weeks earlier, an Argentine C-130 made a genuine forced landing at Stanley Airport, but such was the tension among the Argentines that the Air Force was accused of alerting the British. Although the Dependencies were often overflown by Argentine aircraft, the frequency of flights in March was not seen to be unusual.

Meanwhile, Davidoff had returned to Buenos Aires and was given permission from the British Embassy on 10 March to land forty-one workmen at Leith for four months. They embarked on the naval transport *Bahia Buen Suceso,* which he had chartered from the Argentine Navy and whose commander, Captain Briatore, would supervise the work. Davidoff was reminded that he had to complete immigration formalities at Grytviken. On 15 March, HMS *Endurance* collected the Joint Services expedition and four days later was in Stanley preparing for the long voyage back to Chatham. Three days later, the 2nd Marine Infantry Battalion embarked on a former US Landing Craft Tank (LCT), the *Cabo San Antonio,* and four days later carried out several landings and advances to contact on San Roman beach in the Gulf of San Jose.

When the *Bahia Buen Suceso* arrived at Leith on 19 March, Captain Briatore failed to report to Grytviken, so the BAS Base Commander, Steve Martin, signalled Governor Hunt:

BAS Field Party observed Argentine vessel Bahia Buen Suceso in Leith Harbour and a sizeable party of civilian and military personnel ashore. Field Party reported shots fired, Argentine flag hoisted, notices in English changed to Spanish. They have been told that they should have reported to Grytviken first. The Party have been instructed to inform the Argentines that they have entered illegally and they must report to Grytviken.

A reindeer, a protected species, was also being barbecued. Next morning, Trevor Edwards, the BAS team leader, read a message from London to Briatore:

You have landed at Leith without obtaining proper clearance. You and your party must go back on board the Bahia Buen Suceso immediately and report to the Base Commander at Grytviken for further instructions.

You must remove the Argentine flag from Leith. You must not interfere with the British Antarctic Survey depot at Leith. You must not alter or deface the notices at Leith. No military personnel are allowed to land on South Georgia. No firearms are to be taken ashore.

When Argentina denied all knowledge of the *Bahia Buen Suceso*'s military activities, Governor Hunt persuaded London to send HMS *Endurance* back to South Georgia and evict the Argentines. Lieutenant Keith Mills RM commanded *Endurance*'s ship's detachment. Soon after landing with his Royal Marines at Stanley for ground training and a 'run ashore', he was called to Moody Brook Barracks where he was briefed by Major Gary Noott RM, Officer Commanding NP 8901, on the situation. He was then reinforced with a NCO and eight Royal Marines, which brought his detachment to nearly troop strength, and was instructed to return to HMS *Endurance*. To accommodate the enlarged detachment, Barker put ashore Lieutenant Richard Ball, another officer and nine sailors to complete scientific records gathered during the summer. Early next day, HMS *Endurance* left Stanley.

When Major Noott arrived in March 1981, he had inherited a concept of operations not markedly different from that used by Major Ewen Southby-Tailyour RM, when he commanded NP 8901 from 1977 to 1979. This envisaged:

Disruption of landings.

Conduct a withdrawal to Stanley through three defensive lines at Hookers Point, in the town and the third around Government House.

Government House would be a stronghold.

Moody Brook to be abandoned.

A section on Cortley Ridge had a secondary role to move to a hide stocked with pre-dumped supplies overlooking Port Salvador and provide a point of contact for relief forces.

During the counter-intelligence operation after the Argentine surrender, a Falkland Islander said the plan was well known to the islanders and, most probably, to the LADE (Lineas Aereas del Estado) office, the centre of Argentine intelligence operations.

Although the BAS agreed to pass information to Barker, Steve Martin was careful not to jeopardize their civilian status, nevertheless on 21 March, several scientists established an observation post (OP) on Jason Peak, which overlooked Stromness Bay. They watched *Bahia Buen Suceso* leave on 21 March, apparantly with the shore party, but in fact leaving several Argentines behind. London thought the crisis over until the OP reported their continued presence at Leith.

When HMS *Endurance* arrived unexpectedly at South Georgia on the 24th,

Foreign Minister Mendez advised London that attempts to evict the Argentines would not be tolerated. South Georgia had therefore now become a convenient vehicle from which to escalate the crisis. For the next week, HMS *Endurance*, on reduced rations, continued hydrographic and chart work. The Royal Marines took over the Jason Peak OP and reported next day that the naval transport *Bahia Paraiso* had entered Stromness Bay during the night and had disembarked ten marines. It later emerged that they were commanded by Lieutenant Commander Alfredo Astiz, who was wanted by Sweden and France for the murder of a girl and three nuns at a naval interrogation centre during the Dirty War. Also on board the ship was an Army 601 Combat Aviation Battalion Puma and a 1st Helicopter Squadron Alouette. Because of the difficulty of seeing into Leith, the OP was moved next day to Grass Island, but even this gave only marginal improvement. Mindful of the need for information, Mills and his experienced Detachment Sergeant Major, Sergeant Peter Leach, landed at the foot of Olsen Valley and scouted the abandoned whaling stations of Husvik and Stromness before concealing themselves on Harbour Point, about 600 metres from Leith, to watch the activity.

Meanwhile, Captain Barker joined Lieutenant Commander Tony Ellerbeck and his observer, Lieutenant David Wells, in one of the two 829 Naval Air Squadron (NAS) Wasp helicopters, and landed on Tonsberg Point to observe Leith. Buzzing around the harbour was the Alouette piloted by Lieutenant Remo Busson with orders to shadow HMS *Endurance*. Shortly after the two Royal Marines met Barker's party, Busson, with Captain Trombetta on board, hovered above the five Britons. When Busson then found the Grass Island OP, surveillance was transferred to Busen Peninsula.

Argentina's sabre-rattling was failing to prompt Great Britain to negotiate and her Chiefs of Staff advised the Junta that they did not favour a protracted engagement, particularly as reports from London were indicating British escalation. The naval Exercise Springtrain had been cancelled and the nuclear submarine HMS *Spartan* was despatched to the South Atlantic from Gibraltar. British public opinion was hardening. On 26 March, the Junta decided to invade the Falklands and set D-Day for 2 or 3 April, with the option of bringing it forward to 31 March. During the afternoon, First Lieutenant Oscar Outlon, who commanded A Company, 1st Marine Infantry Battalion, attended a briefing at 2nd Marine Infantry Battalion for an exercise in Tierra del Fuego:

> I knew nothing about Operation Rosario. The only thing I did know was that our Commanding Officer, the Second-in-Command and the Logistics Officer had, for several days, been leaving the Battalion and only returning from time to time. Something unusual was afoot, but I did not even begin to imagine that an operation was imminent. When I arrived at 2nd Marine Infantry, there were a great number of senior ranks in the Command Building. Guards were at the entrance to the first

9

floor and occasionally someone would come down and invite one of us to go upstairs. I realised that something serious was happening and no one was making any comments. Captain Carbajal took me into the planning room of Amphibious Operations. There I was given operational orders in which my Company was to be the Landing Force Reserve and that I would embark on the Almirante Irizar and would, when instructed, land by helicopter. I was not at all clear about the reasoning behind the operation and the mission that my Company had to accomplish. My Commanding Officer took me to one side and clarified all my queries. In short, he told me that I had to prepare a Company platoon of sixty-one men composed of Company HQ, a rifle section, a support platoon of a 81mm mortar group, a medium machine-gun group and a detachment of rocket launchers. I was also instructed to raise two groups of riflemen and a 60mm group and place them under command of Lieutenant Luna.

The Argentine plan depended on preventing NP 8901 entering Stanley from Moody Brook Barracks and from withdrawing into the 'camp' to carry out a guerrilla campaign. The main assault was to land on Red Beach at Yorke Bay, seize the airport and occupy Stanley. The emphatic order was 'Fight without shedding blood' and the defenders had to be convinced that the odds were overwhelming. The Argentine force was divided into five separate elements:

NAVAL AND AIR SCREEN – Task Force 20

Commanded by Captain Sarcona on the aircraft carrier *Veinticino de Mayo* (former Centaur class HMS *Venerable*). On board were the Sea Kings of 2nd Helicopter Squadron. Major General Garcia, who was in command of the newly created Malvinas Theatre of Operations and in overall command, had his HQ on the ex-British Type 42 destroyer *Santisima Trinidad* to co-ordinate the landings and act as air traffic control once the airport had been seized.

PORT STANLEY – Task Unit 40 (TU 40)

Commanded by Rear Admiral Gualter Allara, Chief of Fleet Operations. To transport, protect and provide naval gunfire support for the 874-strong Landing Force.

Landing Force (Task Unit 40.1)

904 Marines and Army divided between ARA *Cabo San Antonio* and ARA *Almirante Iriza,* Commanded by Rear Admiral Busser.

D and E Companies, 2nd Marine Infantry Battalion (TU.40.1.1) – 387 all ranks. To enter Stanley.

1st Platoon, C Company, 25th Infantry Regiment – 39 all ranks. To seize the airport.

A Company, 1st Marine Infantry Battalion (TU.40.1.7) – 65 all ranks. Landing reserve.

1st Amphibious Commando Group (TU.0.1.3) – 92 all ranks. Seize Government House and Moody Brook Barracks. A year earlier, Hunt had given a set of plans of Government House to an Argentine visitor, who, he thought, was an architect.

A Battery, Marine Field Artillery Battalion – 41 gunners manning 4 x 105mm M-56 Pack Howitzers.

1st Marine 105mm Rocket Battery.

1st Amphibious Engineer Company.

1st Marine Anti-Aircraft Battery – 4 x Tigercat missile launchers.

1st Amphibious Vehicle Company – 101 all ranks operating 20 x LTVP-7 and 5 x LARC-5 amphibious tracked vehicles.

HQ and Communications Unit – 42 all ranks.

Logistic support services (TU.40.1.8) – 84 all ranks.

Civil affairs – 41 all ranks.

Special Task Force (TF 40.4.1)

Beach recce and obstacle clearance.

Submarine *Sante Fe* (Baloa-class former USS *Catfish*).

Detachment of twelve tactical divers.

PROJECT ALPHA, SOUTH GEORGIA – Task Unit 60 (TU 60)

Naval transport *Bahia Paraiso*.

A69 corvette *Guerrico*. Commanded by Commander Carlos Alfonso, it was hurriedly withdrawn from dry dock and prepared for sea.

1st Marine Infantry Battalion platoon commanded by Lieutenant Luna.

601 Combat Aviation Battalion Puma helicopter.

1st Helicopter Squadron Alouette helicopter.

Once the intervention force had completed its mission, an Air Force team would prepare the airport for the fly-in of the garrison, 25th Infantry Regiment (Lieutenant Colonel Mohammed Seineldin). Its 1st Platoon would be helicoptered to Goose Green. Seineldin was a fervent Malvinist with a Lebanese background; 25th Infantry Regiment was based at Colonia Sarmiento in the sparsely populated southern province of Chubut and was part of 9 Infantry Brigade, of V Army Corps. When warned for deployment to the Falklands, Seineldin renamed it the 25th 'Special' Infantry Regiment; Argentine journalists later christened it the 'Seineldin Commando Regiment'. In Stanley, he enlarged it to five companies each of about 100 men, mostly commandos and paras, by adding D and E Companies. The regimental shoulder flash, which was designed by his wife Marta, depicted an armed Argentine soldier astride the Falklands Islands.

On 27 March, after Garcia and Busser had approved of his plan, Weinstabl summoned his battalion to barracks. Next day, he attended a briefing in his operations room:

> Captain Gaffoglio gave a full breakdown of information received about Port Stanley, its population's daily routine, details of the selected objectives for its taking at H-Hour, general characteristics about the area around it and information on the general character of the place. This information was extraordinarily useful for all the officers.

Adolpho Gaffoglio was the Argentine representative in Stanley and worked from the LADE offices. On 31 March, he returned to Stanley.

During the morning, the battalion embarked on the assaults ships and joined Task Force 40 assembling in the Rio de la Plata estuary, with the cover story of an exercise with Uruguay. Next day, it departed for the 780-mile passage to Stanley, as Air Transport Command made its final preparations. When, during the day, the *Bahia Paraiso* left Leith and vanished into the South Atlantic, HMS *Endurance* searched for her in atrocious weather amongst the islands, inlets, coves and icebergs of South Georgia, Barker struggling to maintain contact under dogged surveillance from Lieutenant Busson. Barker's attempts to radio Trombetta were unsuccessful.

On 23 March, the British Naval Attaché in Buenos Aires, Captain Mitchell, flew to Montevideo to meet the incoming 1982/83 NP 8901 (Major Mike Norman RM), who were expecting to be taken to Stanley on HMS *Endurance*. When it looked as though the Royal Marines would be stranded, Mitchell recognized their value as reinforcements and arranged for them to be ferried to Stanley on the RRS *John Biscoe*. The use of this research ship gave Argentina the opportunity to claim that she and her sister ship, the *Bransfield*, were engaged in military activities. On 29 March, Norman's men moved into Moody Brook Barracks, while Major Noott's outgoing detachment was billeted in private accommodation, as was the custom.

On 31 March, the British Government deduced from an Argentine newspaper reporting on naval and military preparations that Argentina intended to invade the Falklands and South Georgia on 2 April, but shrank from escalating the dispute. Early in the afternoon, Captain Barker was instructed by Commander-in-Chief Fleet, Northwood to reinforce sovereignty of South Georgia by landing his Royal Marines. Steve Martin was less than happy, however as Magistrate he agreed to a compromise that he would remain in charge as long as diplomacy lasted; if hostilities broke out, Lieutenant Mills would take over.

Initially, London ordered Mills to fight to the end, but as the day wore on, orders became diplomatically phrased emphasizing that if Grytviken was occupied by Argentina, it would be shown to have done so by force. Barker confirmed that the Rules of Engagement were to be based on the Yellow Card used in Northern Ireland and Cyprus, detailing making an arrest, searches and opening fire. Fortunately, Mills and several Royal Marines had completed tours in Ulster and were familiar with the conditions – not that they necessarily agreed. When the Royal Marines moved into Shackleton House and dumped stores in Quigley's House, they disrupted the routine of some BAS scientists yet to grasp the seriousness of the situation. They were reminded of their predicament, however, when they heard Governor Hunt announce on the radio the imminent invasion of the Falklands by Argentina.

Admiral Busser intended that Task Force 40 would approach the Falkland Islands from the south and land early on 1 April, but when a gale blew throughout the 29th and 30th, Garcia and Allara postponed the landing for twenty-four hours and approached from the north. Many of the embarked force were badly seasick. Only Weinstabl and Santillan were privy to the operation:

> The rest of my Staff and my Company officers, even if they imagined, they knew what it was all about, knew nothing of the mission and no details of the plan in particular. I was itching to inform the Company Officers – who were my tools for the success of the operation – in the picture so they might begin the planning of their respective tasks. *(Operation Rosario)*

As the day wore on, London realized that the Falkland Islands and South Georgia were under immediate threat of invasion. At 10.30 am, Governor Hunt told Majors Norman and Noott that the FCO believed that an Argentine submarine had landed a recce party to survey beaches around Stanley. This was something of a shock to Norman because, on 18 March at the FCO, he had been briefed that although negotiations were difficult, Argentina would 'not dare to use force of any kind'. Norman later said: 'We believed that the Argentineans were simply in the niggling game and the submarine was nothing for us to worry about.'

Major Noott sent Corporal David Carr and two Royal Marines to the Cape Pembroke lighthouse, and Lance Corporal Steve Black to an OP on Sapper

Hill with orders that if they saw a submarine, they were to alert the Quick Reaction Force (QRF). This consisted of Corporal Steve Johnson and five Royal Marines in two Land Rovers. It was intended to arrest any invaders. At 9.00 pm on 1 April, Major Norman assumed command of NP 8901 in the belief that the submarine was, like the presence of the scrap metal merchants on South Georgia, just another example of Argentina raising the stakes. The force now consisted of 3 Royal Marine officers, 2 Royal Navy officers, 66 Royal Marines, 43 of whom had just arrived, and 9 sailors. Noott became military adviser to Governor Hunt.

The same day, Weinstabl broke the news of the invasion to his officers and shared the intelligence that NP 8901 had been reinforced by Norman's detachment. With Red Beach at Yorke Bay and the airport now believed to be defended, General Garcia and Admiral Busser amended the orders:

Amphibious Commandos – to land at Mullet Creek, move north across Stanley Common and simultaneously capture Government House and Moody Brook.

The Army platoon – to seize the airport. Its deployment to Goose Green was cancelled.

Crossing the line of departure was timed for 5.30 am on 2 April. Busser then sent a message to the Landing Force:

I am the Commander of the Landing Forces, made up of the Argentinean Marines and Army on this ship, of units aboard the destroyer Santisima Trinidad and the icebreaker Almirante Irizar and the divers on board the submarine Santa Fe. Our mission is to disembark on the Falklands and to dislodge the British military forces and authorities installed there. That is what we are going to do. Destiny has wished us to be the instigators of making good the 150 or so years of illegal occupation. In those islands we are going to come across a population with whom we must develop a special relationship. They live on Argentine territory and consequently they must be treated as though they are living on the mainland. You must be punctilious in respecting the property and integrity of each of the inhabitants. You will not enter into any private residence unless it is necessary for reasons of combat. You will respect women, children, old people and men. You will be hard on the enemy, but courteous, respectful and pleasant in your dealings with the population of our territory and with those we have to protect. If anyone commits rape, robbery or pillage, I shall impose the maximum penalty. And now, with the authorization of the Commander of the Transport Division, I am sure the Landing Force will be the culmination of the brilliant planning other members of the group have already achieved. Thank you for bringing us this far and thank you for landing us tomorrow on the beach. I have no doubts that your courage, honour and capability will bring us victory. For a long time we have been training our muscles and our hearts for the supreme moment when we shall come face to face with the enemy. That moment has now arrived. Tomorrow you will be conquerors. Tomorrow we shall show the world an Argentine force valorous in war and generous in peace. May God protect you! Now say with me Long live the Fatherland! (*Operacion Rosario*)

During the day, the US tried to persuade Argentina to step back, but it was clear that Galtieri did not want to stop Operation Rosario. Governor Hunt then received a signal from the FCO which stated rather quaintly: 'We have apparently reliable information that an Argentine task force could be assembling off Cape Pembroke by dawn tomorrow. You will wish to make your dispositions accordingly.'

He was somewhat taken aback for he believed that South Georgia was the centre of tension, and had not been told that a large amphibious force was bound for the Falklands. Hunt was offered virtually no advice on likely Argentine strategy, probably because it did not exist at the Ministry of Defence. Hunt then told the two majors that the FCO believed that an Argentine invasion force would be off Cape Pembroke by first light next day. He said, 'It looks as though the silly buggers mean it,' and ordered the mobilization of 123-strong Falklands Islands Defence Force.

In assessing Argentine intentions, the Royal Marine officers decided on two possible landing sites: Yorke Bay, which they named Orange Beach, and a beach to the immediate east, Purple Beach. They believed that Orange Beach was the most likely and defended it with a few reels of barbed wire. The airport runway was obstructed with abandoned vehicles, but there was no time to block the approaches to Stanley Harbour. The single 2-inch mortar was cracked.

Chief Secretary Baker, Police Constable Lamb and the nine sailors, commanded by Colour Sergeant John Noone, detained thirty Argentines in the Town Hall, most of whom were employees and their wives of *Yacimientos Petroliferos Fiscales*, the Argentine State Oil Company, as potential fifth columnists. Leaving Lieutenant Ball RN to guard the prisoners, the sailors returned to Government House where they ran an information service. There was no time to interrogate the Argentines. At 8.15 pm, Hunt broadcast the imminent invasion to the people of the Falklands. At 11.00 pm at Moody Brook, Norman briefed NP 8901 that his aim was to inflict casualties, delay progress and buy time for negotiation:

It was the most difficult set of orders in my life. I made it clear that an invasion force was definitely coming; it was likely to be big and we were likely to be killed. I thought they would be depressed and I would have to gee them up a bit but that was a bad estimation because, at the end, they were raring to go – mainly, I think, because it was a slight to their professionalism. Their attitude was that they knew they were going to

15

lose but the Argentineans would know all about it before they did. (Parker, *Commando*)

Corporal Stefan York recalled that although his manner raised morale, everyone knew the odds were stacked against the defenders. 5 Section (Corporal 'Figgy' Duff) defended Stanley Airport. A GPMG with about 1,000 rounds manned by Marines Leslie Milne and Rod Wilcox covered Orange Beach. They had motorcycles for a quick getaway to two canoes, which they would use to paddle to Stanley. Strung out in defensive positions along the road to Stanley were three sections: 1 Section (Corporal Lou Armour) was at Hookers Point; to his west were Lieutenant Bill Trollope and 2 Section, with a Carl Gustav and 66mm Light Anti Tank Weapon (LAW) near the old airstrip; a kilometre to the west was 3 Section, forming the nucleus for a stronghold. The idea was to delay and retire, delay and retire finally to Government House. 4 Section (Corporal Carr) was on Murrell Heights covering the southern approaches. At the Sapper Hill OP was Marine Mike Berry. Across Stanley Harbour on Navy Point was 6 Section (Corporal York) of six Royal Marines defending The Narrows and with the best chance of melting into the camp to 'go covert' until the arrival of reinforcements, or the political situation had been resolved. However, like Corporal Armour's section, they were NP 8901 (1982/83). Norman set up his Tactical HQ on Look Out Rocks, with the remainder of the Royal Marines Defending Government House. The Falkland Islands Defence Force response was disappointing and of the twenty-three who mobilized, most were assigned to a series of OPs. The Canadian Bill Curtis, a former air traffic controller, deactivated the directional beacon at Stanley Airport; Jack Sollis, who skippered the coaster MV *Forrest,* used its radar to scan Port William; the Cape Pembroke lighthouse keeper Basil Biggs switched off the lamp and watched for shipping; Patrick Watts kept the radio station open. The night was calm with a full moon peeping from scudding clouds. By 2.00 am on 2 April, everyone was in position.

After dark, off South Georgia, under orders to return to Stanley, Captain Barker landed his Royal Marines at Grytviken as instructed. Determined to dispense with the attentions of the Argentines, he then darkened ship, slipped the cover of the *Bahia Paraiso* and, keeping close to the coast on radio silence, steamed at best speed toward the Falklands, into an uncomfortable fresh, westerly swell.

Chapter Three

Invasion of the Falklands and South Georgia

Shortly after 9.00 pm on 1 April, the *Santissima Trinidad* hove to in a light swell about 500 metres south of Mullet Creek. After the deck watch had lowered twenty-one inflatables for the ninety-two amphibious commandos commanded by Lieutenant Commander Guillermo Sanchez-Sabarots, and eight tactical divers, an advance guard, led by Lieutenant Bernardo Schweitzer, landed at Mullet Creek. As they did so, the current nudged the main party's inflatables into long entrails of kelp. On Sapper Hill, Marine Berry reported engines being gunned from the south, but Government House believed these to be helicopters. The main party managed to extricate the inflatables from the kelp, and although some engines refused to start, they finally landed near Lake Point before linking with Schweitzer at 11.00 pm.

Following a fence that led past Sapper Hill, it took nearly five hours for Sanchez-Sabarots and the Moody Brook Barracks assault group to cover the 6 miles across ground they assumed to be patrolled:

It was a nice night, with a moon, but the cloud covered the moon for most of the time . . . It was very hard going with our heavy loads. We eventually split up into three groups. We only had one night sight. One of the groups became separated when a vehicle came along the track we had to cross. We thought it was a military patrol. Another group lost contact, and the third separation was caused by a fast pace. This resulted in my Second in Command, Lieutenant Bardi, falling and suffering a hairline fracture of the ankle. He was left behind with a man to help him. We were at Moody Brook by 5.30 a.m., just on the limits of the time planned, but with no time for the one hour's reconnaissance for which we had hoped. It was still completely dark. We were going to use tear-gas to force the British out of the buildings and capture them. Our orders were not to cause casualties, if possible. All our training as commandos was to fight aggressively and inflict maximum casualties on the enemy. We surrounded the barracks with machine-gun teams, leaving only one escape route along the peninsula north of Stanley Harbour. Anyone who did get away would not able to reach the town and reinforce the British there. Then we threw the tear-gas grenades into each building. There was no reaction. The barracks were empty. (*Operacion Rosario*).

The explosions alerted Major Norman on Look Out Rocks. Not expecting an attack on Moody Brook and with his force facing two directions, he decided to centralize at Government House. At Hookers Point, Corporal Armour recalled: 'We packed our kit and started running back to Stanley. Moody Brook had been bombed, over the radio we could hear, "Stanley is under fire" and some Marine casually pulls over in a Land Rover and says "Get in".' (Bilton and Kominsky, *Speaking Out*)

Meanwhile, Lieutenant Commander Pedro Giachino, who was the 1st Marine Infantry Battalion Second-in-Command, and had volunteered for the mission, approached Government House with eight amphibious commandos and the eight tactical divers. From a small hillock, he could see Royal Marines and several vehicles parked in the drive. At 6.15 am, Giachino went ahead with his original plan to attack from both sides. With four men, he broke into the servants' annexe, believing that it was the rear entrance to Government House, only to find it empty. Vaulting a wall into the garden, the five were then cut down at close range by three Royal Marines, Giachino falling badly wounded, still holding a grenade. Lieutenant Diego Quiroga was hit in the arm and the remaining three retreated to the maid's quarters. The Argentine medic, Corporal Ernesto Urbina, was wounded by a grenade while attempting to reach Giachino. Giachino was invited by the Royal Marines to throw away the grenade so that he could be helped, but as he did not understand English and none of those inside Government House spoke Spanish, the wounded Argentines were left. Meanwhile the Royal Marines and the Argentines were exchanging shots.

When Chief Secretary Baker returned from rounding up Argentines, Governor Hunt told him to continue, but without the naval detachment because it was required at Government House. As Baker opened the door to leave, a hail of machine-gun fire tore into the brickwork. Norman, who had only just arrived, ran out to the defensive perimeter shouting, 'Who fired those shots?' Another burst provided the answer. Baker joined Hunt underneath the Governor's desk.

At 11.00 pm the *Santa Fe* surfaced off Kidney Island, which Sollis reported to Government House, and launched ten tactical divers in three Zodiacs, one of which motored to The Narrows to watch activity in the harbour. At about 2.30 am Sollis and Biggs both reported the transport *Cabo San Antonio* and its close escorts, the Type 42 destroyer *Hercules* and A69 corvette *Drummond*, hove to in Port William about a mile north-east of Yorke Bay.

Reveille for the embarked forces had been at 4.00 am. Commander Weinstabl:

In the evening, a Mass was conducted in the ship's Mess. The rough weather we had experienced throughout the crossing had almost completed abated. We were only some ten kilometres from our target. Before evening meal, I gathered my Battalion together in three troop sections and addressed them. I noted a very good spirit and predisposition for the difficult task ahead at the end of the following day. The night was dark but calm and not chilly. The men had breakfast and made themselves ready quickly and quietly. I went to the bridge to check for new information. The ship was sailing slowly and stealthily. Its Commander, Captain Acuna, bore on his head signs of preoccupation but he was moving about exuding strengths of his character. Also on the bridge were the Admiral, Captain Estrada, Lieutenant Colonel Seineldin and Captain Payaba. After a few jokes to break the tension, we wished each other good luck. In the darkness to the right of Port Stanley, noises and explosions started which indicated the Amphibious Commandos had arrived at their target and that the combat had begun. (*Operacion Rosario*)

At Mass, Lieutenant Colonel Seineldin, a devout Catholic, prayed to the Virgin of Rosario to calm the storm and at the final planning meeting, he persuaded Busser to dedicate the operation to the Virgin del Rosario. At about 5.30 am, the Landing Force filed into their amtracs. At 6.26 am, the bow doors opened releasing a cloud of blue exhaust and then the 1st Amphibious Vehicle Company commander, First Lieutenant Forbice, ordered 'Move now.' Controlled by a naval officer using a red lamp to wait and a green one when the ramp was clear, Forbice experienced a surge of patriotism as the amtracs orbited, as follows:

First wave – four LVTP-7s:

Lieutenant Commander Santillan's advance guard.

A platoon from First Lieutenant Carlos Arruani's E Company.

Second Lieutenant Reyes' 25th Infantry Regiment platoon.

Second wave – fifteen amtracs:

First Lieutenant Francisco Di Paola's D Company.

The remainder of E Company.

Busser's HQ.

Weinstabl's HQ.

Third wave:

A LVTP-7 recovery amtrac.

Five LARC-5 loaded with ammunition, medical supplies and other war stores.

Busser's LVTP-7's deflector plate, which controlled the flow of water, failed to engage and the amtrac turned in circles until the driver engaged reverse. Busser, planner of the landings, therefore approached the beaches in Argentina's most high-profile campaign, in ignominious reverse. Santillan picked out the red navigation beacons fixed by the tactical divers and ordered the first wave into assault formation. Weinstabl:

> We were guided by the red light on the rear of the vehicles moving forwards, since visibility was already very reduced. Inside, my men were tense and silent. All that could be heard was the muted purring of the engine and the dull splash of the swell on the front of the vehicle. At 06.30, a bump on the end of the vehicle told us that we had gone up the beach and the caterpillars had found a place where they could get a grip. The most critical period of the whole amphibious operation had happened. They were probably the longest four or five minutes of my life. Fortunately, the beach was not mined and the enemy was not defending the place. At the precise moment of hitting terra firma, I ordered the upper hatches to be opened so that the men could be

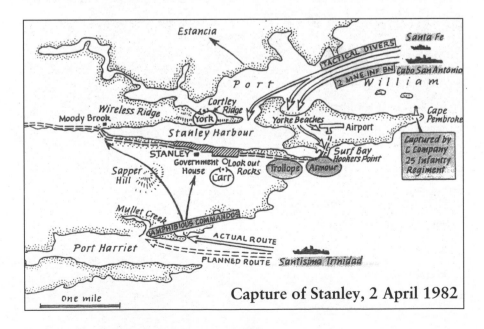

Capture of Stanley, 2 April 1982

afforded their own immediate safety. Visibility had improved rapidly. The stony, upward terrain made the vehicle sway but the tension had already abated noticeably. (*Operacion Rosario*)

Expecting to be ambushed, the amtracs negotiated a defile and reached the airport where the army platoon dismounted, cleared the obstacles and captured the Cape Pembroke lighthouse. Lieutenant Carlos Arruani was in command of E Company with five LVTP-7s:

> While we were overtaking the advance guard, I captured the Airport. I ordered the men to go and form a crocodile. The runway had many obstacles on it – all sorts of vehicles, which I had not foreseen. I ordered it to be cleared for the Hercules bringing in Army units. Given the time it would take to complete the task, the rest of the Battalion continued with the operation under the orders of Lieutenant-Colonel Seineldin. (*Operacion Rosario*)

D Company passed Hookers Point and had reached the old airfield when it encountered several obstacles across the road near the Ionospheric Research Station, including a yellow road repair machine. Lieutenant Trollope describes the action:

> Six Armoured Personnel Carriers began advancing at speed down the Airport Road. The first APC was engaged at a range of about 200 to 250 metres. The first three missiles, two 84mm and one 66mm, missed. Subsequently one 66mm fired by Marine Gibbs, hit the passenger compartment and one 84mm by Marines Brown and Betts hit the front. Both rounds exploded and no fire was received from that vehicle. The remaining five APCs which were about 600 to 700 metres away deployed their troops and opened fire. We engaged them with GPMG, SLR and sniper rifle from Sergeant Shepherd for about a minute before we threw a white phosphorus smoke grenade and leap-frogged back to the cover of gardens. Incoming fire at that stage was fairly heavy, but mostly inaccurate.

Lieutenant Commander Santillan's official post-battle report:

> We were on the last stretch of the road into Stanley when a machine-gun fired from one of the three white houses about 500 metres away and hit the right-hand Amtrac. The fire was very accurate. Then there were some explosions from a rocket launcher, but they were inaccurate, falling a long way from us. We followed our standard operating procedure and took evasive action. The Amtrac on the right returned fire and took cover in a little depression. Once he was out of danger, I told all three vehicles to disembark their men. I ordered the crew with the

Recoilless Rifle to fire one round of hollow charge at the ridge of the roof of the house where the machine-gun was, to cause a bang but not an explosion. We were still following our orders not to inflict casualties. The first round was about a hundred metres short, but the second hit the roof. The British troops then threw a purple smoke grenade; I thought it was their signal to withdraw. They had stopped firing, so Commander Weinstabl started the movement of the two companies around the position. Some riflemen in one of the houses started firing then; that was quite uncomfortable. I couldn't pinpoint their location, but one of my other Amtracs could and asked permission to open up with a mortar which he had. I authorized this, but only with three rounds and only at the roofs of the houses. Two rounds fell short, but the third hit right in the centre of the roof; that was incredible. The British ceased firing then. (*Operacion Rosario*)

Lieutenant Trollope recognized Weinstabl's intent, and after throwing a purple smoke grenade, withdrew along Davis Street before taking up defensive positions after it became obvious Government House was under siege. Awoken by the amtrac drivers revving their engines, the shocked townspeople suddenly found themselves in the middle of a battle. John Smith, who was employed by the Falklands Islands Company, watched from his Sparrow Hawk House:

Everyone up and at the front bedroom windows to see what was going on. A patrol of Royal Marines has just passed along opposite the house, keeping low on the ground past the Fire Station, then – joined by another group a few yards up the road who appeared from the end of King Street at high speed – vaulted the fence into St Mary's Paddock and opened fire up King Street, a pitched battle which lasted a few minutes. It was just like watching a film. We could not believe that this was happening in front us just on the other side of the road. (Smith, *74 Days*)

Santillan's advance guard pushed on toward Moody Brook Barracks and at 7.40 am met Sanchez-Sabarots with his amphibious commandos going to Government House. An anxious Rear Admiral Busser had heard nothing from the amphibious commandos and it was evident that Government House was being defended. At 7.30 am, he ordered Lieutenant Commander Norbeto Barro to send two white anti-submarine Sea Kings from the *Veinticino de Mayo* to the *Almirante Irizar* and lift A Company, 1st Marine Infantry Battalion and Lieutenant Perez's 105mm rocket launchers ashore. Marine Berry reported this to Government House.

On the road back to Stanley in the Land Rover, Corporal Armour was waved down by Corporal Dave Carr, who was in a defensive position outside the Post Office; both then tried to reach Government House but failed:

A lot of tracer started flying down the road and we just scattered, we jumped out of the Rover dived into the gardens, trying to figure what the hell was happening. It was pitch black, we didn't know exactly where they were around Government House. It was all a bit chaotic. (Bilton and Kominsky, *Speaking Out*)

Claudette Mozley was watching this when she saw a Royal Marine crawl into her garden. 'Is that you, Figgy? Would you like some coffee?' To which Corporal Duff replied, 'Get on the floor, you silly bitch! There's an invasion.' Armour and his section tried again:

Dave Carr began returning fire and there was fire being exchanged down the road I had to go along. We got to the hospital and then we had no choice, we had to leap across the football field. Getting into Government House was dodgy because we were frightened of getting shot at by our own guys. We were actually shot at and we ran forward shouting like crazy, 'Marines! Marines! Marines!' My boss, Major Norman said 'Well done' and told me to put the lads upstairs. I was relieved to be among the crowd. (Bilton and Kominsky, *Speaking Out*)

With the intention of joining Corporal York, Carr persuaded Sollis to lower *Forrest*'s dinghy but when its outboard refused to start, the Royal Marines went below to await events.

At Government House, the three Argentine commandos in the maid's quarters were heard by Major Noott who fired into the ceiling, forcing their surrender.

As the 2nd Marine Infantry Battalion advanced through Stanley, Commander Weinstabl arrived at the Town Hall:

The town was silent. Arriving at the place we had chosen as the Battalion Command Post, we found abandoned weapons and packs. I ordered Lieutenant Martinelli to recce the building and within a short while he returned with about thirty men and women who came out of it smiling. They were all Argentines who had been locked in that place the night before. Almost opposite was the Police Station. Inside were six or seven policemen with their Chief and a group of sailors from an oceanographic research ship. I ordered the Police Chief to send the constables home and to tell them not to come out until they were told. (*Operacion Rosaria*)

At about 8.30 am, Governor Hunt realized that further resistance was pointless and telephoned Air Commodore Hector Gilobert, who professed complete ignorance of events. Fortuitously, he had returned to Stanley on 31 March, ostensibly to sort out financial problems at the LADE offices, although he was strongly believed to be an intelligence officer. Major General

Garcia suggested a ceasefire but the white flag had not been packed so several plastic waste-disposal bags were used instead. At about 9.20 am, the party walked to Government House where Rear Admiral Busser introduced himself. Except for the antagonism of the chief military security officer, Major Patricio Dowling, who was of Irish extraction and did not like the British, the negotiations were civil, even though Hunt refused to shake hands with Busser, telling him, 'This is British property. You are not required here.' There was then the inevitable 'We are stronger than you' and 'I have my duty to do' between the two men until at 9.25 am, Hunt instructed Norman to surrender. Norman:

> Surrender, as far as we were concerned, was never an option. The men felt the same. But Rex Hunt ordered me to do so and he was the Commander-in-Chief. I was devastated. My men knew the score. Although we were terribly over-whelmed, they still wanted to fight on. The fact remains, we were not there to defend the Falkland Islands, we were there to defend the seat of government. I gave him three options and none of them involved surrender . . . He told me, 'Mike, I want you to order your men to lay down their arms.' (Parker, *Commando*)

When Norman instructed 6 Section to go 'covert', York booby-trapped their Carl Gustav with phosphorous grenades and radioed that he was going 'fishing', a cryptic reference to a comment he had made earlier to Norman when asked what he would do if the Argentines invaded. The section launched their Gemini and when they apparently found themselves being pursued by a warship, made for the shadows from a Polish fishing factory ship and landed on a small beach. They then melted into the 'camp' with only their fighting order. Their bergens and sleeping bags were still at Moody Brook.

As 149 years of British colonial rule passed to Argentina and an uncertain future, Patrick Watts, Director of Broadcasting, had kept the world informed of the invasion throughout. The victorious Argentines began to round up the Royal Marines. Amphibious Commando Group Sergeant Manuel Batista:

> As we approached Government House, I searched a few houses and took several members of the Civil Defence Force prisoner. I carried on and took two Royal Marines by surprise. Another British Marine was trying to get to a hedge in front of Government House so I covered him with my gun. British Marines were around the outside of the building. I told them to put their hands up. After some hesitation, someone spoke in English and they advanced towards me. Other British Marines also laid down their arms and surrendered. As I went on to the patio of Government House, I found Captain Giachino and two of our wounded commandos, who had been wounded in the firefight. (*Operacion Rosario*)

Giachino died in the hospital soon afterwards. A eulogy entitled 'Recuperacion' (literally translated 'Recovery'), written by an Argentine lady, had been found on many of the captured Argentine soldiers. The time was 9.20 am. Weinstabl reached Government House:

> At the moment we arrived, the English were leaving their hiding places with their hands in the air, having surrendered. Just at that moment, I was informed of the sad news that Captain Giachino was dead and two men were seriously wounded. Our joy at having concluding the operation was dulled by such harsh news. (*Operacion Rosario*)

Noott was escorted to assemble the Royal Marines in Stanley. Not since the Gloucesters had been overwhelmed on the Imjin River in 1951 had there been a mass surrender of British forces. Photographs of Royal Marines and Royal Navy personnel prone on the road, that had been flashed around the world, helped to harden British public opinion. Corporal Armour:

> At the time of the surrender, when Rex Hunt went out to talk to them, I was actually quite pleased we were stopping. I was just glad it was finished. They made us lie down. Suddenly you're in their hands. When we were actually lying down I felt a bit humiliated but I also felt apprehensive about what was going to happen to us. One of the Argentine officers came along and actually struck one of the guards and told us to stand up. We stood up and he shook my hand, a few other guys' hands and said that we should be proud of what we'd done. I liked him. (Bilton and Kominsky, *Speaking Out*)

Euphoric that their aims had been achieved with the minimum loss of life, Major General Garcia and Rear Admiral Allara met Busser at 12.15 pm, and in a short ceremony raised the Argentine flag at Government House. The Argentine Air Force Operation Aries 82, which was the air bridge (*puente aereo*) from the mainland to the Military Air Base, Stanley, began when a C-130 and two F-29 Fellowships left Military Air Base Comodoro Rivadavia with 25th Infantry Regiment personnel and several Air Force specialists. A returning C-130 flew Governor Hunt and his wife, the captured British servicemen and several civilians to Argentina. As the 2nd Marine Infantry Battalion returned to the *Cabo San Antonio*, the night was punctured with firing as the jittery Argentines shot at shadows.

New to the Falklands, 6 Section eventually reached a remote shepherd's cottage near Estancia owned by Mr Watson. Hindered by the lack of local knowledge, without a radio and concerned about the safety of the Watsons if they were captured, on 4 April, York felt that he had no alternative but to surrender. Contacting the Argentine authorities, he used a CB radio to advise them that he wished to surrender. The Royal Marines buried their weapons and awaited their fate; they were not optimistic. Major Dowling, the chief security officer, and a 181 Military Police Company detachment arrived by helicopter and, after searching and tying them with wire, locked them up in Stanley Police Station. Dowling later overstepped his authority on several other occasions and was sent back to Argentina in near disgrace in early June.

Some 600 miles to the east, the Force 10 gale that had delayed the Argentine invasion was blowing across South Georgia. On hearing that Las Malvinas had been liberated, Lieutenant Commander Astiz raised two Argentine flags and declared that South Georgia would now be known as 'Isla San Pedro'. There was one more thing to do – seize Grytviken and complete Project Alpha. Lieutenant Mills heard about the surrender on the radio and knew that the Argentines would soon arrive. Following the departure of HMS *Endurance,* he had lost the ability to fly men to the Jason Peak OP, so to keep an eye on the Argentines, next day he sent Corporal Nigel Peters and three Royal Marines by the BAS launch to man it. Transmissions were kept to a minimum.

Planning the defence of Grytviken with Sergeant Leach, Mills selected a 30-foot-high plateau north-west of Shackleton House, beneath a scree cliff as his position. Four two-man and two three-man trenches dug into the summer tussock grass covered the approaches from Grytviken and King Edward Point. The assault engineer, Marine L. Daniels, helped by Marines R. Porter and L. Church, mined the beaches below the Customs House and wired several houses with improvised explosive devices made from empty ammunition tins and chunks of metal. The jetty was mined with a command-detonated 45-gallon oil drum filled with a cocktail of petrol, paint and plastic explosive. Mills planned to resist until dark and then collect ammunition and rations dumped at Whalers' Church, before withdrawing to the 2,000-foot Mount Hodges and making for Maiviken from where they would conduct a guerrilla campaign. He also knew from a prepared code that HMS *Endurance* would be in a position to help by 3.00 pm the next afternoon. Steve Martin sent three BAS scientists to join the wildlife photographers, Cindy Buxton and Annie Price, who were making an Anglian TV documentary in St Andrew's Bay.

Trombetta and Astiz finalized their plan to fly marines ashore to occupy the BAS accommodation and occupy Grytviken. Second Lieutenant Luna's 1st Marine Infantry Battalion platoon was embarked on the *Bahia Paraiso.* The Royal Marines were preparing their positions when the *Bahia Paraiso* appeared out of a rainstorm and Captain Trombetta radioed Martin that next morning he would receive an important message. When Mills radioed this message to Captain Barker, he was told: 'The Officer Commanding, Royal Marines is not, repeat not, to take any action, which may endanger lives.'

This confused Mills for it contravened the Rules of Engagement to the extent that he was not allowed to open fire; yet, how could he not put up a token resistance?

The next day, 3 April, dawned bright, a gentle breeze barely disturbing the bay. Sergeant Leach and Steve Martin were discussing recovering Corporal

Peters from the OP when Peters radioed that they had photographed a small warship refuel from the *Bahia Paraiso* in Stromness Bay. Marine Ian McCallion, an Ulsterman, who had served an apprenticeship with Harland & Wolff, recognized it as a French Type A69 corvette – the *Guerrico* – her presence giving added impetus to Mills's preparations. When Lieutenant Busson recced the beach south of The Gaol shortly before 5.30 am, in preparation for the army Puma landing the marines, he saw nothing unusual; the Royal Marines remained motionless in their trenches. At about 6.30 am, the *Bahia Paraiso* transmitted on VHF and to the garrison on HF, which enabled *Endurance* to listen in: 'Following our successful operation in the Malvinas, your ex-governor has unconditionally surrendered the Falklands and its dependencies. We suggest you adopt a similar course of action to prevent further loss of life. A ceasefire is now in force.'

Governor Hunt had surrendered the Falklands but not the Dependencies. Needing any delay to buy time, Steve Martin pretended his low-powered VHF set was faulty and repeated the message on his HF set, hoping that Captain Barker's radio operators would pick it up, which they did. He asked for two hours to consider his response. Breaking radio silence, Barker unsuccessfully attempted to release Mills from the Rules of Engagement, however, although virtually every other station in the region heard, he could not raise Grytviken. When Trombetta then radioed that he would be sending marines ashore, Martin told him this was illegal and would be opposed. Unimpressed with this empty threat, Trombetta instructed Martin to assemble everyone on the beach. While Mills issued final orders to his men, Martin assembled the remaining thirteen scientists in the Church.

> As the message came in, the Argentine corvette Guerrico rounded the point and headed into the cove. A helicopter reconnoitred overhead. The Paraiso was then informed that there was a British military presence and that any attempt to land would be repulsed. The Base Commander withdrew to the civilian sanctuary of the Norwegian Whaling Church and Lieutenant Mills moved down to the jetty at King Edward Point to commence negotiations with the Argentine boat landing party, which he assumed would arrive. At the same time the corvette headed back into East Cumberland Bay and he was simultaneously surprised by an Argentine helicopter (the Alouette) disgorging its seven marines near him. As the Argentines took up positions of cover, one of the marines raised his rifle. (Lockett, *HMS Endurance*)

As Mills and Daniels' team sprinted to the defensive position, the Argentines ran into the buildings. First Lieutenant Alejandro Villagra, the pilot of the army Puma, then left the *Bahia Paraiso* with fifteen marines and was approaching Grytviken from Mount Hodges when he was advised by Busson of enemy and to land his stick to link up with his group. However, the Puma was fitted with skis and Villagra needed somewhere flat to land. Mills saw his dilemma and the Royal Marines laced the helicopter with 500 rounds, killing two marine infantry, wounding several others and damaging the hydraulics, however, in a demonstration of fine airmanship, Villagra and his co-pilot, First Lieutenant Eduardo Leguizamon, coaxed the damaged aircraft 400 metres across the bay and crashed-landed near the Hummocks, where it rolled on to its side. A second Alouette was then hit as it landed close to the smoking Puma. Meanwhile, the seven marine infantry were skirmishing toward Shackleton House and Lance Corporal J. Thomson's position but were driven back into cover when, at a range of about 100 metres, Marine S. Holding opened up with his GPMG.

With enemy reported, Trombetta then ordered Alfonso to bombard King Edward Point. *Guerrico* confidently steamed into the bay to support the landing and opened up with her 40mm.

> To the surprise and delight of the defending marines, the ship steamed on her slow relentless course, and only about 300 metres from the base, the Royal Marines loosed off one 84mm Carl Gustav, which dived into the water 10 metres short of the ship, and struck the starboard quarter below the water line. It exploded. The forward 100mm turret was damaged by 66mm and heavy machine gun fire. As the corvette became increasingly under pressure, she turned and retraced her track into the safety of the bay. The battering did not stop, however, and anti tank rockets hit her Exocet launchers. The Argentines disclosed later that 1,275 hits were recorded on the Guerrico. (Lockett, *HMS Endurance*)

Marine David Coombes, normally a steward in HMS *Endurance*'s Senior Rates' Mess, and his Number Two, Marine Stonestreet, had fired the Carl Gustav, but they had also experienced several misfires. Could they have turned the tide of history had the projectiles been more reliable? Marines S.J. Parsons and Steve Chubb fired accurate bursts with their LMG and Sergeant Leach, lying on a table in an upstairs room of Shackleton House, sniped at the bridge. Corporal Peters, standing head and shoulders out of his trench to fire a 66mm, was wounded in the left arm and shoulder by a marine infantryman inside the BAS buildings.

While the contest between the Royal Marines and the *Guerrico* was taking place, Busson's gunner, Petty Officer Gatti, and the Puma loadmaster, Sergeant Jorge Medin, dismounted a MAG from the wrecked helicopter and opened fired across the bay. Frequently under long-range fire from the Royal Marines, Busson flew twenty sorties flying the wounded from the Puma to the *Bahia Paraiso*, returning each time with two marine infantry. By the time the battle was over, he had been flying for three hours.

About 3,000 yards out to sea, the battered *Guerrico* opened fire with her damaged 100mm by training her bows on King Edward Point, four shells in quick succession bracketing the plateau. Mills was in a dilemma. Although the Royal Marines were safe in their positions and had plenty of ammunition,

"BRITISH MARINES.... WHY DON'T YOU GIVE UP.... WE THINK YOU'VE SUFFERED ENOUGH!"

Luna's marine infantry had advanced to Grytviken and were threatening to cut the Royal Marines' escape route into the mountains. He had no idea that HMS *Endurance* was nearby and that Ellerbeck had settled his Wasp on a ridge overlooking Grytviken, where he could offer nothing but moral support and pass information on the engagement back to the ship. Corporal Peters needed treatment. During a lull in the bombardment from *Guerrico* and with the prospect of relief unlikely, when Mills said that he intended to surrender, Sergeant Leach suggested they make for the mountains.

> The OCRM quickly re-assessed the situation and decided that the point had been made; military force had been used to take the island; and little was to be gained by a suicidal defence. Without a surrender flag available, a make shift flag in the shape of a coat was held aloft and the shooting stopped. The two commanding officers met to negotiate the surrender and the 22 Royal Marines put down their arms on condition that good treatment was guaranteed. The civilian scientists were released from their refuge, the most southerly church in the world. (Lockett, *HMS Endurance*)

The Argentines suspected a ruse when they saw the defence consisted of twenty-two men. All the BAS were accounted for except for Steve Martin, who eventually turned up having spent two hours sheltering from the fighting in a cold and wet gully dressed only in shirt and slacks. Astiz landed and, after acknowledging Mills's advice about the mined beach and jetty, invited Daniels to make the areas safe. An Argentine doctor on the *Bahia Paraiso* treated Corporal Peters. Several years later, at a reception at Highgrove House for Falklands veterans in the presence of HRH Prince Charles, Surgeon Commander Rick Jolly gave Peters the X-rays taken of his wounds, courtesy of his Argentine contacts. Meanwhile, HMS *Endurance* was ordered to remain in the region intelligence-gathering and pretending to be an iceberg to avoid radar detection. The Royal Marines and BAS were ferried by landing craft to the *Bahia Paraiso* and accommodated in several cabins below the flight deck. Calling in at Rio Grande, the Argentine dead and wounded, and Corporal Peters, were landed. On 13 April, the prisoners were transferred to an indoor swimming pool at Puerto Belgrano Naval Base. The following day, Peters rejoined the detachment with the news that the Task Force had sailed from the United Kingdom. On the 16th, the captured Britons were driven to an airfield and flown to Montevideo, where they were handed over to British officials. Three days later, they boarded an RAF VC-10 bound for RAF Brize Norton. After a short leave, Mills agreed to return to HMS *Endurance,* which desperately needed her Royal Marines.

Mills was awarded the DSC and Sergeant Leach the DSM. Marines Coombes and Stonestreet were Mentioned in Dispatches.

Chapter Four

Occupation

Day One of seventy-four days of Argentine occupation was 2 April. John Smith kept a diary throughout this time:

> By 10am, the fighting was over. By 10.30am, the Argentine flag is flying over Government House. Constant Argentine military band music being played over the radio; then within half an hour edicts or communiqués broadcast, each preceded by a barrage of Spanish and their national anthem. (Smith, *74 Days*)

In several communiqués, Colonel Esteban Solis, the Chief Civil Affairs Officer, greeted the Falkland Islanders to Argentina and assured them of their civil and freedom of movement rights – this from a country with an appalling human rights record. He confirmed that 'colonial and military instructions of the British Government are effectively relieved of their charges', and, introducing a curfew, residents were to place a white cloth outside the door should a problem arise, which the islanders found abhorrent for it implied surrender. Disobedience to the curfew, public order disturbances, insults to national symbols or any action against the Argentine Code of Law could lead to imprisonment. A forty-strong civil administration team, headed by Air Commodore Carlos Bloomer-Reeve, a former Consul in Stanley, then arrived. He had been involved in the negotiations over the future of the Falklands and was considered to be the ideal choice to represent the islanders. Installing himself in the Secretariat, it was his responsibility to emphasize the justification of the Argentine cause. Next day, Bloomer-Reeve circulated a communication giving an assurance that civil rights would be acknowledged, although some liberties would be withheld because of the mainland anti-terrorist struggle. Then vital CB transmissions were banned with the threat of imprisonment.

Generally, the Falkland Islanders carried on 'as usual', although there was some suspicion about the loyalties of some Anglo-Argentines. On 13 April, several islanders seen to be a threat were repatriated to the UK, where most gave invaluable intelligence debriefs. When the Carrier Battle Group began lurking offshore on 27 April, the Argentines enforced a blackout and a curfew between 6.00 pm and 6.30 am; shops were to close by 4.00 pm. The military security authorities rounded up several islanders thought to be subversive, including Gerald Cheek, who ran the Falkland Islands Air Service and was one of the Falklands Islands Defence Force who responded to Governor Hunt's mobilization:

> On 27 April, I'll never forget that date, they came for me one afternoon and said I was being taken away. I didn't know where to. Four (military police) came in with pistols and threatened my family, saying to me 'You've got to go, you've got ten minutes to pack'. I thought I was being taken to Argentina. They took me and several other people – fourteen in all – down to Stanley Airport. We were taken to Fox Bay and placed under house arrest (with the settlement manager, Richard Cockwell) for the remainder of the war.

The former RAMC doctor, Daniel Haines, the Senior Medical Officer, and his wife, were arrested because he opposed the Argentines using the hospital for Argentine troops. This left Dr Alison Bleaney and Mary Elphinstone to look after the medical needs of Stanley. The only serious confrontation happened on 1 May when a group of civilians sought shelter in a godown after rumours circulated that a British landing was imminent. Major Dowling customarily overreacted by ordering 181 Military Police Company and 601 Commando Company to arrest anyone leaving it. Next morning, Bloomer-Reeve ordered their immediate release, much to the disgust of Dowling. When the International Committee of the Red Cross published a report on 21 May, the day the British landed at San Carlos, Argentina claimed that only five Falklands Islanders had been detained and that three serious crimes by Argentine troops against private property had been dealt with by military tribunals. Argentina claimed that the imposition of the Total Exclusion Zone (TEZ) was obstructing the delivery of supplies to the civil population.

The subsequent frequent air raids and naval bombardments were unnerving for islanders born in the tranquillity of the Falklands. Both sides were careful to avoid civilian casualties. The Argentine authorities even formed a committee to identify robust houses suitable for air-raid shelters and at the end of the campaign, as the Argentines retreated to Stanley, the military government issued an instruction that all inhabitants to the west of the Battle Monument were to leave their houses because of British shelling, and to shelter in St Mary's Church and the West Stores. Nevertheless, three people were killed when a British artillery shell hit a house on 12 June.

The Army, which now occupied the Falklands, had underpinned the struggle for independence. British commercial interests then supported the fledgling economy. Among the patriots who returned from the Napoleonic Wars was the Peninsula War veteran Jose de San Martin. In 1817, he led 5,000 Argentines on an epic march across the Andes and contributed massively to Chilean and Peruvian independence. In 1982, his largely ceremonial 1st 'General Jose de San Martin' Cavalry Regiment sent six machine-gun detachments to the Falklands, which were attached to 1st 'Los Patricios' Infantry Regiment, the oldest infantry unit of the Argentine Army. From 1880, the Army was actively involved in political power-broking and of the eighteen governments between 1930 and 1982, ten were military. When, in 1974, President Peron was succeeded by his widow, Isabel, this sparked two years of inter-faction fighting. Into the void stepped the left-wing revolutionary groups, which then provoked a junta headed by General Jorge Videla, deposing Isabel and ending the Dirty War, in which Argentina had achieved global isolation.

In 1982, the Argentine Army was divided into five corps, with tactical deployment built around two armoured brigades, three infantry brigades defending the Chilean border, plus a mountain brigade and a jungle infantry brigade. 4th Airborne Infantry Brigade was the National Strategic Reserve. Most formations, units and bases had an additional honorary nomenclature – for instance the 3rd 'General Manuel Belgrano' Mechanised Infantry Regiment, so named in honour of the eighteenth-century Argentine soldier and intellectual. Conscription began annually in February with selection based upon the year in which the conscript was born, thus those born in 1963 were conscripted in February 1982 as *Soldado Clase 63*. The Army served for a year and the Navy and Air Force two years. When training ceased in October, conscripts were progressively released to make way for the next annual induction. Most conscripts served near their homes. Most had a firm conviction that *Malvinas es Argentina*. Of an Army establishment in 1982 of 85,000 men, 65,000 were conscripts, about half of whom had only been inducted in February and had barely finished basic training. The only non-commissioned rank achievable to conscripts was *Dragoneante,* which equates roughly to the US Army Private First Class. Discipline tended to be unso-phisticated. Potential regular NCOs attended the 'Sergeant Cabral' School of NCOs, which was part of the School of Infantry 'Lieutenant-General Pedro Eugenio Aramburu' at Campo de Mayo, Buenos Aires. NCOs had little responsibility except for low-level tactics and administration of the conscripts. Even though there were sizeable class, cultural and philosophical distinctions, there was plenty of evidence of '*hermandad*' (brother) between the Argentine officer and other ranks. Telegrams sent by Argentine servicemen to their families through Cable and Wireless from the Falklands were intercepted by HMS *Fearless* at Ascension Island and passed to 3rd Commando Brigade intelligence.

As throughout the rest of South America, most Argentine officers were Roman Catholic and middle to upper class. Cadets attended the National Army Academy, which was modelled on West Point. Officers selected for field rank attended Staff College followed by three years at the Senior Level War School; some attended foreign staff colleges and courses. Argentines were regu-larly seen in the United Kingdom. Peculiar to the Army was the *logia* (lodge), a sort of Masonic lodge, which had been founded by General San Martin and was designed to further the belief that the Army firmly believed in its motto 'Nacion con el pais en 1810' (born with the nation in 1810) and were guardians of tradition. Political disagreement was rife. Brigadier General Jofre not only had to fight the British but also deal with Lieutenant Colonel Seineldin, the commando Major Aldo Rico and other right-wing officers, all of whom under-mined his authority. This rivalry led to the 25th Infantry Regiment, arguably Argentina's best infantry unit, defending Stanley Airport instead of being in the front line. Defeat in 1982 damaged the credibility of politico-officers.

Great Britain has a long military tradition of losing battles and winning wars. Now this conscript South American army was about to take on a regular army that had lost a soldier killed in action every year since 1945, except 1968. When Ruben Moro, a Canberra pilot who took part in the campaign, wrote: 'Although British armed forces had not actually been engaged in a shooting war since the Suez crisis in 1956, Great Britain was nevertheless prepared to meet any contingency arising from its Atlantic Alliance obliga-tions', he had conveniently forgotten British military operations in Kenya, Cyprus, Aden, Borneo and Northern Ireland.

Argentina's euphoria was short-lived. At the UN debate on 3 April, Resolution 502 was passed, demanding the withdrawal of Argentine forces, cessation of hostilities and a political solution. The Junta had three choices:

Raise the crisis diplomatically and force negotiations.

Call Britain's bluff and hope that international mediation would prevail.

Defend the Falklands.

9 Infantry Brigade (Brigadier General Americo Daher) continued to arrive as the 8th 'General Bernardo O'Higgins' Infantry Regiment deployed to Fox Bay on 6 April, where it remained until the Argentine surrender. Most of its soldiers were reservists. Next day, 5th Marine Infantry Battalion deployed straight to Mounts William and Tumbledown to cover the southern beaches – organic to 1st Fleet Marine Force in Rio Grande in Tierra del Fuego, it was well used to the cold of the approaching winter. The Malvinas Theatre of Operations was absorbed into the South Atlantic Theatre of Operations.

Brigadier General Mario Menendez arrived as Military Governor and Commander, Malvinas Joint Command. In a meeting with General Galtieri on 2 March, he had been given three main objectives of: respecting the traditions and property of the islanders; improving their living standards; and integrating them into Argentine life. By nature conciliatory, it was hoped that this personality would help him govern the Falklands during the early negotiations. Menendez:

My arrival on the islands at Stanley was a dream come true for the Argentines. The knowledge of our rights over the Malvinas is a very

34

profound feeling; an ambition and, at the same time, a frustration . . . because the British Task Force had sailed. Above all there was a pride that I was the first Argentine governor of the Malvinas in 150 years. (Bitton and Kominsky, *Speaking Out*)

Told that invasion was not expected, he was tested when he found himself fighting battles after the British landings at San Carlos when a more aggressive military commander was needed. He carried the blame for the Argentine defeat.

In his first Land Forces Argentine Occupied Territories Operations Order, Brigadier General Daher calculated that the British had two options:

1. Special Forces operations to start no sooner than 18 April directed at Stanley, with secondary operations at Fox Bay and Darwin areas. A helicopter assault by about 500 troops in preparation for an amphibious assault by two marine battalions.

2. Special Forces operations, electronic warfare interference and attacks by small, lightly armed and equipped resistance groups in preparation for landings.

Outlining his Concept of Operations, Daher planned an Argentine military presence on the Falklands, even after the British had landed, to give his government a political lever. Stanley, the seat of government, was the centre of defence. Fox Bay and Goose Green were designated as strongpoints from which patrols would dominate the ground. Once ashore, he believed that the British had fourteen possible approach routes to Stanley. San Carlos Water is not mentioned. Daher was complimentary about British abilities: 'Have an excellent standard of instruction . . . morale will be good . . . There will be severe restrictions on their logistics caused by the great distance between their probable bases . . . "high percentage of their personnel are under contract".' He refers to the professional nature of the British, compared to the conscript nature of the Argentine Armed Forces. Quite why the Argentines selected 18 April is not clear. Even sailing at full speed, ships capable of landing troops would take about three weeks to be offshore.

On 7 April, Great Britain posted her intention to impose a 200-mile Maritime Exclusion Zone (MEZ) around the Falklands, South Georgia and the South Sandwich Islands on 12 April with the threat of intercepting any Argentine warships and auxiliaries found inside the zone, the aim being to hinder the reinforcement of the Falklands. The Argentines believed that the Royal Navy would contact the local population either by radio or by landing small patrols. At a meeting on 9 April, Menendez and his security advisers decreed that anyone in Stanley with a 2-metre band CB radio was to hand it to the Security Warehouse in the Town Hall next day. Those outside Stanley were expected to disconnect their equipment. Owners were meant to receive

£200 in compensation. On 12 April, Vice Admiral Lombardo, the newly appointed Commander, South Atlantic Theatre of Operations Command, issued Military Committee Outline Plan 1/82 and told Brigadier General Menendez, 'I will give you freedom of action because you will be isolated.' Reviewing possible British strategies, Lombardo listed naval options open to the British:

Blockade the islands using submarines and deny the use of the airfield.

Attempt total or partial recovery by an amphibious or helicopter assault launched from fifty to 250 miles to the east of the objective. i.e. South Georgia, supported by raids launched from submarines.

Wear down Argentine forces by using nuclear and attack submarines. Since the Beagle Channel conflict was unresolved, Great Britain's actions could encourage Chile to take concurrent action and thereby stretch Argentine resources.

Lombardo recognized that the deployment of Argentine naval surface units would be restricted by nuclear submarines and arrangements were made to extend the Air Transport Command Operation *Aries 82*. The Command flew in 6,712 soldiers, 414 Navy and 863 Air Force personnel and 6,335 tons of Army, 200 tons of Navy and 1,171 tons of Air Force supplies from several Atlantic air bases. In contrast, the British were reliant upon shipping, some already in service but including forty-five merchantmen taken up from trade as transports, repair ships, tugs and hospital ships. They moved over 100,000 tons of war stores, 400,000 tons of fuel and 9,000 men.

When it became clear that UK was assembling a Task Force, General HQ (GHQ) instructed 10 'Lieutenant General Nicolas Levalle' Mechanised Infantry Brigade (Brigadier General Oscar Jofre), which was based at La Plata defending the Atlantic Littoral, to prepare to deploy to the Falklands. Jofre replaced most of the conscripts with reservists summoned by radio announcements, telegram and home visits. With equipment deficiencies made up from other units, the Brigade began arriving by air from 11 April. Because his artillery group was equipped with US 105mm field guns, which were unsuitable for the Falklands, Jofre was assigned the 3rd Artillery Group (Lieutenant Colonel Martin Balsa), although Balsa had not previously worked with the Brigade. The Group was equipped with Italian M56 105mm Pack Howitzers. With two brigades ashore, Menendez reorganized Malvinas Joint Command.

Brigadier General Jofre was appointed Commander, Land Forces.

Brigadier General Daher became Chief of Staff to Menendez.

10 Infantry Brigade assumed responsibility for the defence of Stanley as Army Group, Stanley.

9 Infantry Brigade took responsibility for the rest of the Falklands with orders to reinforce Stanley.

In his threat assessment, Menendez's Chief Intelligence Officer, Colonel Francisco Cervo, identified eleven potential assault beaches; again San Carlos Water was not mentioned. A GHQ assessment gave a detailed organizational and equipment breakdown of the British order of battle, but made some basic errors, for instance that the SAS were based in Aldershot and the decommissioned HMS *Blake* was part of the Task Force and carrying eleven Sea Kings.

By 16 April, 10th Infantry Brigade was in defensive positions, although it would not be until 22 April that its heavy equipment arrived. Believing that the main threat was from Berkeley Sound, Jofre organized Army Group Stanley to face north:

Sector Oro (Gold). 3rd Infantry Regiment covered the southern beaches.

Sector Acero (Steel). 6th Infantry Regiment covered the approaches from the south-west and south. C Company was later assigned to Z Reserve and was replaced by A Company, 1st 'Los Patricios' Infantry Regiment, which was designated C Company.

Sector Plata (Silver). 7th Infantry Regiment on Mount Longdon and Wireless Ridge faced north.

Sector Cobre (Copper). Military Air Base, Stanley.

Sector Victoria (Victory). Airport area. Defended by 25th Infantry Regiment.

Sector Bronce (Bronze). 5th Marine Infantry Battalion on Mount Tumbledown and Mount William covered the south-west approaches.

General Galtieri visited Menendez on 22 April and agreed the British would land at or near Stanley. When Menendez asked for Special Forces and another regiment as his heliborne reserve, Galtieri, without consulting the Junta and the Chiefs of Staff, instructed Major General Garcia to send 3 Mechanised Infantry Brigade (Brigadier General Omar Parada). Usually deployed along the Uruguayan border in the sub-tropical province of Corrientes and part of II Army Corps, when 9 and 10 Brigades left for the Falklands it had joined 11 Mechanised Infantry Brigade in Patagonia defending the Atlantic Littoral and the border with Chile. Although Parada mobilized his reservists, by the time the troop trains were en route to Puerto Deseado for embarkation, his units were under strength and the men mostly conscripts. To replace the 3rd Artillery Group, Parada was given the 4th Airborne Artillery Group from the National Strategic Reserve. At Puerto Deseado, equipment was loaded on board four Naval Transport Service ships, however the *Ciudad de Cordoba*, which was loaded with mortars, vehicles, reserve ammunition, field kitchens and war stores of the 12th 'General Juan Arenales' Mechanised Infantry Regiment, returned to port after hitting a rock. Its soldiers, travelling in light order, arrived in Stanley between 24 and 29 April and were despatched to Goose Green. Conferring with General Herrera at GHQ on 25 April, the day that South Georgia was recaptured, Menendez said that the reinforcements were impacting on his logistics and that more helicopters would ease his problems. Herrera said that heavy equipment would arrive by ship, however the imposition of the TEZ on 1 May proved final. Menendez re-emphasized his need for commandos: 'so that they can become familiar with the islands and its geography in order to be able to operate with the greatest efficiency.'

With three brigades, two with full headquarters, Menendez again reorganized his command. Brigadier General Parada took command of Army Group, Littoral and was ordered to move to Goose Green. His command was:

Sector Plomo (Lead). Task Force Mercedes – HQ, A and C Companies, 12th Infantry Regiment at Goose Green.

Naval Air Base Calderon, Pebble Island. Task Force Marega (1st Platoon, H Company, 3rd Marine Infantry Battalion).

Mount Wall and Mount Challenger. Task Force Monte Caseros (HQ, B and C Companies, 4th Infantry Regiment).

Mount Kent. Combat Team Solari (B Company, 12th Infantry Regiment).

Port Howard. Task Force Reconquest (5th Infantry Regiment). Its commanding officer was traditionally a full colonel; in 1982 this being Juan Mabragana.

Sector Uranio (Uranium) – 8th Infantry Regiment at Fox Bay.

3 Infantry Brigade suffered from lack of acclimatization and a deficiency of the appropriate equipment, clothing and training, however this must be set against the Argentine belief that the British would land in the vicinity of Stanley.

By 2 May, it was clear to Argentina that unless a political settlement was reached, landings near Stanley were likely. Menendez issued his Preparatory Order for the Reserve to Brigadier General Parada to contain the landings around Stanley:

Task Force Reconquest at Fox Bay to transfer to East Falkland.

Task Force Mercedes at Goose Green to deploy to Two Sisters, Mount Tumbledown and Wireless Ridge and destroy enemy penetration.

Task Force Monte Caseros to occupy Mount Wall and Mount Challenger and prevent enemy penetration westwards.

Combat Team Solari, supported by a helicopter company, to block enemy advances from the north.

Nevertheless the question for Menendez was: where and what will the British do if they land? A document compiled in mid-May suggests the British strategy would be to defeat the Argentine forces and recapture as much of the Stanley peninsula as possible. Britain would manoeuvre into a favourable political bargaining position either by a high-risk direct assault against Stanley, or a low-risk amphibious assault north-east of Stanley with a view to recapturing the town once sufficient forces were ashore. San Carlos is mentioned as one of three possible landing zones, the others being at Fitzroy and the St Louis peninsula, however it was considered a disadvantageous option because of the length of time it would take to approach Stanley. It was felt that the British were reliant upon helicopters.

Chapter Five

The British Response

When news of the surrender of the Falklands was confirmed, there was national embarrassment and anger. Confusion reigned as Whitehall and Westminster limited the damage to the reputation of Great Britain. During the evening of 31 March, Admiral Sir Henry Leach, the First Sea Lord, had read intelligence reports given to the Secretary of State for Defence, John Nott, and found incompatibility with one document warning of an invasion and another suggesting that:

> Further naval deployments were unnecessary and undesirable. Endurance would remain on station and be supplied. Here was a clear imminent threat to a British overseas territory . . . What the hell was the point of having a Navy if it was not used for this sort of thing? Even as I decided that the briefs were upside down. I learned that my Secretary of State was being briefed from that at the very moment. (Freedman, *Official History*, Vol 1)

In full uniform, Leach was famously barred from the House of Commons by a police officer until he was rescued by a Whip and taken to a meeting chaired by Prime Minister Margaret Thatcher. Nott was reluctant to escalate the crisis. Leach suggested that any response must be robust, however it would take three weeks to assemble a task force based around the Fleet, its two aircraft carriers and 3 Commando Brigade. Thatcher corrected him, 'Three days, you mean.' Leach's opinions were greeted with scepticism by some Cabinet ministers, nevertheless, by 11.00 pm, he had stopped Easter leave and was assembling a task force, in particular from Exercise Springtrain, although a decision had yet to be made that it would sail. During the famous Saturday House of Commons debate on 3 April, Thatcher acted with characteristic decisiveness when she announced: 'A large task force will sail as soon as preparations are complete.'

Since this was going to be a naval operation, Admiral Sir John Fieldhouse, Commander-in-Chief Fleet, was appointed Commander, Combined Task

Force 317 (CTF 317), with his headquarters at Northwood. CTF 317 was broken down into Combined Task Groups (CTG):

CTG 317.0. Amphibious Task Group. Commanded by Commodore Michael Clapp RN, the in-post Commander Amphibious Warfare at Plymouth. It had three tasks: 1) plan the land; 2) direct inshore operations; 3) support the defeat of the enemy ground forces.

CTG 317.1. Landing Force Group. 3 Commando Brigade (Brigadier Julian Thompson RM) at Plymouth. It was reinforced by the Spearhead Battalion, 3rd Battalion, Parachute Regiment, and several smaller Army and RAF units. It had three tasks: 1) Land; 2) Establish a beachhead; 3) Defeat the enemy's ground forces.

CTG 317.8. Carrier Battle Group (Rear Admiral 'Sandy' Woodward RN). Woodward was Flag Officer, 1st Flotilla. Its tasks were: 1) Establish a naval and air blockade of the Falklands; 2) Defeat Argentine naval forces; 3) Secure British air superiority; 4) Ensure the Landing Group arrived at their destination in one piece.

CTG 324.3 – (Submarines).

18 Group RAF reporting direct to Fieldhouse.

Although Woodward had limited experience in amphibious warfare, he was appointed Combined Commander, Task Force 317, which included all surface units and ground and air forces. Confusion surfaced quickly when Brigadier Thompson and Commodore Clapp, both one-star officers were unsure whether they reported to Woodward, a two-star officer, or had equal responsibilities as commanders reporting direct to Fieldhouse. This tension emerged several times over the coming weeks. The preparations reinforced Britain's intent and the occupied Falkland Islanders were grateful that a country which for decades had ignored them was at last taking an interest in them. In the meantime, international diplomacy mediated to identify common ground between Great Britain and Argentina.

3 Commando Brigade was a highly motivated formation, with some units still returning from the annual three-month winter warfare deployment to Norway. If it had a weakness, its isolation from the Army meant that it was not totally familiar with some aspects of warfare, for instance the all-arms battle. Within four days, elements of the 4,350 men, about 50,000 tons of war stores and sixty vehicles that would make up the Brigade embarked on ships for the passage to Ascension Island. Fears of mixing 1,400 commandos and 600 paras on *Canberra* to be a lethal cocktail proved unfounded. Thompson placed his headquarters on HMS *Fearless*. There was very little intelligence, in spite of the historical threat that Argentina posed to the Falklands.

The disputed territories were 6,700 miles to the south and essential to Great

Britain was a forward operating base. 3,750 miles from the Falklands and 4,225 miles from the United Kingdom, Ascension Island was ideally placed to be that base. With a decent anchorage and Wideawake Airfield, it could be secured cheaply and was screened from the media. Its tranquillity changed overnight on 2 April when Sergeants Macelreavy and Keeping and five Royal Signals from 1st Signal Group at Tidworth arrived by air with Tactical Satellite Communications and Diplomatic Communications radios for Governor Hunt. However, when the surrender interrupted their journey, they embarked on RFA *Fort Austin* on its way to replenish HMS *Endurance*, eventually landing at Stanley on 19 June. Captain Robert McQueen RN was appointed Commander, British Support Unit:

> This was to be the base for the forward logistic support of British Forces on Operation Corporate. There were two more or less distinct parts to our task. First, the support of ships in the South Atlantic involved the transhipment of people, stores, ammunition and helicopters from Support Command and chartered transported aircraft by helicopter and lighter to ships passing the island. Second, the RAF Operations mounted from the island had to be supported and the defence of the island had to be secured. Fitness and weapon training had to be provided for troops in ships which stopped over at the island. (McQueen, *Naval Review*)

The increasing use of Ascension impacted on its limited water supply, a problem solved with desalinators. The demand for aviation fuel discharged from US Sealift Command tankers was resolved when 1 Troop, 51 (Construction) Squadron RE laid a 4-mile aviation fuel pipeline from a storage fuel tank farm to Wideawake Airfield to replace bowsers unable to keep up with demand. The very limited accommodation was enhanced with the tented 'Lunar Bay Holiday Camp' at English Bay, and the loan by 4449 Mobile Support Squadron USAF of thirty-one twelve-man modules for 'Concertina City', which were particularly valuable for the RAF Vulcans and Victors flying their long-range sorties. The redoubtable Royal Engineers and a Cable and Wireless team renovated every disused building, so that by mid-April, about 1,500 people could be accommodated. With their Royal Navy and RAF colleagues, 29 Transport and Movement Regiment, Royal Corps of Transport installed a Movement Control Check through which men and material moved. It also provided 'movers' on ships as liaison officers to arrange the stowage of equipment and stores.

Supplying the ships fell to the Royal Naval Aircraft Servicing Unit (Naval Party 1222) which arrived on 6 April. McQueen:

> Stores were unloaded from the transport aircraft by three RAF teams working twelve hours on and twenty-four off. They were then sorted into and moved into dumps by an assorted team of fork-lift truck drivers, naval supply ratings and soldiers. Luckily there was consider-

able space to the south and east of the dispersal because the stores dumps became very large. (McQueen, *Naval Review*)

Ships taken up from trade and the Royal Fleet Auxiliary (RFA), moved an estimated 9,000 personnel, 100,000 tons of freight and ninety-five aircraft to the South Atlantic. RFA overseas agents were also responsible for arranging the supply of oil for warships, with an estimated 1,200 refuelling-at-sea resupplies. Wideawake Airport became the most stable aircraft carrier in the world and, on 18 April, with over 500 air movements, the busiest airport in the world. Its single runway and two PAN AM air traffic controllers handled 2,500 fixed-wing flights and 10,600 helicopter rotations during Operation Corporate. Commanded by Group Captain Jeremy Price, the RAF contingent handled 5,800 personnel and 6,600 tons of stores using C-130 Hercules, ex-military transport Belfasts chartered from Heavy Lift Cargo Airlines and VC-10 passenger and aero-medical. Ascension Island was defended from nosy Soviet Long Range Air Force Tu-95 Bear C/Ds, first by eight GR3 Harriers from 1 (Fighter) Squadron, a RAF Regiment Wing equipped with Rapier and an early warning radar system installed on Green Mountain; then, from 24 May, when the Harriers joined the Task Force, by 29 (Fighter) Squadron F-4 Phantoms.

While the Task Force was preparing to go south and the Landing Group was assembling at Ascension Island, the recapture of South Georgia was underway.

With her fuel and stocks running low, HMS *Endurance* was ordered on 5 April to rendezvous with the Fleet Replenishment Ship RFA *Fort Austin* (Commodore Sam Dunlop). Her departure from the region left the British blind to Argentine activities, however, the BAS formed themselves into coast watchers and sent their observations to the BAS station on Signy Island, 650 miles to the south-west. It was then relayed to RRS *Bransfield*, copied to the Maritime Communication Centre at Portishead, sent to Cambridge and made available to the Ministry of Defence. Other BAS reported on Argentine activity in Cumberland Bay, ski-patrolled looking for Argentine activity, covering a total of a third of the east coast of South Georgia, and provided valuable intelligence of where the Argentines were not.

By 1981, the SAS were thriving on fame after the Iranian Embassy siege in London and were known, by some, as 'Maggie Thatcher's Own'. One SAS sergeant later claimed the Regiment could have recaptured the Falklands without help! To some extent, the SAS operated in a bubble with their own communications to Director, SAS at the Ministry of Defence via Hereford. As soon as Brigadier Peter de la Billière, Director, SAS, heard that a Task Force was assembling, he lobbied Admiral Fieldhouse for a role and activated his contacts with the US Delta Force:

At the scent of battle our American colleagues were raring to join in the action, but, being prevented from doing so by political considerations, lent us some of their best equipment, including a Stinger, a hand-held, ground-to-air missile system which was just coming into use. It so happened we had an experienced non-commissioned officer in the United States, Corporal Paddy O'Connor; he was rapidly diverted to Delta Force, where he took a crash course on the Stinger. Mike Rose managed to jump the gun, very much as he had done at the start of the Iranian Embassy siege. Without any official permission, he took D Squadron to Brize Norton and got them on board an aircraft; before anyone in authority realised where they were, they had arrived at Ascension island, four thousand miles down into the South Atlantic and half-way to the target. (de la Billière, *Looking for Trouble*)

Lieutenant Colonel Rose was Commanding Officer, 22 SAS. D Squadron (Major Cedric Delves) consisted of a Headquarters, including fourteen 264 Signal Squadron, and 16 (Mobility), 17 (Boat), 18 (Air) and 19 (Mountain) Troops. Flying by a 10 Squadron RAF VC-10, the eighty-strong Squadron arrived at Ascension on 5 April with about 50,000 pounds of palleted equipment. Meanwhile de la Billière: 'Was liaising and advising at the highest level, for some of our operations were highly sensitive, and needed not only military approval but political backing from the top' (de la Billière, *Looking for Trouble*).

In London, the Cabinet view was that while South Georgia was of secondary importance, its occupation was not negotiable. Its recapture would demonstrate political resolve and raise public morale, which was becoming disenchanted with the protracted seesaw mediation by General Al Haig. The leeward coast offered relatively sheltered anchorages for a forward operating base, although the Falklands were 600 stormy miles to the west.

At about 5.00 pm on 6 April, Major General Jeremy Moore RM MC ∎, who was Major General, Royal Marines, told Brigadier Thompson, just as he was about to fly to HMS *Fearless* from HQ Commando Forces in Plymouth, that Northwood needed a commando company group for a classified mission and suggested the 45 Commando detachment on jungle warfare training in Brunei. When Thompson suggested 42 Commando, which had just returned from its annual Norwegian winter deployment, next day, Colonel Richard Preston, Chief-of-Staff, Commando Forces instructed Lieutenant Colonel Nick Vaux, who commanded 42 Commando, to set aside a company group equipped for winter warfare on six hours' notice to move. Vaux:

First, I had to decide who should go . . . One of my rifle companies was to be despatched on an evidently hazardous mission, under someone else's control. I was not happy with the circumstances, and it was then that I first considered putting Guy Sheridan in overall command . . . His qualifications were unique, and instinct also told me that an experienced major like Guy Sheridan was more likely to resolve dissension within a force drawn from several units than a younger company commander.

That decision taken, it was easier to choose the company commander for the South Georgia party, since I could afford to retain the two most experienced for whatever awaited us elsewhere. As it happened, I had not the slightest doubt that Captain Chris Nunn, who had just success-fully completed his first winter in command of M Company, was the right choice . . . We agreed upon a company group that included a precious section of the unit's Reconnaisance Troop, who were all tried and trained specialists in mountain and arctic warfare. We decided to include two of the six 81mm from Support Company but also asked for a naval gunfire support team. (Vaux, *March to the South Atlantic*)

Major Sheridan, Vaux's Second-in-Command, was an inspired choice. A former member of the British Olympic Biathlon Team, he was a very experi-enced mountaineer and had served in Aden, Borneo and Oman. Joining M Company were four Signals Troop and three medics, including Surgeon Lieutenant C. Swinhoe, giving a total of 132 all ranks. Confined to the gym-nasium, M Company were forbidden to contact their families. Moore briefed Sheridan at HQ Commando Forces and told him that although a political solution to the crisis might preclude a landing, he, Sheridan, was Landing Force Commander for the recapture of South Georgia. It would be 'quick, easy and attractive'. Sheridan wanted the Mountain and Arctic Warfare Cadre, Royal Marines, but was told to expect Mountain Troop, D Squadron.

On the same day, Captain Brian Young, who commanded the County class destroyer HMS *Antrim* in Gibraltar, was ordered by Admiral Fieldhouse 'to proceed with despatch' to Ascension with the Type-12 frigate HMS *Plymouth* (Captain David Pentreath) and the Fleet Oiler RFA *Tidespring*, and join HMS *Endurance* to form CTG 317.9 (Task Force, South Georgia). Young was nominated as Task Force Commander, an appointment that was a touch surprising – whereas Captain Barker had a wealth of polar experience, Young was a naval aviator with no practical experience of the South Atlantic or working with amphibious forces.

On 8 April, RFA *Fort Austin* arrived at Ascension. M Company arrived next day and were met by Major Jonathan Thomson RM, who commanded the SBS and had been instructed to attach 2 SBS to the Landing Force; the Company embarked on RFA *Tidespring* (Captain Shane Redmond). Meanwhile Major Delves had persuaded Captain Young and Major Sheridan that in view of current intelligence about Argentine strength on South Georgia, D Squadron should join the Task Force and embark on RFA *Fort Austin*, a suggestion that was supported by Northwood. There was actually nothing to suggest that the Argentines had reinforced South Georgia since 3 April and Sheridan had not asked for the reinforcements. The SAS then lost some credibility when some doubted Major Sheridan's expertise. They also placed a severe strain on the Royal Navy's ability to administer the soldiers. In any event, D Squadron knew they had a boss lobbying on their behalf 'at the highest political level'. More usefully, Sheridan was joined by Naval

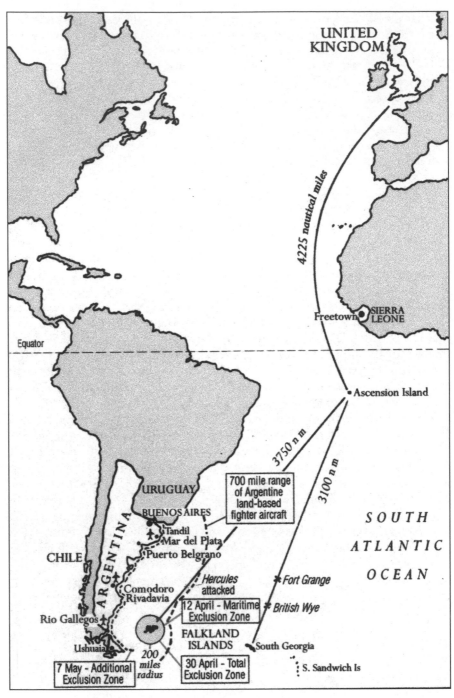

The South Atlantic

Gunfire Forward Observation Party 1 (NGFO 1) (Captain Willy McCracken) and NGFO5 (Captain Chris Brown), 148 (Meiktila) Commando Observation Battery. In overall command of this unit was Lieutenant Colonel Keith Eve RA, a highly experienced commando and parachute gunner.

Admiral Fieldhouse regarded the recapture of South Georgia, named Operation Paraquet, after the long-tailed parrot, as an important statement on intent. Initially planned by HQ 3 Commando Brigade, it was renamed Operation Paraquat, after the industrial rat poison. As far as Thompson and Commodore Clapp were concerned, the operation was an opportunity to rehearse an amphibious assault. Intelligence on the Argentines was scarce but they were thought to be platoon strength. Organization, tactics and weapon configuration were not known. If armed, the scrap metal merchants, still assumed to be at Leith, would give the Argentines about two platoons. There was no evidence of interference with the BAS field parties or two wildlife photographers, Lucinda Buxton and Anne Price.

Task Force, South Georgia, with RFA *Tidespring* carrying two 845 NAS Wessex HU 5 assault helicopters and M Company, left Ascension on the 11 April. Next day, HMS *Endurance* replenished supplies from RFA *Fort Austin* and the remainder of the Task Force left Ascension. On the 13th, since it had become apparent in the early planning that D Squadron needed to be dispersed, there followed a long and complex operation, which was hampered by weather, with Squadron HQ, 16 (Mobility) and 18 (Air) Troops cross-decked to a very crowded HMS *Antrim*, while 19 (Mountain) and 17 (Boat) Troops joined HMS *Plymouth*, an event that took all morning. Sergeant Peter Ratcliffe, of Mountain Troop:

> There was little for us to do aboard Plymouth except play cards and drink beers. Much smaller than Fort Austin, but with a larger crew, there simply wasn't room for us to run round decks, and even less space below. The hardest problem was finding a bed. Since Plymouth had no room for us, we used the petty officers' bunks while they were on watch; when they came off duty, they would tap us on the shoulder and say 'Please can I have my bunk back'. We would then wander around until each of us had found another empty bed. (Ratcliffe, *Eye of the Storm*)

On 14 April, after Task Force Georgia had had an emotional reunion with HMS *Endurance*, Captain Barker joined the planning group, bringing with him a mass of knowledge and experience about South Georgia. He soon found the traditional secrecy of the SAS frustrating and allegedly commented, 'It's not exactly as busy as Brighton Front round here, you know.' On the 15th, a No. 42 (Torpedo Bomber) Squadron Nimrod, flying from Ascension, dropped formal operational orders, dated 12 April, from Admiral Fieldhouse to Captain Young, ordering him to reoccupy South Georgia with 21 April set as D-Day. Captain Young then gave his orders to Major Sheridan:

Recapture Grytviken and Leith.

Neutralize Argentinean communications.

Capture or kill Argentinean military and arrest Argentinean civilians.

The plan was to insert SAS and SBS recce patrols north and south of Grytviken and then land M Company either as reinforcements or an assault group. No one seems to have suggested inviting the Argentines to capitulate. Major Sheridan felt operational difficulties were being underestimated by the SAS when Delves instructed that Mountain Troop (Captain John Hamilton) would be delivered by helicopter 20 miles south-east of Stromness:

1. To recce Leith, Stromness, Husvik and East Fortuna Bay for a Squadron-sized attack.

2. To find routes across Fortuna Glacier, Breakwind Ridge and Konig Glacier.

As soon as Argentine strengths and dispositions were known, the Troop would deal with the enemy in the knowledge that D Squadron could reinforce them. Barker was not convinced that Delves appreciated the risks of landing on Fortuna Glacier. The weather was unpredictable and experience counted for little. When Barker suggested that the SAS approach a few miles from north-east of Leith, Delves conceded that his plan was unwise but insisted the best place to land was on Fortuna Glacier. Virtually everyone disagreed. Major Sheridan: 'I gave him the job and could not tell him how to do it. I advised against the Fortuna route but they thought they could do it.'

In a show of the tensions emerging within the planning group of 'experts with influence' versus local knowledge, Delves consulted with two SAS in UK who had climbed Mount Everest but had never been to South Georgia. Barker certainly felt that his information was undervalued and one BAS scientist later described the SAS attitude as 'We're the SAS, we can walk on water.' With the spirit of de la Billière hovering in the background, a Royal Marines operation was fast becoming a SAS operation. The SBS plan was simple and the best option – land three patrols at Hound Bay, cross Cumberland Bay East by Gemini dropped by helicopter and find an OP on Brown Mountain to overlook Grytviken.

On 17 April, HMS *Fearless* anchored off Georgetown and when Brigadier Thompson and Commodore Clapp met with Admiral Fieldhouse on board HMS *Hermes* for a strategic conference, not only did he tell them to forget Operation Paraquet, but that 5 Infantry Brigade was also being mobilized. Thompson:

I was told that the Commando Brigade would be reinforced by a further Parachute Battalion, the 2nd Battalion, The Parachute Regiment (2

48

Para) . . . This was good news indeed. The addition of 2 Para to 3 Commando Brigade merely increased the feeling that existed already among all ranks in the Brigade that the team getting ready to go south was the First XI. Military common sense dictated that if pitched battles were to be fought against what was estimated to be a total of 10,000 Argentine soldiers in the Falklands, including a reinforced Brigade defending Stanley, at least another brigade's worth of troops should be on hand. When asked, I said that five battalions or commandos was as much as I would wish to handle in battle. So 5 Infantry Brigade with another Brigade Headquarters would be needed. This would necessitate a Divisional Headquarters. (Thompson, *No Picnic*)

When Major General Moore was appointed as Commander, Land Forces, Falkland Islands (CLFFI), CTU 317.1 (Landing Group) was sub-divided into:

CTU 317.1.1. 3 Commando Brigade.

CTU 317.1.2. 5 Infantry Brigade.

This was the first time that a Royal Marine had commanded a division since the Second World War and although there were many army officers with divisional experience, Moore's appointment reflected the amphibious nature of the campaign. Arriving from the Royal College of Defence Studies, as his deputy and spare brigade commander, was Brigadier John Waters (Gloucesters), who was described by one senior naval officer as 'a total brick' – steady, reliable and robust. Colonel Brian Pennicott RA, who had commanded 29 Commando Regiment when Moore had commanded 3 Commando Brigade, joined as Commander, Royal Artillery. Lieutenant General Sir Richard Trant, Commander, Southern District, took over as Military Deputy to Fieldhouse and took Colonel Christopher Dunphie MC from a tedious logistics appointment as his Chief-of-Staff. At the conference, the Task Force commanders presented their courses of action to Admiral Fieldhouse with Rear Admiral Woodward opting for a beachhead and airstrip on West Falkland, while Brigadier Thompson and Commodore Clapp favoured an amphibious landing on East Falkland and an advance against Stanley. The Woodward versus Thompson and Clapp camp would affect strategy throughout the war.

Rear Admiral Woodward's ships began leaving Ascension on 14 April and the Landing Group spent the next three weeks restowing men and equipment, and training. Concern for her vulnerability to an increasing Argentine Navy and Air Force activity led to the RRS *Bransfield* leaving the region the same day. This was a crushing blow to the BAS field parties who had hoped the ship would collect them.

*   *   *

Meanwhile, US Secretary of State Al Haig failed to persuade Argentina to evacuate the captured territories and warned the Junta to expect military action against South Georgia within days. The planners were unaware that an early decision by the Junta was for the defence of South Georgia to be minimal. The Cabinet authorized approval for its recapture and operational command was passed to Captain Young, by now well inside the 200-mile South Georgia Maritime Exclusion Zone imposed by Great Britain in early April.

Early on 20 April, Squadron Leader John Elliot, carrying out a Maritime Radar Recce sortie in a Victor, covered 150,000 square miles of the South Atlantic, including South Georgia, in a 14 hours and 45 minutes flight that established the record for a long-range operational recce. Later, Young sent HMS *Plymouth* and HMS *Endurance* to the south-east of Cumberland Bay while HMS *Antrim* and RFA *Tidespring* loitered off Stromness. However, a Force 11 gale 'left everyone wishing they had never left home'. Next day, HMS *Endurance* slipped into St Andrews Bay and Lieutenant Commander Ellerbeck flew ashore to warn the BAS field parties and two women of military action. They had not seen any Argentines. Peter Stark, whose knowledge was desperately needed, joined the planning team and was replaced ashore by Chief Petty Officer Tommy Scott, but his opportunity to share his knowledge disappeared when he was led away by an SAS model maker constructing a facsimile of Grytviken and Leith.

Next day at 5.30 am, 10 miles off Stromness Bay, Lieutenant Commander Ian Stanley RN, flying HMS *Antrim*'s anti-submarine warfare Wessex HAS-3, 'Humphrey', flew a weather recce, and in spite of driving sleet and a strong wind on Fortuna Glacier, Young decided to proceed with the operation at 7.00 am. Mountain Troop emplaned on 'Humphrey' and Stanley led the two Wessexes to the glacier, however deteriorating weather and ice forced him to abort. Two hours later, the helicopters again lifted off, and in spite of freezing squalls and whiteout whipping in from the Antarctic, landed Mountain Troop on Fortuna Glacier. At about 5.30 pm, four 2 SBS were landed by Wasp from HMS *Endurance* at Hound Bay. Two of them recced the area, during which one of them trod on the tail of a large sleeping elephant seal, before meeting two startled BAS in a hut where they were treated to a cup of tea. No Argentines had been seen.

As Barker and Stark had predicted, Mountain Troop found Fortuna Glacier a challenge.

I have seen some terrible weather during my service, but nothing as bad as that on South Georgia – I didn't even go to the glacier. Three times the naval pilots flew between the ships and the shore, before finally succeeding in setting down on Fortuna Glacier. Within minutes, however, the whiteout was back as gale force winds whipped the glacier. Carrying their bergens, each weighing 77lbs and dragging four pulks (sledges), each weighing 200lbs, in five hours Mountain Troop covered about half a mile – and these men were the cream of mountain warfare experts. (Ratcliffe, *Eye of the Storm*)

The Royal Marines would probably not agree on Ratcliffe's last assessment! Crevasses, frozen weapons and GPMG feed trays were blocked by spindrift and Hamilton sought sanctuary.

> With light fading fast, they tried erecting two-man Arctic tents behind an outcrop of ice to provide some shelter. But savage winds, by now gusting in excess of 100 mph, blew away one tent like a paper hand-kerchief and snapped the tent poles of the others. Five men crawled into one tent while the rest huddled for shelter under pulks in sub-zero temperatures as winds that had now reached storm force clawed at the glacier. (Ratcliffe, *Eye of the Storm*)

An attempt by Ellerbeck to land another SBS patrol at 11.00 pm at Hound Bay failed when his Wasp was almost blown into the heaving seas. Captain Barker then took his ship to within 800 yards of the shore and, in a brief window of tranquillity, launched the SBS in two Geminis. Cold after landing through heavy, freezing surf, the SBS walked through packs of seals and penguins and contacted the patrol already ashore, before settling down for the night at Dartmouth Point. Meanwhile, Squadron Leader Seymour undertook a second radar search. As dawn broke, so did the storm.

On Fortuna Glacier, the condition of Mountain Troop was deteriorating and, when, at about 7.00 am, Captain Hamilton signalled 'Unable to move. Environmental casualties imminent', the HMS *Antrim* sick bay prepared to receive cold-weather casualties. Hindered by snowstorms gusting between 70 and 80 knots, at about 8.00 am, the helicopters left.

> Three Wessex helicopters set out for the glacier, but couldn't find the SAS patrol and returned to refuel. On their second attempt, they reached the men through a fifteen minute, clear weather window at 13.30 (9am) and embarked them and their equipment. But minutes after lift-off, one of them (piloted by Lieutenant Tidd) crashed in a blinding whiteout, although miraculously, of the seven on board, only one was injured. They and the crew of the crashed aircraft were split between the two remaining helicopters, but in whiteout conditions, one (Lieutenant Andy Pulford) hit an ice ridge and also crashed, luckily without serious injury. In one of the greatest single feats of the entire war the pilot of the third helicopter, Lieutenant Commander Ian Stanley, embarked all SAS and aircrew aboard his aircraft and managed to lift off the glacier, although most of the patrol's equipment had to be abandoned with the two wrecked Wessex. With himself and fifteen men and their weapons aboard, Stanley's helicopter was seriously overloaded. Because of the weight, he was unable to hover Antrim's deck, and therefore decided to

51

crash-land instead, slamming the aircraft down with the rotors at full power to slow the descent. Ian Stanley was awarded the DSO, the only one granted to a pilot in the campaign. (Ratcliffe, *Eye of the Storm*)

The remainder of the Troop was rescued later in the day. Lieutenant Parry was Stanley's observer: 'The SAS are a strange lot. Before the events of the last two days, they barely spoke to us. Just now, all of them, including the troopers invaded the wardroom and insisted that we had a drink with them. (Winton, *Signals from the Falklands*)

Meanwhile, the SBS had crossed Sorling Valley with the intention of launching the Geminis at the foot of Nordenskjold Glacier, but found Cumberland Bay East icebound. A Wasp helicopter flew in two Geminis but their outboards failed and then when severe weather set in, the SBS were stranded for the next three days. So far, Operation Paraquat had achieved nothing: the 21 April deadline had been missed; D Squadron had ignored local knowledge resulting in the loss of two valuable helicopters; Mountain Troop had lost most of its equipment. The SAS had potentially compromised the recovery of South Georgia.

Shortly after midnight on 22 April, in a second attempt to land the SAS, Captain Young nosed HMS *Antrim* to a mile east of Grass Island to disembark the fifteen-strong Boat Troop (Captain Tim Burls) in five Geminis and establish an OP on Grass Island to overlook.

The specially silenced outboard motors had been warmed up in a tank on board Antrim only half an hour before the boats were launched. Nevertheless, once in the water, two of the engines wouldn't start. At the time, it didn't seem any great setback, since the other boats could easily tow the unpowered craft to Grass Island – or so we thought. Once Antrim had departed, however, there was a swift and astonishing change in the weather. The wind that had, until then, been little more than a breeze rose to gale force in seconds. White-capped waves smashed over the Geminis and the Troop was scattered in the Antarctic darkness all over Stromness Bay. The two towed Geminis broke loose and were swept away. The crew of one (Gemini 'Bravo') paddled with their mess tins, but even so were in danger of being swept far out to sea, when next morning, Ian Stanley picked up the signal from the emergency beacons and winched them aboard his Wessex. The others made it to Grass Island, where they set up a camouflaged OP from which to watch the settlements. (Ratcliffe, *Eye of the Storm*)

With Gemini 'Delta' missing, Boat Troop reported little activity in Stromness Bay. Shortly before midnight on 22/23 May, the nine SAS on Green Island attempted to land near Stromness but again the outboards failed. Intercepted communications between an Argentine C-130 and an Argentine submarine then suggested that the latter was close to South Georgia.

Constructed during the Second World War specifically for Pacific Ocean operations against the Japanese, the Balao-class diesel submarine *Santa Fe* (formerly USS *Catfish*) (Lieutenant Commander Hugo Bircain) was underway to South Georgia from Mar Del Plate Naval Base with eleven naval technicians and nine 1st Marine Infantry Battalion anti-tank gunners with their Bantam anti-tank missile launchers. She was commanded by Lieutenant Commander Lagos, who had been sent by Vice Admiral Lombardo in response to a request for reinforcements by Captain Trombetta. As Captain Young and Major Sheridan were preparing to land, signal intercepts suggested the submarine was a threat and although his destroyer was trained to hunt nuclear submarines, at 11.00 pm on 23 April, Young was instructed by Northwood to disperse his ships out of the South Georgia Maritime Exclusion Zone, except for HMS *Endurance,* which remained near Hound Bay. Northwood then ordered the frigate HMS *Brilliant* and nuclear submarine HMS *Conqueror* (Chris Wrexford-Brown) to join Task Force Georgia and hunt the Argentine submarine.

During the night, after Boat Troop landed near Stromness, a SAS patrol followed the track taken by Lieutenant Mills and Sergeant Leach to Harbour Point to look down on Leith. Everything was quiet. At dawn, they plotted the two marine infantry sections during stand-to. When the *Santa Fe* tied up in the morning, the patrol plotted the marine infantry occupying the trenches dug by Mills's Royal Marines. Observations by Lieutenant Commander Bircain confirmed Argentine suspicion that an attack was imminent.

The following morning, when a 1st Air Transport Group Boeing 707 flew over South Georgia searching for the Task Force, Argentina was informed that the British Rules of Engagement permitted the shooting down of any Argentine aircraft. A month earlier, a Boeing from the Group had been at Stanstead loading military stores from Royal Navy lorries. During the day, HMS *Brilliant* joined CTG 317.9 and gave Young two more Lynx helicopters.

The next morning, 25 April, *Santa Fe* left Grytviken and, at 8.55 am, was about 2 miles off Banff Point heading north-west when her radar signature was picked up by Lieutenant Commander Stanley, who was hunting for her. Bircain could not submerge because of a damaged hatch and in the first attack by the Royal Navy on an enemy submarine since April 1945, Stanley dropped two depth charges. The first damaged the aft ballast tanks and steering planes, while the second clanged off the deck into the sea. This attack was followed by a Lynx from HMS *Brilliant* dropping a Mark 46 torpedo and machine-gunning her. Still unable to submerge, *Sante Fe* reversed course and was attacked a third time with AS-12 missiles launched by the Wasps from HMS *Endurance* and *Plymouth*, the missile fired by Lieutenant Wells exploding inside the submarine's distinctive fin. Ellerbeck made a second attack, his AS-12 flying through a fibre-glass section of the fin and exploding on contact with the sea. Commander Sandford in HMS *Antrim*:

We were very anxious, professionally, to ensure this submarine stayed on the surface; we didn't want it to go to the bottom. War hadn't even been declared, but, if we could force him to beach at Grytviken, it would be game, set and match. We came out of the mist and saw South Georgia, breathtaking in all its glory, for the first time. It was sheer exhilaration. We had hoisted the battle ensign and were thundering along at 30 knots. It was a sunny Sunday morning. The Padre came up and asked what time could we have church. (Middlebrook, *Operation Corporate*)

As Bircain shepherded his battle-damaged submarine back to Grytviken, the second Lynx from HMS *Brilliant* machine-gunned her. When Bircain tied up alongside the King Edward Harbour jetty, he unloaded his only casualty, a steward who had been badly wounded while feeding ammunition to a machine gun.

Meanwhile, Major Sheridan was instructed by Northwood to complete the recapture of South Georgia. Unfortunately, M Company was 50 miles away on RFA *Tidespring* and his naval gunfire support was out of position. Available, he had D Squadron, his Tactical HQ, two 81mm mortars and the two NGFO teams. Forced to wait three hours until 1.30 pm, while Captain Young and his officers dissected the attack on the *Santa Fe*, at 1.45 pm Sheridan gave orders and set H-Hour for 10.45 pm. Lieutenant Colonel Eve controlled the fire support provided by the 4.5-inch guns of the Royal Navy. Major Sheridan:

I had about seventy-five men – about half the opposition we expected; so it was a gamble! The three Troops of about twenty men were commanded by Major Delves, Captain Nunn and Lieutenant Clive Grant RM with Surgeon Lieutenant Crispin Swinhoe RN in my tactical headquarters. I had two 81mm tubes and each man carried two high explosive bombs.

At 10.00 am, HMS *Antrim* and *Plymouth*, reacting to Captain Brown's observations from a Lynx, shelled the landing site at Hesterleten, a grassy patch 3 miles south of Grytviken. It was exactly sixty-seven years since the first aerial spotting for a naval bombardment at Gallipoli in 1915. At 10.30 am Lieutenant Commander Stanley led the two HMS *Brilliant* Lynxes, with eighteen D Squadron on board and, after being forced to orbit the north end of Cumberland Bay until the bombardment finished, landed the troops at 10.45 am. Stanley's landing was unconventional – a commando assault from a geriatric ASW Wessex and two of the latest ASW Lynx flown by pilots untrained for amphibious warfare.

The traditional controlled rush from 'Humphrey' was prevented by the Anti-Submarine Warfare equipment, so the SAS squeezed out one at a time and waited while the loadmaster, Petty Officer Aircrewman David Fitzgerald, handed down their equipment. Over the next forty-five minutes, the Composite Company Group and the SBS, commanded by Captain Nunn, landed with the two mortars and started registering possible targets on Brown Ridge, much to the annoyance of Major Delves who wanted his intended route mortared. Major Sheridan landed and, annoyed about this disagreement, issued orders that 'Everyone must sort themselves out and get on with it.' The two destroyers meanwhile shifted their fire onto the track to Grytviken. When Sheridan then discovered that D Squadron had not seized Brown Mountain because the summit might be an Argentine position, he instructed the SAS to lead the advance to contact. A 'main position' that was machine-gunned turned out to be a cairn and a wooden spar masquerading as an antenna. Two Milan missiles destroyed another 'position' near Penguin River – several seals, relaxing on the banks.

When Captain Brown asked HMS *Antrim* to stand off the entrance of Cumberland Bay East to give close fire support – remembering what had happened to the *Guerric* – Young reluctantly agreed. By 1.00 pm, Sheridan was overlooking The Hummocks and the wrecked Argentine Puma. Two white flags were flying on the BAS buildings and an Argentine flag on a flagpole. Cancelling the third landing by the SBS and Mobility Troop at Bore Valley Pass, and to demonstrate future resistance was pointless, he radioed Young for the two warships to show themselves. As HMS *Antrim* entered Cumberland Bay with Young inviting the Argentines to surrender, a marine infantry signaller replied, 'No shoot! No shoot!' and mentioned a wounded man without legs. The post-Operation Paraquet report later stated: 'Consider NGS effect devastating and surrender indicated before fire plan completed. Demoralisation by NGS absolute.'

More white flags appeared from the Argentine position at King Edward Point and about fifteen minutes later the defenders filed out of Discovery House and paraded underneath their flag. Sheridan ordered the advance to halt, but Delves' radio had apparently become defective and he and three SAS advanced past the crashed Puma and into Grytviken. 'There was then a mad dash to see who could be the first in to raise the flag. It was actually Mountain Troop.' (Ratcliffe, *Eye of the Storm*)

Lieutenant Bircain then radioed HMS *Antrim* that the garrison was surrendering, they had wounded, one seriously, and that the helicopter pad and the track from Grytviken were mined. This information was passed to Delves, whose radio corrected itself. Frustrated by the SAS initiative, Sheridan left Mountain Troop on Brown Mountain and, after ordering Nunn's Troop to advance into Grytviken, landed in an HMS *Endurance* Wasp on King Edward Point a few minutes after Delves had raised the Union flag. At about 1.15 pm, Sheridan accepted the surrender of Grytviken from Lieutenant Commander Lagos. At 1.30 pm, Captain Young radioed London: 'Be pleased to inform Her Majesty that the White Ensign flies alongside the Union Flag at Grytviken, South Georgia. God save the Queen.'

Without an exchange of fire, 129 captured sailors and marines were captured. The wounded Argentine steward, whose leg had already been amputated by *Santa Fe*'s surgeon, was flown on to RFA *Tidespring* for further treatment. One British soldier had slightly twisted his ankle. Bircain and Lagos signed the formal surrender on HMS *Antrim,* although Leith was still occupied. When Major Sheridan asked Bircain to persuade Astiz to agree terms, Bircain replied, 'Astiz says he will not surrender. He will fight to the death.'

In a show of force, at 2.15 pm, Captain Pentreath took HMS *Plymouth* and HMS *Endurance* with Sheridan, 2 SBS and Air Troop to Leith. At about 6.45 pm, while Barker and Pentreath were discussing their options, Surgeon Lieutenant Neil Munro, HMS *Antrim*'s doctor, took a call from Astiz offering to surrender. Barker told Astiz to muster next morning. After dark, Air Troop landed on Harbour Point and met 2 SBS and Boat Troop. Next morning, the British watched the scrap metal workers assemble and marines parade. HMS *Plymouth*'s helicopter then collected Astiz to sign for the Argentine surrender of Leith. Lockett:

> We returned to HMS Endurance with eight Argentine prisoners, the remainder came on board later. Their arrival caused consternation as members of the Troop were forced to leave Number One hold . . . and to add insult to injury then had to guard the prisoners who didn't appreciate their new lodgings. The two SAS who were sharing the ship's one man cell complained so bitterly about moving, they were allowed to stay. The refugees from Number One Hold moved upstairs to join the comparative luxury, thereby increasing the number in the First Lieutenant's cabin to ten. (Lockett, *HMS Endurance*)

Soon after the surrender, the three SAS from Gemini 'Delta' strolled into Leith. Their outboard swamped, they had paddled ashore and sheltered in a cave at Cape Saunders, the last landfall before the vast grey mass of the South Atlantic; much to their credit they had not activated their rescue beacons, in case it compromised the British presence to the enemy. A disappointed M Company arrived the following day to garrison South Georgia and guard the 151 naval and marine prisoners and thirty-nine civilians held on HMS *Endurance*. Leith was littered with improvised devices and the prisoners agreed to dismantle them and mark out minefields.

The same day, three 2nd Air Brigade Canberras, led by a Boeing 707 guide, left Rio Grande Naval Air Base to attack Grytvikven but were prevented from doing so by bad weather. When the prisoners transferred to *Tidespring*, which was to return to Ascension, Astiz was kept separately on HMS *Antrim*. Argentina claimed that South Georgia had been subjected to a naval blockade and that a submarine landing provisions, mail and medical supplies had been attacked. Subjected to a sustained assault by armed helicopters, the small naval force had held out gallantly. The recapture of South Georgia was greeted with some relief in London with Prime Minister Thatcher fobbing off questions with: 'Just rejoice at the news and congratulate our forces and the marines. Rejoice.'

On 27 April, the *Santa Fe* was moved from the jetty with the help of several Argentine sailors guarded by Royal Marines with instructions to ensure that the boat was not scuttled. As the submarine moved, it suddenly lurched, and under orders from an Argentine officer, Petty Officer Felix Artuso operated a switch, which had been listed as forbidden, however he ignored warnings and was shot dead. A court of inquiry chaired by Captain Young and attended by Bircain cleared the Royal Marine. The *Santa Fe* was immobilized by explosives and, after slowly flooding, she settled with only her fin showing above the freezing water. Artuso was buried with full honours in the cemetery at Grytviken. Unfortunately, his widow is unable to visit his grave.

On 2 May, RFA *Tidespring* left with the prisoners and the BAS for Ascension and was met by a Joint Forward Interrogation Team. The prisoners were repatriated to Argentina via Montevideo on 14 May. When Lieutenant Mills and his detachment arrived at Ascension Island, they had the satisfaction of guarding Astiz on the RFA *Tidespring*. Because of the allegations against him, Astiz was detained at the Royal Military Police barracks in Chichester until 10 June when he was repatriated. On 25 May, Mills and his detachment rejoined HMS *Endurance* at Grytviken.

Commanded by Brigadier Matthew Wilson OBE MC, with Brigade HQ at Aldershot, 5 Infantry Brigade was converted from a mixed Regular/Territorial Army home defence formation, in January 1982, into an all-Regular one with the Leading Parachute Battalion Group role, through 2 Para. It also took over several 6th Field Force units including 3 Para and 1st Battalion, 7th (Duke of Edinburgh's Own) Gurkha Rifles (1/7th Gurkha Rifles). The Brigade lacked artillery. On 2 April, at a 10 Field Workshops parade, Major Brendan Lambe, the Chief-of-Staff, learnt that the Brigade was earmarked for the South Atlantic.

At a HQ United Kingdom Land Forces (HQ UKLF) conference at Wilton to juggle deployments for Northern Ireland and the Falklands, while maintaining its NATO Priority One commitment, to replace 3 Para, Major General Sir Desmond Langley KCVO MBE, General Officer Commanding, London District, offered one of his three Guards battalions, namely: 1st Welsh Guards, which had just handed over as Spearhead Battalion; 2nd Scots Guards, which was on Public Duties and providing a military presence in London to the Irish Republican threat; and 2nd Grenadier Guards, which had recently returned from West Germany and was mechanized warfare-minded. The controversy surrounding the deployment of the Guards was largely media inspired, and by others who felt that a 1 Infantry Brigade battalion, in particular 1st Queens Own Highlanders, should be earmarked for the Falklands and that the Guards should fill in the empty slots in the unlikely event of hostilities against the Warsaw Pact.

On 4 April, 1st Welsh Guards (Lieutenant Colonel Johnny Rickett) brought

5 Infantry Brigade back to three battalions. Meanwhile, Lieutenant Colonel Hubert 'H' Jones, the 2 Para Commanding Officer, was returning from skiing in France and was determined that his Battalion should join the Task Force, and not go to Belize as planned. Using his knowledge of unit tasking from a staff posting at HQ UKLF, he suggested his Battalion should join the Task Force so that 3 Commando Brigade would have two identically organized parachute battalions as opposed to an airborne and an infantry battalion. Coincidentally, Brigadier Thompson, on his way to Ascension, had calculated that he needed another battalion. When, on 15 April, 2 Para was placed on three days' notice, Jones formed a battle group consisting of:

2 Para.

29 (Corunna) Field Battery from 4th Field Regiment RA.

Two Blowpipe detachments, 32nd Guided Weapon Regiment RA.

2 Troop, 9 Parachute Squadron RE.

Advanced Detachment of three Scout helicopters from 656 Squadron AAC.

Parachute Casualty Clearing Troop, 16 Field Ambulance RAMC.

When it seemed that protocol would ensure that 1/7th Gurkha Rifles (Lieutenant Colonel David Morgan MBE) would not be deployed, the King of Nepal gave permission for it to join the Task Force. Told about this, Prime Minister Thatcher is said to have commented, 'Only one [Gurkha] battalion?' Argentina then accused Nepal of supplying mercenaries to the British. It so happened that the UN Ad Hoc Committee was considering a draft definition that a mercenary would:

Not be a member of the regular armed forces of a country.

Be paid more than a member of the regular forces of that country.

Not be bound by treaties between two countries.

The Gurkhas had been part of the British Army since 1816 and although Argentina was instructed to quit her accusations, she continued to accuse the Gurkhas of barbaric warfare, of going into battle high on drugs, of eating their prisoners and using their kukris to chop up the enemy. Anxious Argentine conscripts compared their machete with the kukri.

On 7 April, when the Ministry of Defence reduced the notice to move from the standard seven days to three days, 5 Infantry Brigade cancelled Easter block leave. Two days later, as SS *Canberra* sailed with 40 and 42 Commando and 3 Para sailed from Southampton, Brigadier Wilson held a conference. Lieutenant Colonel Rickett:

5 Infantry Brigade's role was never spelt out. We were just another brigade sent south probably with the intention of using it as a garrison in due course. However, it must have been obvious to anyone from the start that given the number of Argentine forces on the islands, one brigade would not have been enough to have won back control on its own. Our understanding was that we were going to fight from the outset and we carried out countless appreciations during the voyage south on what would be our initial tasks. Why spend an awful lot of money and time on exercising the brigade in South Wales prior to actual notice to move unless it wasn't going to be used to fight?

When 2 Para was given notice to move on 15 April, this again left 5 Infantry Brigade a battalion short and London District was instructed to transfer one of the two remaining Guards battalions. Major General Langley selected 2nd Scots Guards (Lieutenant Colonel Michael Scott). Converting his Battalion into a wartime establishment, Scott instructed Major The Hon. Richard Bethell MBE, who, after about twelve years with the SAS, was commanding Headquarters Company, to reform Recce Platoon from the Drums Platoon and volunteers. Scott:

Interestingly, our role did, of course, change as the days went on, really up to the very last minute when it was ultimately decided that the Commando Brigade could not do it all entirely by themselves. However, I am convinced that, initially, we were going to be the garrison when the war was won. We would be there for a 4-month tour when everyone else had left for home and glory. But what a perfect role for Foot Guards – guarding things. You can almost see the Staff thinking how clever they had been. So it probably didn't matter that we weren't brilliantly trained, straight off the gravel of the Forecourt of Buckingham Palace. At the last conference down at Aldershot, Field Marshal Bramall came to give us words of encouragement and I asked him point-blank whether we were to be the garrison and, of course, wily old bird, he denied it. Naturally, I made absolutely no mention of my concerns to the Battalion. As far as they were concerned, they were going to get stuck in.

The HQ and Signals Squadron (Major Mike Forge) had the mammoth task of converting the Brigade from the Larkspur range of radios to Clansman, no mean task when some equipment never arrived, in particular drums of cables that enabled users to operate remotely from their radios. Stationed in Aldershot was 4th Field Regiment (Lieutenant Colonel Tony Holt). Had it not been for the persistence of Holt, 5 Infantry Brigade might well have sailed south without artillery. Equipped with 105mm light guns and with 29 (Corunna) Field Battery supporting 2 Para and 88 (Arracan) Field Battery having just returned from Belize, only 97 (Lawson's Company) Battery was available for deployment. To make up a shortfall of forward observation officers for the three battalions, Major Roger Gwyn, from 49th Field Regiment, and Major Fallon, of 132 (The Bengal Rocket Troop) Field Battery, Support Regiment, Royal Artillery at the School of Artillery, formed a third battery commander and two parties. Neither had ever worked with 5 Infantry Brigade. On 22 April, Holt formed 41 Battery of two Forward Observation Officer teams to support 3 Para. That an artillery regiment went to war with a hotchpotch of organizations must be unusual, as was its inability to train with 5 Infantry Brigade. Holt pointedly mentions that the Brigade was 'unfamiliar with 4 Field Regiment but with regimental gunnery as a whole, having no precedent for a gunner Tac HQ and its services within the headquarters . . . The failure to train (with the infantry) was a disadvantage on operations. (4th Field Regiment post-operation report)

9 Parachute Squadron, Royal Engineers was commanded by Major Chris Davies RE. 2 Troop with 2 Para was replaced by 20th Field Squadron (Captain David Foxley) as 4 Troop. For light helicopters, 5 Infantry Brigade was usually supported by 658 Squadron, which was below strength. When Lieutenant Colonel Jones asked for an advanced detachment from 656 Squadron – the 1 Infantry Brigade Air Squadron, with whom his Battalion had established a relationship on exercise in Kenya in 1981 – three Scouts were absorbed into 3 Commando Brigade Air Squadron. The remainder of 656 Squadron and its Air Maintenance Group were transferred to 5 Infantry Brigade at the expense of 658 Squadron.

Major Lambe encountered entrenched Ministry of Defence bureaucracy when he was offered reversible white/brown winter warfare waterproofs until he reminded the Ministry that with summer approaching in Europe, the United Kingdom Mobile Force would not require their winter warfare clothing for several months. He acquired 4,000 pairs of overboots and consequently no one in 5 Infantry Brigade suffered trench foot, which is more than can be said of 3 Commando Brigade. The Brigade also unearthed several M2 .50 Brownings and 112,000 rounds of Korean War vintage ammunition and then persuaded several Royal Armoured Corps gunnery instructors from the Bovington armoured training school to train the battalions en route to Ascension. When 1/7th Gurkha Rifles converted its MT Platoon to a Heavy Machine Gun Platoon, the drivers were delighted until they realized that the machine guns and ammunition had to be carried. Lambe doubled the number of GPMGs per platoon, which allowed the eight-man infantry sections to break down into two 'fire teams' each built around one machine gun.

With 5 Infantry Brigade hosting strange units, on the instructions of Lieutenant General Trant, Colonel Dunphie organized the two-week Exercise Welsh Falcon at Sennybridge. The first week honed basic military skills and the second week included a simulated landing with real timings from 'ships' (three Welsh barracks) using 'landing' craft (lorries) and helicopters (RAF Pumas). 1st Green Howards provided the enemy and casualties were practised, but not prisoners. Unfortunately, an unexpected heat wave wrecked conditioning. The Scots Guards found the exercise very useful. Tac HQ, let alone Main, had not exercised for several years. Lieutenant Colonel Scott:

> We did not even have a current set of Standard Operating Procedures. Major Iain Mackay-Dick, the Second-in-Command wrote them overnight. This is no reflection on my predecessor, Johnny Clavering, who was a superb and much loved CO, and the Battalion was brilliant under him in Northern Ireland where the scene was entirely different. I do not think the Battalion had done a set piece night attack on its feet for years. Apart from the armoured version in Germany, my own experience was as a lieutenant in Kenya in 1963! But perhaps that is nothing to be proud of.

Shortly before the traditional final attack, Brigadier Wilson was told by HQ UKLF that his Brigade was to embark for the South Atlantic on 12 May. Exercise Welsh Falcon finished on 29 April with one observer commenting, 'They've a hell of a way to go', implying the Brigade was not yet ready for combat. If correct, this was hardly surprising – a home defence formation cobbled together with several units new to its order of battle and the first time that Brigadier Wilson had exercised the Brigade. Few British brigades in modern times have been so badly prepared. Blame should not be levelled at Wilson. Returning to barracks, the Brigade received lorries filled with supplies as peacetime constraints on stores issues were lifted on receipt of a telephone call. Several hundred bergens were purchased from Blacks of Reading. Jones then flew to Ascension Island to wait for the Royal Marines while his Battalion embarked on the P&O North Sea ferry MV *Norland*, which sailed from Portsmouth on 26 April.

Chapter Six

Approach to Battle
8 to 20 May

The three weeks that 3 Commando Brigade stayed at Ascension was a hectic period of restowage of equipment, command post exercises, landings and fishing competitions. The occasional shark's fin deterred swimming from the ships. Tests confirmed that the Scorpions and Scimitars of the Blues and Royals could provide close fire support from landing craft. Fitness training allowed some to climb Green Mountain. On 24 April, the appearance of the Argentine merchantman, *Rio de Plata*, caused a mild panic when it was thought she was carrying human torpedoes, prompting Operation Awkward. While some ships carved out a racecourse during the day, in others, naval sentries patrolled upper decks and seamen in whalers circled their ship dropping small depth-charges. Divers inspected the hull. At night, the anchorage was abandoned. Censorship of mail was introduced for a short time when classified documents drifted ashore.

The most important activity was planning the landings, a process that began when Admiral Fieldhouse arrived at Ascension on 17 April. Current intelligence was desperately short on detail, largely because most came from signals intelligence sources and the classification prevented wide distribution.

While Peru mediated, Great Britain imposed the TEZ on 30 April and next day opened its offensive when, in Operation Black Buck I, 44 Squadron Vulcan XM 607 piloted by Flight Lieutenant Martin Withers left Ascension and approached Stanley at sea level for 250 miles, to avoid the Argentine Skyguard radar. Withers:

> When we thought we had 40 miles to run, I took control and 'popped up' to 10,000 feet to start the run in. Bob (Flight Lieutenant Wright on radar) found his aiming point on the headland, and stuck with it, as 'offsets' he looked for did not show up clearly. Approaching the release point, all was calm and steady. We could see lights on the airfield through broken cloud, a couple of miles away. We shed about ten tons of bombs and climbed for home. (South Atlantic Medal Association)

After a flight of 15 hours 45 minutes and 23-air-to-air refuelling 635,000lb of fuel from 18 Victor tanker sorties, XM 607 landed at Wideawake. Twenty-two bombs had been dropped on Military Air Base, Stanley, but only one hit the runway and it was quickly repaired by 601 Combat Engineer Group. However, the raid had strategic value in that Stanley was denied to Argentine fighters, and squadrons of Mirages were deployed from southern Atlantic coast bases to defend the north. Sea Harriers attacking Stanley and Goose Green prompted the BBC correspondent Brian Hanrahan to announce to the world, 'I counted them all out. I counted them all in,' effectively a breach of operational security, suggesting that Argentine air defence had failed. 44 Squadron RAF carried out three more raids and anti-radar missile attacks, which led to Argentines switching off their radars

"CARAMBA PABLO... IF THATS THE SIZE OF THEIR PLANES... JUST HOW BIG IS THEIR AIRCRAFT CARRIER"

when an aircraft was seen approaching within 40 miles, which allowed the Harriers to get underneath Argentine air defence. (XM 607 is the only Vulcan to have dropped bombs in war and took part in the three Black Buck missions. It is now the gate guardian at RAF Waddington.)

In their intelligence assessments, the Argentines had calculated that 'distraction' forces would appear before any landings. After Brigadier Thompson and Commodore Clapp had selected Advanced Forces tasking, several G Squadron SAS patrols were helicoptered ashore. Captain Aldwin Wight (Welsh Guards) was instructed to establish an OP overlooking Stanley and monitor helicopter activity, because it was strongly suspected the Argentines were heavily reliant on the Huey UH-1H Iroquois of 1st Combat Aviation Battalion, and CH-47 Chinooks of 7th Counter Insurgency Squadron. SBS patrols recced Berkeley Sound, San Salvador Water and San Carlos Water. Coastal reconnaissance tends to be more risky than inland operations; patrols were typically a two-night approach march, three days in the target area and two days to the pick-up point.

At sea, next day, HMS *Conqueror* torpedoed the 6-inch cruiser *General Belgrano* (former USS *Phoenix*, launched 1938), with the loss of 321 sailors, when it presented a threat to the Task Force and launched a controversy that still simmers. Two days later, two Super Etendards ambushed HMS *Sheffield* and she later became the first ship to be lost to enemy action since 1945. Exploding Exocet fuel killed twenty men and wounded twenty-four. During the afternoon, Sea Harrier pilot Lieutenant Nick Taylor RN was killed by ground fire while attacking Military Air Base Goose Green. Later in the day, warships bombarded Stanley Common, the first of many. Lieutenant Colonel David Comini, who commanded 3rd Infantry Regiment covering the southern beaches, reported that the combination of the bombardments, the need to remain alert, the jamming of communications and sixty days in foxholes adversely affected morale. Inadequate food, the difficulty of keeping weapons maintained and inadequate clothing did not help. In spite of the 50x1,000lb, 153x500lb, nine cluster bomb attacks and 1,200 naval shells impacting in their area around the airfield, 25th Infantry Regiment and a School of Military Aviation security company suffered only three killed and eighteen wounded. 601 Commando Company investigated reports of landings. During the morning of 9 May, two 800 Naval Air Squadron Sea Harriers launched from HMS *Hermes* were prevented by low cloud from bombing Military Air Base Stanley and were diverted to attack the trawler *Narwal,* which had been identified several days earlier tailing the Carrier Battle Group. The crippled trawler was seized by a SBS section, which found evidence of intelligence gathering. A prize crew boarded her but she sank next day while being towed by HMS *Glasgow* to South Georgia.

On 25 April, the cargo ship *Rio Carcarana* reached Stanley after breaching the MEZ. On 10 May, some of her cargo was transferred to the coaster *Isla de Los Estados,* which left to resupply Fox Bay and Goose Green, but soon after midnight she was sunk by HMS *Alacrity,* which had scouted into Falkland Sound. The consequence of this incident was that Lieutenant Colonel Italo Piaggi, who commanded 12th Infantry Regiment at Goose Green, was instructed to establish an OP on Fanning Head, which overlooks the northern approaches of the Sound and the narrows into San Carlos Water, and to report any British activity. Summoning First Lieutenant Carlos Esteban, who commanded C Company, 25th Infantry Regiment, he outlined the sinking of the *Isla de Los Estados* and told him to man the OP from Port San Carlos. Esteban selected sixty men, most from Second Lieutenant Reyes's 1 Platoon, which had landed on 2 April. The force was named *Equipo Combat Guemes* (Combat Team Eagle). Esteban had arrived in Goose Green on 3 April and, this being his first independent command in a combat zone, he was determined to make a success of it. As the settlement developed into an important garrison and air base, he imposed a strict regime to ensure that the 114 Falkland Islanders in the settlement complied with his administration, leading to him being described by one islander as a 'real soldier'.

By now the British intelligence assessment was that Argentina had decided to defend the Falklands in order to drag Great Britain to the negotiating table.

The Argentine Navy had lost the sea battle and both air forces were operating from distances – the Task Force limited by the two carriers and Argentina by the distance from the mainland. Argentine jets were unable to use Stanley because of the unsuitability and vulnerability of the runway. While the Argentines could air refuel and keep their aircraft flying longer, the Sea Harriers had limited loiter time over the battlefield. Argentina considered strengthening West Falkland with 4 Airborne Brigade, however the Air Force did not have enough aircraft for a mass drop and could not guarantee a lengthy period of air superiority.

On 12 May, Major General Moore plus his Headquarters and 5 Infantry Brigade sailed from Southampton, after an impressive fanfare, on the Cunard liner *Queen Elizabeth II*, designated as a 'Landing Platform Luxury (Large)' – only to stop off the Isle of Wight to repair a boiler. After the exercise in Wales, the Brigade and its attachments set about preparing for the passage south, however, when it became evident that only the *Queen Elizabeth II*, the two RoRo ferries, *Baltic Ferry* and *Nordic Ferry*, and *Atlantic Causeway* were available to transport the 4,000 men and their equipment and supplies, the force was reduced by about 1,000. Northwood also issued its six-phase Operation Order for Operation Sutton, which was the recovery of the Falkland Islands:

> Carrier Battle Group to maintain blockade within the TEZ.
>
> Carrier Battle Group to conduct Special Forces recces and direct operations prior to landing.
>
> 3 Commando Brigade and Commodore Amphibious Warfare to conduct main amphibious landings.
>
> Land operations by 3 Commando Brigade prior to arrival of Major General Moore and 5 Infantry Brigade.
>
> Major General Moore to establish HQ LFFI on HMS *Fearless* and landing of 5 Infantry Brigade.
>
> Repossession of the Falklands by Landing Forces supported by naval forces.

Moore then issued his strategic directive to Brigadier Thompson:

> You are to secure a bridgehead on East Falkland, into which reinforcements can be landed, in which an airstrip can be established and from which operations to repossess the Falklands can be achieved.
>
> You are to push forward from the bridgehead area, so far as the maintenance of security allows, to gain information, to establish moral and physical domination over the enemy and to forward the ultimate objective of repossession.

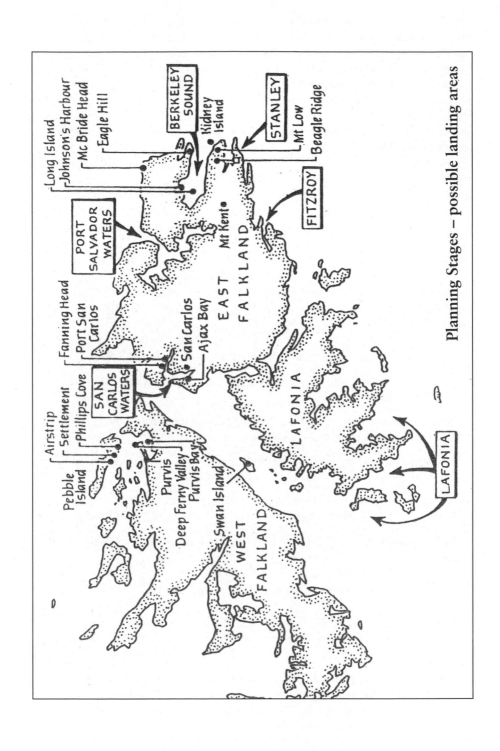

Planning Stages – possible landing areas

You will retain operational control of all forces in the Falklands until I establish my Headquarters in the area. It is my intention to do this, aboard Fearless, as early as practicable after the landing. I expect this to be approximately on D+7.

It is then my intention to land 5 Infantry Brigade into the beachhead and to develop operations for the complete repossession of the Falkland Islands.

Admiral Fieldhouse had recommended to the Chiefs-of-Staff that the landings were to be made between 19 May and 3 June. En route to Ascension Island, Commodore Clapp and Brigadier Thompson identified three possible beaches:

Steveley Bay on West Falkland, which was a long distance from Stanley.

San Carlos on East Falkland.

Berkeley Sound, a few miles to the north of Stanley.

At the 17 April meeting at Ascension, Brigadier Thompson preferred the San Carlos option, while Rear Admiral Woodward suggested a West Falkland beachhead for the purpose of building an airstrip for C-130 Hercules and F-4 Phantom aircraft. When Admiral Fieldhouse indicated that he wanted to land on East Falkland and then attack Stanley, the San Carlos Water option was selected.

Named after a Spanish ship which entered it in 1768, San Carlos Water provided a sheltered anchorage which could be defended by the Royal Navy closing the entrances to Falkland Sound against enemy surface and submarine attacks. Since the beaches lay 50 miles over very rough ground from Stanley, Argentine counter-attacks would be limited by the number of assault helicopters. Finally, the high ground surrounding San Carlos Water would prevent Argentine aircraft from using their feared Exocet at the ships in the anchorage. Interestingly, in the 1930s, a British naval task force had recommended using San Carlos Water as the best landing site in the Falklands, but there were disadvantages: the surrounding hills would restrict rapid acquisition of low-flying aircraft threats until they emerged over the high ground, and therefore a naval air defence screen would be needed to the west; the narrowness of the anchorage gave ships little manoeuvring room.

In the Wardroom lounge aboard HMS *Fearless* on 13 May, Brigadier Thompson issued his orders. A terrain brief given by Major Southby-Tailyour was followed by Captain Viv Rowe RM, Thompson's Intelligence Officer, giving the intelligence assessment:

9 Infantry Brigade with two infantry units at Port Howard and Fox Bay. Morale was reportedly low.

3 Infantry Brigade with Task Force Mercedes at Goose Green.

10 Infantry Brigade defended Stanley.

An Army helicopter base, which gave the Argentines a battalion-sized lift capability with gunship escort, was on Mount Kent.

A strategic reserve of unknown composition was thought to be around Darwin.

Air intelligence was less clear with several fundamental questions still to be resolved, such as loiter time of mainland-based aircraft over the Falkland Islands without refuelling. The indications were that they could not.

Thompson stepped up to the dais:

> Mission. To land at Port San Carlos, San Carlos and Ajax Bay to establish a beachhead for mounting offensive operations leading to the recapture of the Falkland Islands . . . Design for battle. A silent night attack by landing craft with the object of securing all high ground by first light. The individual Tasks for each Commanding Officer were then given by me, addressing each Commanding Officer by name and prefacing him orders by the phrase 'I want you to . . . (Thompson, *No Picnic*)

The Royal Marines, as befits their role would lead the three-phase assault:

First wave

40 Commando. To land on the shingly Blue Beach at San Carlos.

45 Commando. To land on the sandy Red Beach at Ajax Bay and secure Sussex Mountain. The frozen sheep refrigeration plant would be the Brigade Maintenance Area (BMA).

Second wave

2 Para. To pass through 45 Commando and secure Sussex Mountain.

3 Para. To land at Green Beach and secure Port San Carlos.

Floating Reserve

42 Commando. On Canberra. To land after the air defence and artillery were ashore and then patrol in the general area of Teal Inlet.

Diversions

D Squadron. To convince Task Force Mercedes that a regiment – 'noise, firepower but no close engagement' – was attacking.

Operation Tornado. Activities and spoof signals along the south coast of East Falkland to suggest a landing in order to keep Army Group, Puerto Argentino occupied.

London was to act as if nothing was happening.

If the opportunity for exploitation arose to advance on Stanley, without waiting for 5 Infantry Brigade, it was to be made. The Brigade Chief-of-Staff, Major John Chester, then issued co-ordinating instructions. Thompson:

> He pointed out that the timings of H and L hour, and indeed the date would follow in the signal known as OPGEN Mike, to be sent by the Commodore when the firm details were known. He reminded them that in an amphibious operation, H-hour was the time that the first wave of landing craft would beach and L-hour was the touchdown time for the first wave of helicopters. Easy to remember, he said, because, illogically, H-hour was for landing craft and L-hour for helicopters, which drew a laugh. (Thompson, *No Picnic*)

Two Commodore Amphibious Warfare officers gave a complex landing plan, which drew one delegate to comment, 'Although I am sure they understood it, I had the general impression no one had a clue what they were talking about.'

After Major Gerry Wells-Cole, the Deputy Chief-of-Staff, had explained the logistic plan that ranged from resupply to burial of the dead, Thompson said that the killed and wounded were to be left, otherwise the impetus of the assault would be lost. So explicit were the orders that there were no questions. Thompson concluded, 'May I remind you that this will be no picnic. Good luck and stay flexible. See you on the beach.' He was one of the few to know that if the landings were to take place, the first opportunity would be between 16 and 25 May.

Next day, 601 Commando Company was flown to Port San Carlos by 601 Combat Aviation Battalion to check out the area ready for the insertion of Combat Team Eagle. No evidence of British activity being found, the OP was established on Fanning Head, a tussock-covered feature rising steeply to 768 feet. Arriving at Port San Carlos, Lieutenant Esteban immediately sent Second Lieutenant Reyes with a platoon of twenty men, an 81mm mortar and a 105mm recoilless rifle to the OP. However, their arrival had been identified by British signals intelligence and was then confirmed by a SBS patrol near Port San Carlos. The following day, when the Brigade Intelligence Section analysed the deployment of '*EC Guemes*', it was initially greeted with alarm and then assumed to be related to 12th Infantry Regiment at Goose Green. It quickly became known as the 'Fanning Head Mob'. A member of the Intelligence staff:

> The immediate concern was that no one knew what the initials 'EC' stood for in the signals until Captain Rod Bell solved the problem. 'That's easy. EC stands for "Equipo Combate" which translates into "Combat Team".' Half the problem was solved; we assumed there was a company strength unit on Fanning Head. Shortly afterwards, we received another report that the EC Guemes patrol base was at Port San Carlos. Another assumption could now be made that the unit probably had infantry support weapons to control the neck of San Carlos Water.

Captain Bell was the Adjutant, HQ and Signal Squadron, 3 Commando Brigade. Born in Costa Rica to a British UN official, he spoke better Spanish than English when he joined the Royal Marines. Brigadier Thompson:

> The reports of the strategic reserve north of Darwin worried me more. If they got an inkling of the landing, even on the night of D-day, and moved fast, they could get up on to Sussex Mountain, which overlooked the whole of the eastern arm of San Carlos Water, containing the major anchorages and three of the four beaches. Clearly, Sussex Mountain must be seized as soon as possible, so I changed the order of landing. (Thompson, *No Picnic*)

First wave

2 Para. To land on Blue Beach One at San Carlos.

40 Commando. To land on Blue Beach Two at San Carlos.

Second wave

45 Commando. To land on Red Beach at Ajax Bay, as briefed.

3 Para. To land at Green Beach and secure Port San Carlos, as briefed.

Floating Reserve

42 Commando. On *Canberra*.

Fanning Head

3 SBS. To neutralize the 'Fanning Head Mob'.

Diversions

Goose Green – no change.

Operation Tornado – no change.

London – no change.

Some Royal Marines were less than impressed that their traditional amphibious first-ashore role had been usurped by the Parachute Regiment, in particular the ubiquitous late arrivals, 2 Para.

Intelligence staff at Northwood had detected increased Argentine air activity on Pebble Island after a Sea Harrier pilot returning from a Goose Green sortie was said to have registered an Elta radar emission on his avionics. Pebble Island lies to the north of West Falkland. The two principal features are Marble Mountain Peak at the eastern tip of the island and First Mountain, which overlooks the settlement. The terrain is low, particularly to the east where there are several lakes and large ponds. In 1982, its approximately twenty-five inhabitants were involved in shepherding 25,000 sheep. A track ran west from the settlement to a croft on the lower southern slopes of Marble Mountain Peak. A Royal Engineers briefing map dated April 1982 listed two airstrips, a grass runway to the east of the settlement and the other on the sheltered southern beaches of Elephant Bay.

On 24 April, when Captain Gaffoglio, the senior Argentine naval officer on the Falklands, had authorized the establishment of Naval Air Station Calderon on Pebble Island, ground crews despatched in a Coastguard Skyvan requisitioned the sheep-shearing shed, the guesthouse and an unoccupied house. The Argentine Air Force, however, were unimpressed by the remoteness of the island and deployed its Pucara ground-attack operations to Goose Green. The Navy pilots, complaining of the poor state of the Goose Green runway, declined to join the Air Force. Three days later, 1 Platoon, H Company, 3rd Marine Infantry Battalion (Lieutenant Ricardo Marega), arrived as Combat Team Marega, with four 75mm recoilless rifles. Insisting that settlement life should not be disrupted, Marega imposed a curfew between 9.30pm and 7.30am and commandeered all Land Rovers. The requisitioned Falkland Islands Company coaster *Forrest* arrived two days later with heavy equipment, ammunition and aviation fuel, and was then followed by four 1st Naval Air Squadron T-34C Mentor trainers (Lieutenant Commander Batlori). Although slow, the Mentor can operate from grass strips and is a steady bomb, rocket and 7.62mm machine-gun weapon platform. Naval Air Station Calderon was declared operational, with the first patrols investigating reports of British helicopters. When Military Air Base Condor was raided on 1 May, the six Pucaras were diverted to Pebble Island and Air Force South and Naval Air Command agreed to use Naval Air Station Calderon as an alternative. However, the weather turned nasty and when the runway became waterlogged on 5 May,

Batlori declared it non-operational to fixed-wing operations. The dejected Pucara pilots, separated from the relative civilization of Goose Green, were now confined to an inhospitable, windswept island. A heavy overnight frost on 7 May allowed the Mentors to patrol.

Since the island was only nineteen minutes' flying time from San Carlos Water and was a threat to the anchorage, Rear Admiral Woodward had asked the SAS on 10 May if D Squadron could neutralize the threat, ideally by the 15th. The SAS liaison officer replied that some preparatory work was needed.

'How long do you have in mind?' asked Woodward.

'Three weeks.'

'No good,' replied Woodward. He knew that SAS operations depend on meticulous planning, but Pebble Island needed to be dealt with quickly. 'What about five days?' he asked as optimistically as he could, later recalling that the SAS officer looked at him with one of those 'Who does this bloke think we are?' looks.

'I'm sorry, Admiral, that may not be possible. We need three weeks to get it right.'

'I'm afraid it's got to be in five days. It's 15 May or never.' Helicopters were not available after that date. When the SAS agreed, the stage was set for a traditional SAS raid straight out of the Second World War. Captain Hamilton was placed in command with all D Squadron at his disposal with three insertion options:

Helicopter direct to the east of Pebble Island – rejected in case the Elta picked up the aircraft.

Gemini – rejected because D Squadron had lost confidence in the outboard engines at South Georgia. Also difficult to hide the Geminis.

Klepper canoes – accepted for a recce team, followed by the assault force being delivered by helicopter.

The plan was to drop an eight-man Boat Troop patrol commanded by Captain Burls with four Kleppers at Purvis Bay during the night of 10/11 May. They would then paddle to Deep Ferny Valley and find a lay-up position from which to watch Pebble Island before crossing the 2km stretch of sea. The raid was planned for 2.30 am on 15 May, however bad weather delayed the recce patrol deployment until the following night. The recce radio operator:

If the sea was too rough to paddle safely, we had an alternative drop-off point. The sea was very rough, so we used this one. We dismantled the canoes and manpacked them over to Deep Ferny Valley. The original plan was to establish the observation post on the same night we arrived. However, by the time we had dismantled the canoes, humped them over to Deep Ferny Valley, with our own personal kit needed two journeys. We were quickly running out of darkness. So, we all lay up in

Deep Fern Valley during the daylight of the 12th and having not established observation onto Pebble Island, we were a day behind. But, as it worked out, it didn't matter. On the night 12/13 May, we all moved to an OP position from which we could observe the east end of Pebble Island, in particular we watched the area around Phillips Cove, which was our intended point. (Ramsey, *SAS: The Soldier's Story*)

The only enemy seen was a 7th Counter Insurgency Squadron CH-47, which flew at low level over them. When the vicious winter squalls then gave way to an almost serene evening, the patrol returned to their canoes in Deep Fern Valley. The radio operator:

We assembled the canoes and paddled across to Phillips Cove. There was a tide race of between 10 and 15kph running through the straits and, in fact of this, Admiral Woodward had advocated using Geminis. We used the canoes without his knowledge and were not affected by the tide race because we avoided the straits and crossed well to the south. Once we had beached in Phillips Cove, we split into two four-man patrols. One patrol stayed in Phillips Cove to dismantle and hide the canoes. The other patrol moved along to have a look at the airfield and settlement. When we got past the trig point, we began to have difficulty with communications back to the patrol in Phillips Cove. We decided to split the patrol. I and one other returned to the trig point to act as a relay for our Troop Commander, and the others who went to set up an OP closer to the settlement. At first light, the OP was in position and they saw eleven aircraft dotted around the airfield. (Ramsey, *SAS: The Soldier's Story*)

Caching their bergens, the pair recced the airfield. The SAS radio operator:

I had no comms with the patrol in Phillips Cove, and I could hear the OP patrol but they were not receiving me. The OP patrol, believing they had no comms with anybody, decided that they would move back to Phillips Cove in daylight to enable them to report to HMS Hermes, remembering, of course, that if we didn't get the Squadron in on that night, there would be a three to four hour delay because of helicopter unavailability. Because the terrain was so bare, the OP patrol had to leave their heavy kit in the OP position and they had to crawl out of the area on their stomachs. Anyway, eventually they made their way back to Phillips Cove, then we returned from the trig point to join them. We had great difficulty in establishing comms with the Hermes because we were using a directional aerial and we didn't know where the Hermes was. The other problem we had was that there were a number of other stations sending long messages from other parts of the island back to Hermes. (Ramsey, *SAS: The Soldier's Story*)

Eventually, radio operators on HMS *Hermes* picked up:

Squadron attack tonight.

LS GR (in code) . . . . Phillips Cove.

11 aircraft at GR (in code).

Probably real.

No further details on enemy or radar.

Confirm ETA.

'Probably real' insinuated that the patrol believed the aircraft to be real, not decoys. Major Delves could hardly believe his luck and after radioing the message 'ETA Squadron 22.30 hrs', he instructed Captain Hamilton to raid Pebble Island. Rear Admiral Woodward detached HMS *Hermes,* the destroyer HMS *Glamorgan* and the frigate HMS *Broadsword* from the Carrier Battle Group to steam at best speed for Pebble Island. The plan was for Mobility Troop to raid the airfield, while Air Troop cleared the settlement of Argentines. Mountain Troop was in reserve with the 60mm mortar detachment. Accompanying the raid was Captain Brown's NGFO5 from 148 (Meiktila) Commando Forward Observation Battery, giving a total of forty-five men. H-Hour would be signalled when HMS *Glamorgan* opened fire. At about 8 pm, the heavily-laden soldiers filed across the gently swaying flight deck of HMS *Hermes* to four darkened Sea Kings, however the combination of their weight and the fuel load was too much for safe flying and forty-five precious minutes were spent burning off the fuel. Sergeant Ratcliffe was with Mobility Troop:

> At last we lifted off, flying low level across the sea in blackout conditions, occasionally gaining fleeting glimpses of the sea below . . . To be part of the largest SAS raid since the Second World War was something that I would not have missed for anything, especially when I remembered that I should have been back in a Birmingham drill hall completing my two-year stint as an instructor. (Ratcliffe, *Eye of the Storm*)

At 11.45 pm on 14 May, an hour behind schedule, the helicopters swung into Phillips Cove and after being briefed by Burls, Hamilton briefed the men that speed to cover the 7,000m was more important than tactics. They set off in single file at a fast pace toward the trig point, where Air Troop diverted to the settlement. However, as always happens when a fast pace is set, Mobility Troop, at the rear, lost touch with Mountain Troop and Hamilton was forced to change the plan with Mountain Troop attacking, while Mobility Troop went into reserve with the 60mm mortar. Air Troop was to provide fire support. Bang on time, HMS *Glamorgan* bombarded the western edge of the runway, the direction from which the Argentines were expected to launch a counter-attack. Lieutenant Marega ordered stand-to. An Argentine marine recorded: 'There was a heavy bombardment which was probably the softening up for a major amphibious assault on the airfield. Fires were seen burning at the far end of the runway. A patrol then reported that fuel had caught fire and two aircraft were on fire.'

When Lieutenant Marega thought that an aircraft had caught fire and despatched a fire-fighting piquet, the SAS saw the Argentines with their extinguishers, and opened fire. The marines, not unnaturally, retreated into cover from where they returned fire. Mountain Troop then advanced and, reaching the western edge of the airstrip, became involved in a brief firefight with two Argentines in a bunker. 'David' was with Air Troop:

> Then our own mortar opened up, lighting the whole place up like it was a bright daylight. The mortar man was having a lot of trouble. Every time he fired the bloody thing, the whack of the pie was kicking the base plate further into the ground. There was virtually no enemy fire on us, so the boys got stuck into the planes. They split into seven two-man teams. It was a bloody big trip and they had a lot of ground to cover. It's not as if the planes were all parked in a neat row. They were all over the strip. And all the time the boys were running against the clock. Five planes were destroyed using the explosive charges that they had with them. The Pucara was the tallest of the aircraft. As they approached each plane, one bloke would give the other a leg up on to the wing. Once up, he then leaned down and hauled the other one up to join him. The Skyvan was not a problem. The Mentors were very small, and with one great leap, the guys got themselves on the wings. (Ramsey, *SAS: The Soldier's Story*)

Mountain Troop vandalized other aircraft by ripped out wiring and then shot them up to puncture fuel lines, followed by a grenade. Just as Trooper Armstrong was placing explosive on the last aircraft, Marega ordered that a charge halfway along the runway be detonated. The explosion caught the SAS as they were withdrawing, concussing a corporal, who had also been injured on Fortuna Glacier. When another corporal was accidentally shot by a colleague, his patrol commander administered first aid. Under desultory fire from Combat Team Marega, who were still puzzled as to what was happening, the SAS withdrew fifteen minutes behind schedule, at 3.45 am and were on board HMS *Hermes* at about 5.30 am, just as dawn was lining the horizon. Naval medical assistants treated the casualties, one of whom recalled that 'we were looked after admirably.' Next day, air photos showed that the raid had accounted for one Pucara with serious damage, three with minor damage, another had shrapnel damage, while the sixth could still fly. One Mentor was destroyed, another was badly damaged, and the third had minor damage. The Coastguard Skyvan was destroyed. The raid removed part of the air threat to the landings, although there were still aircraft at Goose Green. Marega's men remained in their positions expecting an enemy attack at first light:

> When none came, a patrol despatched to clear the area found live and spent 7.62mm and 5.56mm rounds, confirming the enemy had indeed landed. While I requested an air recce of the island, which was refused, Air Force and Coastguard personnel checked the damage. While we were warned to receive reinforcements, the Air Force were told to prepare to evacuate Pebble Island.

The following midday, when a CH-47 carrying fifty Army commandos landed, several Air Force and Coastguard pilots and ground crew made 'an undignified rush' to the helicopter. Convinced that the islanders were implicated, the settlement was searched but only an illegal CB was found. Nevertheless, the islanders were detained in the house of Griff Evans, the settlement manager, where they remained for the next month in difficult conditions and still suspected of passing messages to British warships. When the Argentines cut down the CB antenna, a clandestine one was rigged. On 17 May, a heliborne commando section carried out an inconclusive search of the island. Life then developed into boredom and occasional excitement as Sea Harriers bombed the useless runway. On 28 May, a Twin Otter evacuated sick and wounded Air Force and then on 1 June, two Naval Air Command Sea Kings, specially adapted with additional fuel tanks, flew from Comodoro Rivadavia and evacuated several naval personnel, but no marines.

Meanwhile Major Ian Crooks, 22 SAS Second-in-Command, had arrived with B Squadron on Ascension with a proposal to raid Argentine naval and air bases in Patagonia, as part of the strategy to weaken Argentine air capability. Sympathetic to Great Britain and Chile, the province was a security nightmare for Argentine counter-intelligence officers. British intelligence often relied on Argentine agents to report military aircraft activity, several using telephone boxes outside military air bases to call London with details of sortie departures, giving the Task Force about thirty minutes warning. Principal targets were the Exocet-carrying Super Etendards operating from Military Air Base Rio Grande, which had sunk HMS *Sheffield*, and the Hotel Santa Cruz, which provided accommodation for Mirage, Skyhawk fighter and KC-130 tanker pilots at the Rio Gallegos Military Air Base. One ambitious plan was to land two Hercules at night, 'Go in with a big brass neck, like the Israelis at Entebbe', and shoot up dispersal areas with a troop of 'Pink Panther' heavily armed Land Rovers.

Six B Squadron parachuted into the sea near the Carrier Battle Group and then on the night of 19/20 May, left HMS *Invincible* in a 846 NAS Sea King, specially adapted for long-range flight and piloted by Lieutenant Richard Hutchings. Their target was Rio Grande. Sergeant Ratcliffe had been tasked to look after the aircrew but was withdrawn by Rear Admiral Woodward to lighten the payload. Several years later, he met Hutchings:

> Having arrived safely and undetected over the landing point in Argentina, after an epic flight by anyone's standards, he called the troop commander forward to tell him that they had reached their destination. The officer, however, had refused to believe him and demanded that they fly around for another fix. The Sea King pilot emphasized the point by indicating their position on the map. Yet the troop commander had again refused to believe it. (Ratcliffe, *Eye of the Storm*)

When Hutchings landed, that was the last he saw of the SAS. Instructed to ditch the helicopter, he landed on a beach near Agua Fresco, about 11 miles west of Punta Arenas, near the border with Chile. He later told Ratcliffe: 'Despite punching holes in it, the aircraft would simply not sink, so we left it half-submerged.' (Ratcliffe, *Eye of the Storm*)

The Argentine 11 Mountain Infantry Brigade deployed a twenty-strong commando unit to support counter-intelligence officers searching for the infiltrators; however the SAS and three aircrew slipped through the net and surrendered to the Chilean authorities. The failure of the raid and its media attention embarrassed the SAS, and the troop commander and his sergeant left soon afterwards. Sergeant Ratcliffe:

> For a long time I thought [SAS] Selection might be the toughest course in the world, but it doesn't tell you everything you need to know about a man. That patrol blew it. Instead of heading for the enemy airfield, they hightailed it to Chile. They didn't even bother to look at the target and judge how difficult it would be to achieve a successful mission, deciding to call the operation off without taking a single pace toward the danger area. To my mind, the damage to the Regiment was much more severe than the loss of its members. (Ratcliffe, *Eye of the Storm*)

"I DON'T CARE WHAT BRIAN JAMES SAID ABOUT US IN THE 'DAILY MAIL' ~ NO WAY AM I JUMPING OUT OF A PLANE WITH THIS LOT!"

Meanwhile, SBS patrols were checking the five assault beaches at Ajax Bay, Bonners Bay, San Carlos and Port San Carlos. A patrol had its hide disturbed when a helicopter hovered overhead and another had the unusual experience of a helicopter landing close by so that the pilot could relieve himself. In readiness to lay on naval gunfire, on 16 May, NGFO 2 (Captain Willie McCracken) landed from HMS *Alacrity* in Ajax Bay and set off for Sussex Mountain. Tailend Charlie, Bombardier 'Jacko' Jackson, thought that they were being followed, called for all-round defence and watched as a mumbling figure appeared over the ridge, and then another until it grew into a file of penguins. Next night, a SBS patrol landed from HMS *Brilliant* at Middle Bay and confirmed that Combat Team Eagle was occupying Fanning Hill. By the 18th, all patrols were withdrawn, except one covering Ajax Bay. G Squadron monitored activity at Port Howard and Fox Bay. In a decision that would have far-reaching consequences for the Argentines, 1st and 2nd Sections, 601 Commando Company, landed to help the two garrisons find enemy patrols strongly believed to be operating on West Falkland.

While 3 Commando Brigade was finalizing its plans, during the evening of 18 May, a signal arrived on Brigadier Thompson's desk from Major General Moore that necessitated a third change in plans. By any stretch of the imagination, this decision was extremely late and a nuisance. Lieutenant Colonel Vaux of 42 Commando:

> While the Task Force wallowed through steadily increasing seas, CINCFLEET's staff in Northwood suddenly signalled that 40 Commando and 3 Para must transfer from Canberra into the two amphibious ships, Fearless and Intrepid. Although no-one disputed our vulnerability, the order caused consternation among the embarked staff. They had evaluated the options during planning at Ascension, and had concluded that the risk of landing most of the Brigade from Canberra had to be taken. An LPD has 'overload' capacity to carry up to 700 troops for very limited periods. Both units now comprised almost that number, but both Fearless and Intrepid were overloaded already. The lines of communication smouldered in the heat of last-minute argument. (Vaux, *March to the South Atlantic*)

On the same day, the BBC again helped Argentine intelligence with another habitual breach of security when it announced that 'the troopships have now joined the main force of warships.' No decision could be made on crossdecking until the weather improved. Commodore Clapp:

> We delayed making any further decision on cross-decking until dawn on the 19th, when, by sheer chance, Julian and I looked over the side and unbelievingly, were able to say to each other, 'It's on!' I could tell Northwood that the sea was quiet enough to use landing craft and that we go ahead as best as we could. (Clapp and Southby-Tailyor, *Amphibious Assault Falklands*)

In broad daylight in the middle of the South Atlantic, 40 Commando and 3 Para slid down ropes into wallowing landing craft that rose and fell in the long swell and were ferried to the two LPDs, HMS *Fearless* and HMS *Intrepid* respectively. An Army NCO on HMS *Fearless* described conditions:

> With 1,400 troops on board, life promised to be uncomfortable. Several 40 Commando SNCOs were stretched out in the Mess. I checked my kit for the final time, stowing my seaman's bag with clothing I would not need in a corner of the Tank Deck. There were no more reports of enemy activity in the San Carlos area. Everything seemed quiet as we awaited political approval to enter the TEZ and then, at 22.14 hours, Captain Larken announced an alteration of course and Action Stations was broadcast. No undressing for bed now and no reasonable meals in prospect, just Action Messing of a bread roll and a mug of soup. Galley cookers were extinguished, just as they had been in Nelson's time. Our Mess was deserted of its Navy members, all of whom had closed up, and a First Aid party headed by the Ship's Paymaster prepared the space for the reception of casualties. Those Embarked Force not at work carried out their final preparations and turned in.

Tragedy struck in the afternoon when a 846 NAS Sea King, on its last lift transferring twenty-seven men from HMS *Hermes* to HMS *Intrepid*, smashed into the sea, killing eighteen SAS from D and G Squadrons, the one RAF fatality of the war, and a Royal Marine loadmaster. One of the SAS killed was Corporal O'Connor, formerly Welsh Guards, the Stinger 'expert'.

When Northwood signalled that no political agreement had been reached with Argentina and the landings were to proceed, Brigadier Thompson ordered Captain Mike Samuelson, his Operations Officer, to signal 3 Commando Brigade with 'OPGEN Mike' giving D-Day as Friday, 21 May and H-Hour as 2.30 am local time. Next day, the Carrier Battle Group joined forces with the Landing Force for the first time. An Army NCO of Brigade HQ on HMS *Fearless* recalled:

> 20 May (D-1) broke with grey skies and the prospect of bad weather. The wind droned and whistled through the rigging and stanchions. Our convoy was grouped in a close air defence formation with warships, LPDs, LSLs and merchant ships pushing through the deep waves. Ahead, Canberra nonchalantly cast aside the seas while Fearless lurched, bows lifting high and then crashing down, throwing aside great sheets of water, the buried stern straining to lift as the bows bit deep into the next waves. "Goffers" [waves] smashed into the bridge and the Oerlikon gunners on the bridge wings sheltered as salt water poured into scuppers and streamed aft. Watch keepers in foul-weather gear scanned the distant horizons. Bright signal lamps flashed from distant ships shrouded in mist; it would have reminded Atlantic convoy veterans of their youth.

Breakfast was an unappetising mug of meat and beans with a roll, hardly meriting the wait in the queue. There was no obvious enemy reaction to our proximity to the Falkland Islands. Would we get away with it? There was nothing to do except monitor enemy activity. Radio silence had been imposed anyway and dissemination of information was impossible. FTV showed Benny Hill and 'Saturday Night Fever'. I dozed on my bunk. Lunch was bread and soup, another unappetising gruel, and I was getting hungry. It would be good to eat compo rations when we were ashore. All enemy submarines had been accounted for except one, which was said to be in the TEZ. Night fell and the gale blew itself out. Nothing further to report in the Intelligence Section, so I returned to my refuge, my bunk, and went to sleep.

Chapter Seven

The Landings and Beachhead
21 May to 3 June

After dark on 20 May, the Landing Group crept into Falkland Sound and lurked outside the narrows guarding San Carlos Water – after seven weeks and 6,700 miles at sea.

While the Royal Marines and paras filed into landing craft, the heroic Wessex 'Humphrey', which had been fitted with a thermal image camera, was sent to recce Fanning Head. Captain Hugh McManners, of NGFO 1, later wrote: 'The sweep along Fanning Head showed clusters of bright glow worms in pairs and in all about fifteen. There were several of these groups to the north of the Head and a group actually at the top of the feature. We had found our heavy weapons company.' (McManners, *Falklands Commando*)

At about 1.00 am, after being briefed from the video on HMS *Antrim*, 3 SBS, joined by the Spanish-speaking Captain Bell with a battery-driven loud-speaker, climbed into a Sea King but, as had happened prior to the Pebble Island raid, it could not take off because it was overloaded. After the fatal ditching of the helicopter the day before, no chances were being taken and after slightly chaotic reorganization, four lifts later, at 1.40 am, the thirty-five strong force was crouched 3,000m south-east of Fanning Head. On Fanning Head, Second Lieutenant Reyes was woken by a sentry reporting helicopters and ordered the 105mm Recoilless Rifle to be fired speculatively into the narrows. There was no reaction, nevertheless he radioed Lieutenant Esteban at Port San Carlos about the reports and then dozed. 1,000 yards short of Fanning Head, McManners radioed HMS *Antrim* for ranging shots:

> It takes some time to get a ship ready to fire and she hit a snag with one of her twin turreted 4.5-inch guns. The rest of the patrol had never had anything to do with ship's guns (or any other big guns) and became impatient. We had a small mortar with us and the mortarman was very keen to use it (lightening his load in the process). Unfortunately im-patience got the better of prudence and about twenty bombs were loosed off in rapid succession to absolutely no effect whatever. Their impact

could not even be heard let alone observed. When the ship reported ready, I ordered her to fire and the twin salvoes were bang on target. Nick had some trouble with communications but by standing about 15-metres away from the patrol, we were able to get through. I had ordered the patrol to lie down when the ship reported to me that the round had been fired and were on their way. We could see the faint flash of Antrim's guns out in the Sound as the remainder of the twenty salvoes were fired. Then followed silence, then an eerie whistling sound and a brief silence. I had ordered airburst (which explodes 500-feet above ground) and as it arrived, it turned night into day. The crash of the explosions came second later. I felt a bit like Merlin unleashing the forces of darkness. (McManners, *Falklands Commando*)

The bombardment persuaded the Argentines to concentrate on survival. In intervals between the shelling, and unable to contact Esteban, Reyes abandoned the OP and led his men into Partridge Valley in the lee of Fanning Head. McManners:

The night was very cold and we rapidly chilled when we stopped. The heavy work of moving caused perspiration which made us colder still when we stopped again. We got to our ridge position, moving very care-fully with snipers out in front. Initially there was no sign, but then silhouetted against the spur on north Fanning Head we could see six or seven men digging in. I opened up well beyond them (800m) and crept the fire backwards to them. (Not only did I not want it to hit them, but I did not want it to hit us!) The bright red figures on the imager ran around, lay down or just stood still when the shells came down. Then a strange thing was seen – a line of two parallel files of men marched over the spur and lined up on our side, appearing to decide what to do next. We decided that this was the time to try and get the loudspeaker into action. It was very windy, blowing from the enemy towards us. A stream of tracker was aimed using an Armalite with a night scope and then we opened up using one GPMG with a burst of tracer over their heads. The loudspeaker, that had been so carefully devised, packed and carried, failed to work. Rod Bell tried something about 'Royal Marine desperadoes' but even if they heard, it must have seemed something like the voice of an angry god, after the shelling and machine-gun fire. (McManners, *Falklands Commando*)

Four Argentines surrendered but a larger party led by Reyes sneaked back to Fanning Head and opened up with a MAG, confounding the theory that the Argentines would not fight. The Squadron Sergeant Major growled, 'This, gentlemen, is not the way to do business.' When the SBS then tried to shepherd the Argentines back to the main group and failed, they shot to kill. McManners:

Rod's sympathy showed through at this stage and he became very angry. He shouted out that he was going to try and stop them from all being killed and that he was going down the hill to talk to them. I urged that a section with a radio be sent to protect him. So, in this highly tricky situation, we let our humanitarian instincts get the better of military logic and we split our forces in the darkness. (McManners, *Falklands Commando*)

As dawn approached, Bell had failed to find any of the enemy. McManners:

With great reluctance, we decided that as they were not surrendering, we would have to shoot to kill. We were beginning to feel like butchers, but the knowledge of what was going to happen later and the thought of what might happen if they got to their mortars, guns and anti-tanks guns tempers my remorse. (McManners, *Falklands Commando*)

The Argentines then began to surrender and signalled the destruction of the 'Fannning Head Mob'. Four wounded were evacuated to a ship. Those who escaped spent the next three weeks in the San Carlos area. Reyes and a small group were captured by a 40 Commando patrol on 8 June, suffering from trench feet, frostbite and hunger after surviving on cormorants and sheep.

Meanwhile, on HMS *Fearless*, 40 Commando had embarked into landing craft, relieved after the long passage but tempered by the possibility of an opposed landing. The ballast pump mechanism, which controlled water levels on the tank deck, failed, leaving the LCUs high and dry. Captain Larken ordered the dock gate to be lowered and the sea poured in. 'Retract the LCUs' and the four LCUs went astern into the darkness of Falkland Sound.

Norland had not replied to the OPGEN Mike signal and it later emerged that the ship's decoder was broken. As signal transmissions were liable to intercept, HMS *Broadsword* was despatched with a copy of the signal. As she approached *Norland*, a lamp flashed: 'Do you know something we do not?' *Broadsword*'s yeoman replied: 'Yes, stand by for line!' When the signal was taken to Lieutenant Colonel Jones, he told his officers that the Battalion had four hours to occupy Sussex Mountain and prepare defensive positions for a possible counter-attack from Goose Green. Within eleven minutes of HMS *Intrepid* anchoring off Fanning Head, her four Tango LCUs set off to find *Norland* but, with radio silence in force, Colour Sergeant Davies on Tango One was forced to identify each ship with a shielded signal lamp. When he eventually went alongside, there were no mooring points and he had to manoeuvre the landing craft constantly to keep it alongside. The paras discovered clambering into a landing craft at night and in battle conditions an entirely different prospect from filing into a wide-bellied Hercules on a well-lit airfield. Private Mike Curtis was a GPMG gunner in 5 Platoon, B Company:

At Ascension Island we'd all practised disembarking from the ship into landing craft, but that had been in calm seas during daylight. Now, in the South Atlantic in the early hours of the morning, the waves were horrendous. Nearing the door, I saw flashes of automatic weapons in the distance and could make out the shape of the hills, lit intermittently by explosions. Fanning Head was being attacked by naval gunfire. Suddenly the landing craft was about 6-feet beneath me and pitching up and down in the swell. The guy despatching us, a Marine, held my webbing and I handed down my bergen. The trick was to wait until the landing craft rose up on a swell and then jump. In front on me, 'Cautious Bob' mistimed and fell more than 10-feet. I timed it right but still landed with a whack. Picking up my bergen and GPMG, I scrambled into stick formation and waited. We were all so knackered, Jimmy crashed out and started snoring. (Curtis, CQB)

The Battalion loading plan collapsed when B Company, which was in reserve to the first wave, embarked instead of A Company, C Company and Tactical Headquarters. To add to the confusion, a soldier crushed his pelvis when he fell in between the landing craft and the ship's side. Lieutenant Colonel Jones reshuffled his landing plan. The confusion induced delays and the inevitable inter-Service rivalry. Major Mike Ryan, an experienced para, commanded Headquarters Company: 'The main lack was no beach assault training. RMs running the LCUs were ill-disciplined and noisy, shouting and lights.' (Adkin, *Goose Green*)

Not for the only time in the campaign would 2 Para offer advice on military and naval matters about which they knew little. Jammed in landing craft, some paras cocked their weapons and the stillness of the night was shattered by an accidental discharge. Major Southby-Tailyour, who would guide the landing craft to the beaches, ever the gentleman, acknowledged their inexperience in amphibious warfare. The leading assault companies were meant to cross the Line of Departure at 1.45 am but the confusion on *Norland* had caused anxieties at Brigade HQ. Brigadier Thompson:

I was asked if I wanted to let 40 Commando go ahead in their craft without waiting for 2 Para, but rejected the suggestion because Major Southby-Tailyour was to lead 40 Commando's and 2 Para's craft in one formation into San Carlos Water down the western side before splitting into two groups a few hundred metres or so east of Ajax Bay and leading 2 Para's craft into Blue Beach Two, before ordering 40 Commando's craft to Blue Beach One. Any tinkering with the plan at this stage, in the dark and the need to keep radio chatter to the minimum, might bring all manner of unforeseen chaos in its train. (Thompson, *No Picnic*)

Thompson slipped the timetable by an hour. Two LCUs each carried a Scorpion and Scimitar for close fire support and the third had a Combat Engineer Tractor.

When, at last, LCU Tango Four, coxswained by Sergeant Garwood, motored alongside *Norland* to collect B Company, Southby-Tailyour found an anxious Lieutenant Colonel Jones on LCU Tango One and commented that if they left without Garwood and steamed at full speed, they would only be forty minutes behind H-Hour. Jones was quick to reply, 'Let's go!' Southby-Tailyour instructed Garwood to follow at best speed. Assembling the seven LCUs and eight LCVPs into a line astern, he ordered them to switch off their navigation lights. Sixty-five minutes behind schedule, the column motored into San Carlos Water and hugged the shadows of the shoreline for the 5-mile approach to the assault beaches. HMS *Plymouth* 'rode shotgun' to provide immediate naval gunfire support. Nearing Bonners Bay, Major Southby-Tailyour identified the wooden jetty below San Carlos on Blue Beach Two and ordered the 40 Commando landing craft to heave to while he guided 2 Para to Blue Beach One. Shaking into line abreast assault formation, while HMS *Intrepid*'s landing craft approached the beach, Southby-Tailyour searched for the tiny red spot indicating the beach centre marked by the SBS. He had arranged torch signals in morse – Alpha – Beach safe; Bravo – Be careful; Charlie – Enemy on beach; no light – Cock up or enemy on beach. Nothing. In a quandary because he implicitly trusted the SBS, he returned to the bridge and found that Lieutenant Colonel Jones had issued 'Prepare to beach'. Jones told him that although the SBS had not been seen, neither had any enemy and therefore he intended to land. Colour Sergeant Davies tried to beach twice but each time was thwarted by rocks. Meanwhile, Sergeant Garwood had arrived with B Company in Tango Four. Running in close to the waterline, at 3.30 am the ramps of the LCUs splashed into the water about 5m from the beach. Private Curtis:

> I looked up and saw the stars, thousands and thousands of them glittering in the black velvet, and occasionally a shooting star, all so bright and low that it seemed possible to reach out and touch them. Imagine finding beauty on a night like that. The adrenalin was pumping so hard that I didn't feel the cold. Huddled together, no-one said a word until the ramp went down and water came pouring around our feet. 'Troops out!' No-one moved. 'Troops out!' I couldn't believe it. We were still 10 yards from the beach and they wanted us to wade ashore with all our kit. The landing craft was supposed to drop us on the beach, but there was no way these guys were going in that far; they were shitting themselves and just wanted out. 'Troops out! Troops out!' Reluctantly we moved. I jumped and sank up to my waist in water that was so cold it took my breath away. 'Little Mouse' Walker almost drowned. If he had fallen over, the weight of his bergen would take him straight under. (Curtis, *CQB*)

On the landing craft with Major Chris Keeble, the Second-in-Command, no one moved on the order 'Troops Out!' until a sergeant major shouted 'Go!' to which someone in the well-deck cynically commented 'This is supposed to be an invasion.' Sergeant Barry Norman was Jones's bodyguard: 'We stepped off on what we thought was beach. We went straight nearly up to the waist in water, which, being the South Atlantic was quite cold. I was not amused. Even at this stage, people thought it was like an exercise: We're wet, wet, wet when we are on exercise.' (Adkin, *Goose Green*)

As the paras splashed ashore, they heard from the darkness, 'Who the hell are you?'

'2 Para. Who are you?' replied Major John Crosland, the B Company Commander.

'3 SBS. God, we thought you were coming on the 24th.'

'Par for the course,' replied Crosland, already thoroughly dissatisfied with the arrangements, although the encounter did explain the absence of torch signals. The landing order was still chaotic and so Jones broke radio silence and encouraged his company commanders to sort the Battalion out.

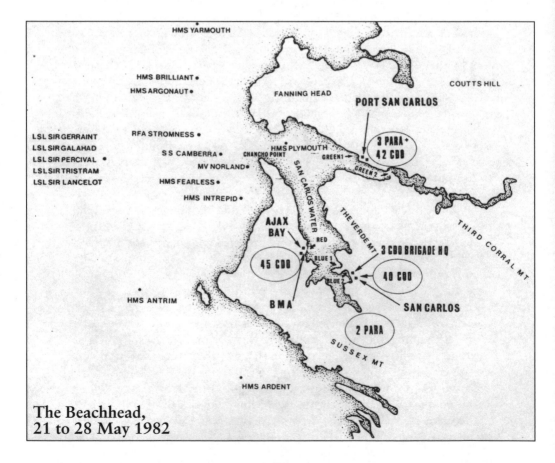

The Beachhead,
21 to 28 May 1982

Eventually, C Company led off and, in a long snake, began the eight-kilometre 'tab' up the 900-foot-high Sussex Mountain. The 43 Battery, 32nd Guided Weapons Regiment RA section carrying the cumbersome Blowpipe launchers had particular difficulty in keeping up. The planned figure of one kilometre per hour at night for heavily laden men was greeted with disbelief at Northwood – they should be faster.

40 Commando and the CVR(T)s landed on Blue Beach Two a few minutes later and dug in around San Carlos and on the western slopes of Verde Ridge. C Company raised the Union flag at San Carlos settlement. At about 5.30 am, two hours behind schedule, 45 Commando and 3 Para were collected from RFA *Stromness* and HMS *Intrepid* respectively. Landing on Red Beach, the Royal Marines cleared the refrigeration plant and 'yomped' up the northern slopes of Sussex Mountain in depth to 2 Para. 3 Para (Lieutenant Colonel Hew Pike) in four LCUs, two of them carrying Scorpions and Scimitars from 4 Troop, The Blues and Royals approached the unexplored Green Beaches near Port San Carlos. Wary of mines, Major Southby-Tailyour navigated to Green Beach One, however as the landing craft fanned into assault formation, Foxtrot Four (Colour Sergeant Brian Johnston) grounded in about 3 feet of water 20 yards short of the beach. Seeing that the beach had been secured by a SBS patrol and believing it nonsense to ask men to wade ashore at the beginning of a winter campaign, Southby-Tailyour signalled the four LCVPs to cross-deck the companies from the grounded LCU. The other LCUs then found a dry landing across a stony beach about 500 yards to the west. Inevitably, the grounding induced the customary rivalry between the paras and landing-craft crews to erupt, not all entirely polite. A clear dawn had sprung from the east and all was peaceful. It was about 7.30 am.

Meanwhile, two 1 (Fighter) Squadron Harriers, guided by Captain Wight's G Squadron patrol, bombed the 601 Combat Aviation Battalion helicopter hide on Mount Kent and damaged a CH-47 Chinook, a Puma and a UH-IH Iroquios, undermining the Argentine ability to move troops quickly. Wight was awarded the MC for this patrol. At about 9.00 am, Flight Lieutenant Jeff Glover was shot down in a lone Harrier attack on Port Howard. Badly wounded, he was hauled from the sea and spent the rest of the war as a prisoner in Argentina.

Hearing the shelling, but not small-arms fire, from Fanning Head, First Lieutenant Esteban attempted to contact Reyes for nearly three hours, but without success. When no runner appeared and having no idea what was happening, he ordered Grey Alert at 6.30 am. As dawn crept over the hills to the east, he deployed observers to overlook the misty surface of San Carlos Water. At about 7.10 am, sentries reported that they could see a large white ship and three warships in Falkland Sound. Climbing to high ground, Esteban saw warships and, ten minutes later, a landing craft leaving the side of the white ship. As the mist dispersed, he saw more landing craft full of troops 'travelling in all directions'. Radioing 12th Infantry Regiment that landings were underway, he requested air support. At 7.30 am, Esteban received reports of Royal Marines, in fact 3 Para, advancing from the west and concluded that resistance was futile. Closing down his signals link to Goose Green, he and his forty-two men collected essential items and withdrew to high ground east of the settlement in order to avoid being cut off.

In Port San Carlos, the settlement manager, Alan Miller, had heard the shelling of Fanning Head and, when dawn broke, he climbed a hill and saw *Canberra* in the distance with landing craft approaching Sand Bay. Miller, his son and a friend alerted the settlement and were running to Green Beach waving a white handkerchief when they were surprised by Major David Collett standing up from behind a gorse bush and bidding him, 'Ah! Good morning, Mr Miller!' Collet commanded A Company. Much of the information about Port San Carlos had been prepared by Brigade Intelligence after Mrs Miller had been debriefed in UK. Miller warned Collett that there were Argentines to the east of Port San Carlos.

In response to Esteban's request for air support, the 1st Naval Attack Squadron was tasked by Naval Air Command to investigate the reports. Shortly after 7.00 am, Lieutenant Guillermo Crippa left Stanley in his MB-339 light attack aircraft. Mist and sun causing glare, he approached from the north. Crippa:

As I came over San Carlos itself, I came face to face with a Sea Lynx helicopter. I was going to attack when I saw the ships in the distance. I decided to forget about the helicopter and go for other targets. I flew straight to the first ship, which was lying at anchor. I don't know which of us was more surprised. I came under attack and they started firing at me. I was taken aback by the number of ships there were in the area and I thought to myself: If I go back and tell them there are so many ships they'll never believe me. I circled and came back trying to hug the terrain and I drew a little map on my knee-pad before I returned to Puerto Argentino. It was strange because it was a beautiful day, very peaceful and the Islands looked lovely. It was incredible to think there was a war going on. (Bilton and Kominsky, *Speaking Out*)

Few who witnessed Crippa's gallant flight are likely to forget it. His rocket and 30mm cannon attack on the frigate HMS *Argonaut* damaged a Seacat missile deck and wounded two sailors. Under fire from rail-mounted GPMGs and a Blowpipe on *Canberra*, a Seacat fired from HMS *Intrepid* and HMS *Plymouth*'s 4.5in main armament, his aircraft was just slightly damaged as he jinked over the ships. For this sortie, Crippa was awarded Argentina's highest award for gallantry.

Meanwhile, D Squadron had been helicoptered during the night to high ground north of Camilla Creek House, about two miles north-east of the Darwin Peninsula. The frigate HMS *Ardent*, 12 miles offshore in Grantham Sound, was ready to shell Military Air Base Goose Green, however the NGSO team could not give corrections because their codes were invalid. When the

SAS opened fire on the 12th Infantry Regiment Recce Platoon (First Lieutenant Morales), Morales reported that he was under fire from a strong force, which was exactly what D Squadron wanted him to believe. Meanwhile, Tigre Flight of the Pucara Squadron Malvinas was briefed to search for helicopters apparently landing troops at Port San Carlos. Just as the first pair rolled, HMS *Ardent* bombarded the runway and only Captain Jorge Benitez succeeded in taking off. Searching Bombilla Hill, he then flew west towards San Carlos Water and the reports of warships, and was lining up to attack a column of troops when a Stinger missile fired by an Air Troop SNCO hit his aircraft. Benitez ejected and walked to Goose Green. The Stinger kill was more luck than judgement as the same NCO missed other aircraft with several missiles. Meanwhile, the second Pucara pair had just shot up a SAS position overlooking Darwin when they were jumped by two 801 Naval Air Squadron Sea Harriers flown by Lieutenant Commanders Nigel Ward and Alisdair Craig. Major Carlos Tomba was shot down, however First Lieutenant Juan Micheloud found cover in cloud. The SAS broke contact and marched to Sussex Mountain. When Piaggi advised Brigadier General Parada that he was under attack, he was told that there was no intelligence to suggest that a landing on Darwin was imminent.

At 7.00 am, two C Flight, 3rd Commando Brigade Air Squadron Gazelles left RFA *Sir Galahad* to recce locations for the Rapier sites and, after clearing two positions, split up to protect Sea Kings bringing stores ashore. At about 7.40 am, Sergeants Andrew Evans and Edward Candlish, both Royal Marines, met up with Lieutenant Ray Harper RN lifting off from *Canberra* with an underslung load of mortar bombs and carrying a Rapier recce party. When Harper flew toward Hospital Point and Port San Carlos, First Lieutenant Esteban, believing that he was about to be attacked by heliborne troops, ordered his men to fire at the helicopters; in his hand-written report, he identified the Gazelles as Sea Lynxes. Realizing that he had overshot the leading 3 Para company, Harper dropped his load and warned Evans that he had come under ground fire. Esteban then came under fire from the paras, who had reached the Community Centre. Meanwhile Evans approached the Argentine position at a height of about 40 feet and fired six rockets before he then banked to follow Harper, however the Argentines fired at the helicopter, hitting the rotor and gear box. Mortally wounded, Evans ditched about 50 yards from a jetty, however, the floatation gear had been removed to reduce the payload for the GPMG mount and the helicopter began to sink. Ashore, Esteban ordered a ceasefire, but it does seem some troops either failed to hear or ignored the order. Under fire and wounded, Candlish inflated the lifejacket of the barely conscious Evans and dragged him downstream about 500 yards to Port San Carlos where he hauled him onto a beach. Some islanders took them to the settlement bunkhouse where Thora Alazia, a cook, and the schoolteacher, Suzanne McCormick, treated Evans, but he died.

That the two sergeants had been shot at while in the water quickly spread and it was feared that the conflict would develop into a nasty affair. As events turned out, this was an isolated incident of inexperienced conscripts caught up in the maelstrom of battle. As an Argentine sergeant later said, 'What is the difference in shooting men struggling in the water to being under naval gunfire and cluster bombs while struggling to survive on the ground?' Whatever the sentiments of this soldier, both sides generally stuck to the Laws of Armed Conflict.

The action was marked by a thin wisp of smoke and marked an aiming point for 3 Para's mortars. Esteban moved east to The Knob. To his astonishment, another Gazelle appeared. Crewed by Lieutenant Ken Francis and Lance Corporal Brett, also both Royal Marines, they had been sent to gather information on the Argentine unit. Arriving at about 7.45 am, Francis overflew Cameron Point at very low level and then as the helicopter banked to pass over Port San Carlos, it was struck on the starboard side by ground fire and crashed upside down near Clam Creek, very near the Argentine position, killing both crew instantly. Esteban claimed that his men had come under fire from its GPMG and they had shot it down as it manoeuvred to fire rockets. 3 Para were under pressure to clear Port San Carlos and 79 (Kirkee) Commando Battery, in positions near San Carlos, fired the first fire mission of the war. The Scimitars and Scorpions of the Blues and Royals were not let loose in the mistaken belief that they could not negotiate soft ground. Lieutenant Esteban shifted east and yet another Gazelle, crewed by Captain Robin Makeig-Jones RA and Corporal Roy Fleming RM, appeared. Believing that it was about to direct naval gunfire on to their positions, the Argentines opened fire and the helicopter veered away to RFA *Sir Galahad* with superficial damage.

These attacks were the first in a conventional war scenario since Confrontation (the war with Indonesia, 1963-66). Esteban had noted that the helicopters were exposed long enough for small arms to be directed at them. For most of the rest of the campaign, air observation and armed action by light helicopters was largely abandoned in favour of casualty evacuation, communications and moving light loads over secured ground. The actions had not paralysed his men, as Esteban thought it might, and they slipped away under intermittent mortar fire. Apart from those missing after Fanning Head, Combat Team Eagle had suffered no casualties, although their problems were only just beginning as they struck out east toward Douglas, which they reached four days later.

While 3 Para were clearing the Argentine withdrawal, mistakes at Battalion HQ resulted in a friendly fire clash between A and C Companies, in which the Mortar Platoon shelled the 'battlefield', two Scimitars opened fire on C Company and a helicopter evacuating two wounded paras was damaged.

Fanning Head and Port San Carlos were the only clashes on 21 May. During the six hours of daylight the Argentine Air Force and Naval Air Command launched eleven raids of two to four aircraft each. Using high ground to shield their approach, they gave the British air defences precious few seconds to react. The T (Shah Sujah) Air Defence Battery Rapiers were early versions. Sensitive weapons, they had experienced several moves during the passage south. A critical factor was the daily 'tests and adjustments' to ensure that the firing systems were calibrated. The firing units had barely been landed before the summons 'Take Post!' Gunner Edward Denmark:

> The noise of the gunfire at the opening to the bay grew once more into a crescendo as every man and his dog fired at the incoming Skyhawks. It was impossible to keep track as they criss-crossed each other, trying to avoid the tracer arching up towards them. The Skyhawks fired their cannons as they swept over the hills. The smell and smoke of cordite from the thousands of weapons being fired drifted across the bay. There was a huge bang and a roar, as one of the missiles fired off the beams (launching pad) of the Rapier. Stewart (Sergeant Stewart Burton) had his target and I watched in an almost trance-like state as the glowing missile hurled across the sky in pursuit of a fleeing missile. A man was fleeing for his life and we all stood there hoping for it to end in repayment for the destruction he had just wreaked upon us. It was not to be. The Skyhawks dropped behind a hill and the missile exploded. Now out of range he lived to fight another day. (Denmark, *Not for Queen and Country*)

Although the gunners had not fired their Rapiers for about a year, they quickly altered their tactics to match the Argentine attack profiles. Junta member Lami Dozo was visiting Air Force HQ at Comodoro Rivadavia when the landings were reported and debriefed some of the pilots. Returning to Buenos Aires, he suggested the beachhead should be attacked, however Brigadier General Menendez cited insufficient assault helicopters. Although Goose Green was vulnerable, his intelligence officer, Colonel Cervo, was convinced that only part of 3 Commando Brigade was ashore and 5 Infantry Brigade had not yet landed. By the end of 21 May, Secretary of State for Defence John Nott was able to report: 'Seven weeks after the Argentine aggression, British troops are tonight firmly established back on the Falkland Islands.'

Although ground force casualties were low, the frigate HMS *Ardent* had been sunk with the loss of twenty-two officers and men. Surgeon Commander Rick Jolly rescued two men from the sea when a Wessex helicopter in which he was a passenger went to assist survivors. For the next ten days, San Carlos Water was the scene of courageous flying and stubborn defence, the frigate HMS *Antelope* being sunk in there in dramatic circumstances.

In London, Prime Minister Thatcher now needed to show that Great Britain meant business. Mindful of Major General Moore's 12 May directive, Thompson rejected attacking Fox Bay and Port Howard because they involved the complexities of amphibious. On 22 May, Thompson: 'A battalion raid on the Argentine garrison of Darwin and Goose Green looked the most promising way of fulfilling Moore's directive to 'establish moral and physical domination over the enemy' . . . 2 Para was the logical choice . . . I therefore warned Jones that is was likely he would carry out the raid.' (Thompson, *No Picnic*)

By 24 May, Argentine Intelligence had concluded that 5 Infantry Brigade landing near Stanley was remote. The Joint Chiefs of Staff concluded that although Goose Green was likely to be attacked, their favoured option was to target the British logistic link to Ascension Island and isolate 3 Commando Brigade, however poor weather precluded this. With 5 Infantry Brigade expected to land between 28 and 30 May, the Joint Operations Centre suggested to Menendez that, since the Navy and Air Force had already made their sacrifices, it was now time for the Army to destroy the beachhead. But Menendez could not attack. The Air Force had not won air superiority and the attack on the Mount Kent helicopter hide had limited his ability to deploy troops. Most of the Argentines were ill prepared to march long distances over rough terrain and then fight. Menendez proposed developing Special Forces operations, threaten the beachhead with 12th Infantry Regiment and reinforce Stanley and Goose Green with 4 Airborne Brigade.

Thompson and Clapp agreed that opening up a southern flank along the Darwin to Stanley track was risky because the coast was full of inlets in which patrol craft could hide and was a navigational nightmare, particularly at night. Thompson favoured 5 Infantry Brigade securing San Carlos Water and Darwin Peninsula, which would release 3 Commando Brigade to break out of the beachhead, when he had enough supplies and:

Occupy the high ground from Long Island Mount through Mount Kent to Mount Challenger in preparation for a night assault on the Argentine Outer Defence Zone:

45 Commando to take Two Sisters.

42 Commando to tackle Mount Harriet.

3 Para to seize Mount Longdon.

If there was sufficient darkness and casualties had not decreased combat effectiveness, the Brigade was to continue the advance with:

3 Para taking Wireless Ridge

45 Commando assaulting Mount Tumbledown

42 Commando in immediate reserve.

40 Commando and 2 Para to be Brigade reserve.

The Brigade would then break out on to the flatter ground of Stanley Common into a thoroughly demoralized Argentine army.

Thompson:

> At about 6pm on the evening of 25 May the R Group with Chester, Wells-Cole and Dixon, the Officer Commanding the Headquarters and Signal Squadron, were at the usual evening conference with me in the small tent behind my bandwagon making the final adjustments to plans to get the Brigade forward. We were interrupted by Captain Edington, the GSO 3 Signals, who stuck his head through the tent flaps and told us that a signal had just arrived saying that the Atlantic Conveyor had been sunk, taking all but one helicopter, a Chinook, to the bottom of the sea. Earlier in the evening the bad news that HMS Coventry had been sunk had also been received, making 25 May a black day. I ordered a full staff conference for the following day to include the CO of 22 SAS, the Commander of 846 Squadron, Commander Thornewill and Major Minords from Clapp's staff. They were to be tasked with investigating what, if anything, could be done to salvage the wreck of the plan using the existing helicopter and landing craft assets. As the R Group dispersed, somebody said, 'We'll have to bloody well walk.' (Thompson, *No Picnic*)

The *Atlantic Conveyor* had fallen victim to an Exocet, taking with her to the bottom of the South Atlantic three Chinooks and five Wessex assault helicopters, and depriving the ground forces of a massive amount of ammunition, equipment and stores, including the balance of the Army's Crimean War era Soyer cooking stoves. 3 Commando Brigade was now reliant on the stores and equipment waiting to be unloaded and in the bergens of the troops.

After the conference, Lieutenant Colonel Rose discreetly mentioned to Lieutenant Colonel Vaux that G Squadron patrols on Mount Kent believed the feature to be vulnerable to a coup de main. Would he care to convince Brigadier Thompson that 42 Commando should seize the feature? Thompson did not need much convincing, except that he was facing increasing political pressure to support 2 Para's raid on Goose Green. Task Force Mercedes was a threat but it had made no move to attack the beachhead. Mount Kent, a feature of uneven ridges and valleys about 14 miles from Stanley, held the key to the defence of Stanley. During the night of 24/25 May, Major Delves and three D Squadron recced Mount Kent on the assumption that the rest of the SAS would arrive within twenty-four hours. By now, Thompson had decided that since 8 (Alma) Commando Battery had completed a night-flying programme in Norway, it should take the place of 29 (Corunna) Battery in the 2 Para battle group. Major Tony remained as Battery Commander to his normal Forward Observation Officers. 2 Troop, 9 Parachute Squadron RE was replaced by Recce Troop, 59 Independent Commando Squadron

RE (Captain Clive Livingstone). Thompson reviewed his options and scrubbed moving the three guns to Camilla Creek House to support 2 Para:

> The raid was not a starter without artillery support so, to Jones's intense annoyance, I cancelled it. It was either that night or not at all, as far as I was concerned. The main objective was still Stanley, so establishing a strong force on Mount Kent and the nearby feature was the most important task. (Thompson, *No Picnic*)

London was unimpressed with the lack of movement. Thompson was seen by the War Cabinet to be excessively cautious and Northwood was instructed to order him to move out of the beachhead, even though his logistic lifeline was in tatters. Northwood suggested, even though he was the commander on the spot, that he did not need recces to seize Mount Kent and did not need guns to assault Goose Green.

Although Argentine patrols were suspected of overlooking San Carlos Water, it was not until 25 May that evidence emerged when Marine Corps Lieutenant Commander Dante Camiletti was captured inside the perimeter by 40 Commando. Arriving with the Amphibious Support Force, when Brigadier General Daher resurrected Operation Cameleon, a plan to neutralize British air defences thought to be north of Mount Usborne, Camiletti had volunteered. Shortly after dawn on 23 May, two Iroquois helicopters landed his Marine patrol on Chata Hill. Two days later, the ten men reached Mount Verde area. When a recce patrol reported helicopters, Camiletti installed himself on Mount Verde and was then captured hiding underneath a rock. On the same day, two more exhausted 'Fanning Head Mob' were captured. Further suspicions of Argentines in the hills bore fruit on 30 May when a Sea King deposited three bedraggled but armed Argentines outside Brigade HQ. There was no capture report, however interrogators established that the prisoners were from the School of Military Aviation tasked to man an aircraft directional radar beacon on Verde Mountain. Running out of rations, they had tried to surrender to passing British patrols several times. Unfortunately, the Sea King crew could not be traced and an opportunity to examine the radar post was wasted.

One of the first tasks of 59 Independent Commando Squadron RE was to select firm ground with a natural ski jump near Green Beach as Harrier Forward Operating Base. Christened by the RAF as 'West Wittering', it was commanded by Squadron Leader Brian 'Sid' Morris AFC and was better known as 'Sid's Strip'. The Fleet Air Arm christened it HMS *Sheathbill*, after a seabird. On 23 May, 1 Troop set up the Emergency Fuel Handling Equipment, however, the frequent air raids and a faulty design of two pumps meant that the transfer of fuel was painfully slow. 2 Troop, 9 Parachute Squadron began to build the strip until, on 24 May, 11 Field Squadron (Major Bruce Hawken), a specialist airfield construction unit, landed from RFA *Bedivere*, although it had no equipment because 500 tons of equipment destined for 'West Wittering' were on the *Atlantic Conveyor* at the bottom of the South Atlantic. The Commando sappers had been unable to land their stores and vehicles from RFA *Sir Lancelot* because it had been hit by two bombs, both of which failed to explode but were still thought to be dangerous. However, on RFA *Stromness* were Pre-fabricated Surfacing Airfield panels for repairing bomb damage and building a vertical take-off and landing pad. Some were flown ashore while others were hauled from Green Beach, using vehicles loaned by Alan Miller. By 2 June, 11 Field Squadron had built an 850-foot runway complete with dispersal areas and had redesigned the fuel-handling system to pump ashore 40,000 gallons of aviation fuel. No sooner had the weary sappers laid down their tools, when the downdraught of the one remaining Chinook landing close to the runway buckled several panels. With no spares available, the Royal Engineers then re-laid most of the runway. Poor weather prevented flying until 5 June when Squadron Leader Bob Iveson led a pair of Harrier GR 3s from HMS *Hermes*. Iveson had been shot down over Goose Green the day before the battle and evaded capture until 30 May. Thereafter, two Harriers and two Sea Harriers arrived from the Carrier Battle Group at first light and remained ashore for the day. The 150(+) operational sorties flown from 'Sid's Strip' during the period 5 to 14 June helped the British maintain air superiority. The Royal Engineers managed 'Sid's Strip' until it was eventually taken over by the RAF in August.

Gradually, the British gained the upper hand and the San Carlos Water beaches became the logistic funnel through which men and supplies were fed. Meanwhile, Brigadier Thompson was under political pressure to do something about the Argentine garrison at Goose Green.

Chapter Eight

The Battle of Goose Green
28 May

In 1982, Goose Green was the largest settlement in the Falklands, its 127 settlers dependent on sheep farming. About 5 miles to the north is Darwin with about twenty-five inhabitants. Both settlements were serviced by an airstrip, which the Royal Engineer briefing map listed as 400 yard long and graded as 'good, fairly firm'. The settlement had been occupied by C Company, 25th Infantry Regiment since 3 April. From air photographs, documents captured at Port San Carlos, a 25th Infantry Regiment prisoner, the Cable and Wireless telegram intercepts and reports from a G Squadron patrol overlooking the settlement from the east, HQ 3 Commando Brigade had good intelligence on Goose Green. The defence of Goose Green was built around the 643 men, mostly conscripts, of the 12th 'General Arenales' Infantry Regiment, which had arrived on 28 April with three missions:

Provide a reserve battle group, known as Task Force Mercedes, to reinforce Army Group, Stanley.

Occupy Goose Green.

Defend Military Air Base Goose Green.

The Military Air Base (Air Commodore Wilson Pedrozo) housed four 7 Counter Insurgency Squadron CH-47 Chinook helicopters and, from 29 April, twelve aircraft of the Pucara Squadron Falklands. Shortly after daybreak on 1 May, in what turned out to be a fortuitous move, Pedrozo ordered the CH-47s to be parked in the settlement. Although several civilian and non-operational aircraft were dispersed around the airstrip to deceive British air photo analysts after three 800 NAS Sea Harriers destroyed a Pucara and damaged two others, Pedrozo declared the base non-operational. He censured Captain Braghini's gunners for not being alert. Using the excuse of ensuring their safety, Pedrozo confined the settlers to the Community Centre. Three days later, Braghini's gunners, alerted by the early warning radar at

Stanley, shot down Lieutenant Taylor's Sea Harrier, which slewed to a stand-still near the eastern perimeter of the airfield.

The main defence line stretched across the isthmus from Darwin Ridge to the ruins of Boca House and was defended by A Company (First Lieutenant Jorge Manresa). In depth, covering the approaches from Lafonia was C Company (Second Lieutenant Ramon Fernandez). Recce Platoon (Lieutenant Morales) provided a screen. In reserve was a composite platoon raised from HQ Company (Second Lieutenant Ernesto Peluffo). 7th Platoon, C Company, 8th Infantry Regiment (Second Lieutenant Guillermo Aliaga) covered Salinas Beach. C Company, 25th Infantry Regiment (Lieutenant Esteban) minus Combat Team Eagle, remained at the Schoolhouse. The artillery was provided by A Battery, 4th Airborne Artillery (First Lieutenant Carlos Chanampa). Two Pack Howitzers were being ferried to Goose Green on the Coastguard cutter *Rio Iguazu* when it was attacked in Choiseul Sound by two Sea Harriers on 22 May with one gun damaged beyond repair. The remaining two arrived from Stanley by helicopter. In addition there were the two 35mm Oerlikons and six Air Force Rh-202 20mm cannon defending the airfield. Two Air Force School of Military Aviation security companies defended the western beaches.

Piaggi was an experienced soldier, however, under command he had troops from three regiments from two brigades from different corps, none of whom had ever worked together and varied in quality. His support weapons were left in Argentina after the *Ciudad de Cordoba* hit rocks and was then stranded by the imposition of the TEZ. He had one 105mm recoilless rifle with A Company and of ten 81mm mortars, eight were damaged. He was short of radios and the loss of B Company (Combat Team Solari) to the Reserve meant that he was fourteen MAG machine guns short. 9th Engineer Company laid minefields covering Salinas Beach, the north end of the airfield, on both sides of the inlet north of the Schoolhouse and between Middle Hill and Coronation Ridge. The Regimental Chaplain, Father Mora, later wrote: 'The conscripts of 25th Infantry wanted to fight and cover themselves in glory. The conscripts of 12th Infantry Regiment fought because they were told to do so. This did not make them any less brave. On the whole they remained admirably calm.'

As we have seen, Brigadier Thompson had been under significant political pressure to demonstrate British resolve. On 24 May, after he had issued formal instructions to 2 Para to raid the Darwin Peninsula, Lieutenant Colonel Jones and his Intelligence Officer, Captain Alan Coulson, flew to Brigade HQ where they were given the latest intelligence. A member of the Brigade Intelligence Section:

> I was already aware that the SAS had made an assessment of the enemy strength at Goose Green, but if 2 Para chose to believe the SAS, the deeper they penetrated toward Goose Green, the more unknown they

would face. The intelligence gained from the interrogation of the Argentine sergeant was the most recent available.

Over the next two days, Jones reviewed his options. Brigadier Thompson initially told him that helicopters were required for the SAS seizure of Mount Kent. A night amphibious landing on Salinas Beach was rejected because of navigational difficulties and warships were needed to defend San Carlos Water. Marching the 15 miles to Goose Green was the only option. 2 Para also faced another difficulty – no patrolling: 'The activities of the SAS were particularly frustrating. SAS operations both before Darwin/Goose Green and Wireless Ridge inhibited the Battalion's own patrolling activities and yet no proper debriefing of the SAS patrols was ever made available to the Battalion.' (2 Para post-operational report)

When Jones sent C Company to recce a route to Darwin, near Canterra House, it reported an Argentine company and a troop carrier. 12 Platoon (Lieutenant Jim Barry, Royal Signals) was lifted by helicopter to investigate, however it took four hours to navigate across trackless moorland before finding the house to be empty. Jones then briefed his company commanders that the Battalion would raid Goose Green early on the 26th and would have three 105mm Light Guns from 8 (Alma) Commando Battery in support. At last light, D Company (Major Phil Neame), tasked to secure the start line, descended Sussex Mountain, collected 12 Platoon and set off for Camilla Creek House. Meanwhile, D Squadron recce patrols had been inserted on Mount Kent and Thompson was concentrating on reinforcing them with 42 Commando and a 105mm Light Gun battery by Chinook helicopters expected from the *Atlantic Conveyor*. However, when news of the sinking of the ship arrived, believing that attacking Stanley was more militarily important than a political demonstration, Thompson scrubbed moving the three guns to Camilla Creek House. Unaware of the difficulties faced by Thompson, Jones was livid: 'I've waited twenty years for this, and now some fucking marine's cancelled it.' 12 Platoon returned to Canterra House and D Company snaked back to Camilla Creek House. Jones then arranged for helicopters at 6.00 am next day to lift D Company to Camilla Creek House but was first told that only one aircraft was available, and then none – bad weather again. This did little to soothe his impatience. 12 Platoon arrived back at 2 Para, cold, hungry and tired.

Although Goose Green was not a threat, on 26 May Thompson was summoned to speak to Admiral Fieldhouse: 'As clear and unequivocal were the orders from Northwood. The Goose Green operation was to be re-mounted and more action required all round. Plainly the people at the backend were getting restless. (Thompson, *No Picnic*)

The instructions contravened Major General Moore's 12 May directive, nevertheless when Lieutenant Colonel Jones was told by Thompson that the raid was back on, he was delighted, as was 2 Para. C Company occupied Camilla Creek House followed by the rest of the Battalion. Initially, the pace was an unrealistic Aldershot 'tab' and it was only after a soldier in A Company collapsed that the stop-go, stop-go march changed into a practical pace. Thompson refused to allocate the Blues and Royals to the attack because he did not believe that light armour could negotiate soft ground.

During the day, Brigadier General Menendez instructed Brigadier General Parada to command 3 Infantry Brigade operations from Goose Green; however the duty flight commander refused to accept Menendez's orders, as they had not been ratified by Air Force headquarters. Naval and air force headquarters often refused to implement his orders until they had been ratified by their own staff. Parada then instructed Piaggi:

> Task Force Mercedes will reorganize its defensive positions and will execute harassing fire against the most advanced enemy effectives, starting from this moment, in the assigned zone, to deny access to the isthmus of Darwin and contribute its fire to the development of the principal operation. The operation will consist of preparing positions around Darwin for an echelon defending the first line, and occupying them and from there putting forward advanced combat and scouting forces, as security detachment, supporting the principal operations with harassing fire against Bodie Peak-Canterra Mount-Mount Usborne.

Although A Company was in defensive position on the high ground of Darwin Ridge behind the minefields, Piaggi instructed First Lieutenant Manresa to move his Company into unprepared positions on Coronation Ridge north of the minefields. Manresa was concerned that his half-trained conscripts were leaving the security of their positions, which were taken over by Second Lieutenant Peluffo's platoon. During the night, Chanampa's guns registered on to targets, most astride 2 Para's route, which brought some discomfort to the paras. Shortly before dawn on 27 May, 2 Para were crammed into the house and ten outbuildings that made up Camilla Creek House. When the Signals Platoon tuned into the 10.00 am BBC World Service news and heard 'A parachute battalion is poised and ready to assault Darwin and Goose Green', there was stunned silence at the enormity of this breach of security. No one has ever owned up to the leak but political expediency from within Thatcher's War Cabinet is suspected. A furious 'H' Jones ordered his Battalion to disperse, which made co-ordination difficult. The Argentines believed the announcement to be a hoax because they believed that no one in their right mind would broadcast an attack.

Two Recce Platoon (Lieutenant Colin Connor) patrols clashed with Lieutenant Morales's Recce Platoon. At about 12.30 am, three Harriers arrived to support Lieutenant Connor, however, Captain Braghini's gunners shot down Squadron Leader Iveson. Bailing out over Paragon House, he was rescued three days later by a 3 Commando Brigade Air Squadron Gazelle. When Morales was ordered by Piaggi to investigate activity north of Camilla Creek House, Morales and three soldiers driving along the track to San Carlos in a commandeered blue Land Rover were captured and,. under interrogation, they admitted the Argentine garrison was alert to an attack. Unfortunately, they were not sent to Brigade HQ for more expert interrogation.

Jones called an Orders Group for 11.00 am, however with the Battalion spread out it was not until 3.00 pm, with the light fading fast, that his officers assembled. Lieutenant Coulson was midway through the crucial intelligence briefing when Jones's impatience prevailed and he interrupted him, consequently denying the Battalion all the intelligence available to them. Jones planned that the raid had developed into an all-out 'six-phase night/day silent/noisy battalion attack':

Phase One

Support Company to establish a firebase at the western end of Camilla Creek.

C Company to secure the Start Line at the junction of Camilla Creek and Ceritos Arroyo and then become Battalion reserve.

Phase Two – 2.00 am

A Company to attack the right flank of 12th Infantry Regiment toward Darwin Hill.

B Company to attack the left flank around the derelict foundations of Boca House.

Phase Three – 3.00 am

A Company to attack Coronation Point.

D Company to deal with a platoon position on high ground 1,000 metres north of Boca House.

Phase Four – 4.00 am

B Company to attack Boca House.

Phase Five – 5.00 am

A Company to exploit to Darwin.

C Company to push through B and D Companies to clear the airfield.

Phase Six – By 6.00 am

A Company to take Darwin.

B Company to attack 25th Infantry Regiment platoon at the Schoolhouse.

C Company to move into a blocking position south of Goose Green,

D Company to liberate Goose Green.

The fourteen hours of darkness would be used to cover the 6,500 yards to Goose Green, with nine hours for battle preparation and the move to the Start Line, leaving five hours to advance against an enemy in depth over unknown ground. Jones concluded his orders: 'All previous evidence suggests that if the enemy is hit hard, he will crumble.' So far, there was no suggestion that they would. Time was short and some company, platoon and section orders lacked some detail. After two sleepless nights and an exhausting approach, the paras were tired.

During the late afternoon, 5th Fighter Group launched the first mission against British positions when two Skyhawks attacked the 40 Commando positions at San Carlos, killing Sapper Pradeep Ghandi, of 59 Independent Commando Squadron RE. One pilot forced to eject from his Skyhawk was returned to Argentine forces by local islanders. Two other Skyhawks attacked Ajax Bay with parachute-retarded bombs and six Royal Marines were killed. Thompson:

> Three 400kg hit the Field Dressing Station itself without exploding, one passing through the roof and bouncing on the ground outside. The two others remained in the Dressing Station until after the end of the war. The bombs that did explode in the BMA started fires among the piles of ammunition stacked close by, mainly 81mm mortar ammunition and Milan. These exploded all night a hundred metres or so from the Dressing Station and Logistic Regiment Headquarters, sending shrapnel whining through the darkness and destroying all of 45 Commando's Milan firing posts. The netted loads of gun and mortar ammunition waiting to be lifted forward to 2 Para were also destroyed. These had to be replaced quickly before 2 Para's battle (at Goose Green) started. (Thompson, No *Picnic*)

At 10.00 pm, C Company and Recce Troop, 59 Independent Commando Squadron RE cleared the route to the start line, which included the unlucky sappers wading waist deep in freezing water checking three bridges for obstacles. Phase One was complete except that Recce Platoon had secured a fence about 400m north of the correct start line. In Grantham Sound, HMS *Arrow* opened fire, in support of A Company's attack on a suspected

101

Argentine position at Burntside House. Bullets smacked into the buildings, showering Mr and Mrs Morrison, his mother, a friend and a dog with wood, glass and debris. A Company skirmished to a fence 350m beyond the building, however the Argentine patrol had retired. Phase Two was complete, but for many paras experiencing battle for the first time, the reorganization was chaotic. A 2 Platoon section commander: 'Nobody knew where we were. The rest of the Platoon didn't know where my section was, and I didn't know where the platoons were. One of the platoons, if I remember correctly, crossed over one another. I wasn't quite sure who was in front of them, but knew it wasn't the enemy.'

B Company was delayed in crossing their start line until 11.11 pm, much to Lieutenant Colonel Jones's frustration, by A Company's difficulties. Crosland:

> I was walking around my leading platoons and the atmosphere was very like the tension before a parachute descent – but underlying this, quiet confidence. At 3am, the word was given and the Company rose as one to start our long assault. My orders were clear – advance straight down the west side, destroying all in the way. We contained a lot of firepower. This was going to be a violent gutter fight, trench by trench – he who hit hardest won. (Adkin, *Goose Green*)

Supported by HMS *Arrow*, bayonets fixed, B Company quickly overran Manresa's conscripts. The advance of 6 Platoon (Second Lieutenant Clive Chapman) on the left was initiated by reports of a 'scarecrow', which then moved and said 'Por favor'. Chapman:

> There was a lot of light in the air at the time from our Schermulys and from our 2-inch mortars. I remember thinking at the time that the field-craft of the troops as they attacked was fantastic. They were weaving left and right, covering in bounds of moving men and really getting stuck into the fight. There was little need to hit the ground and people generally knelt between moves. It was a very dark night, and we had crossed to about 20 to 40 metres from the Argentines when the fight began. Just about every trench encountered was grenaded. Kirkwood [Private Ian, Chapman's radio operator] and myself even took out a trench. There was continuous momentum throughout the attack and it was very swiftly executed. The success of the attack had an electrifying impact on the platoon. (Adkin, *Goose Green*)

At about 4.30 am, Manresa's A Company broke contact and reorganized with 7th Platoon (Lieutenant Horacio Munoz-Cabrera) on Coronation Ridge. B Company advanced through the Argentine positions on Burntside Hill, briefly reorganized and then ejected the Argentines from Coronation Ridge. Private Curtis:

I was breathing hard, exhaling to calm my nerves and gritting my teeth. With eyeballs on stalks, I scanned left, right and in front of me. Increasingly the ground began to slope up on the right. This had the effect of channelling 4, 5 and 6 Platoons slightly towards the flatter ground. To my front and left, a blaze of firepower exploded out of the darkness. 6 Platoon had come under attack. We all went to ground initially and then 4 Platoon opened up on all fronts. As ordered, 5 Platoon held, ready to support or go to either flank. Squashed flat against the frozen ground, I could feel my heart pounding despite the incredible noise. Then during a lull in the gunfire, I heard voices to my right. Although muffled, I could have sworn they were Spanish. We were using classic infantry tactics – just like we'd practised over and over again on Salisbury Plain and at Sennybridge. But everything you do on exercises, even in the darkness, is all neat and précis; when it comes to doing it for real, it's incredibly confusing. The text drill of dash – down – crawl – sights – observe. And fire control goes out of the window. As you start taking real live ammunition and rounds are zipping about your helmet as you crawl along, you can find yourself firing with your head down, not always looking where the rounds are going. I knew it was bad practice but it was very hard to avoid. (Curtis, *CQB*)

The Argentines were shaken by the controlled ferocity of B Company. Several were killed, and a few, still huddled in sleeping bags in their trenches, were captured. Chapman later credited that the success of the attack was profound faith in Major 'Black Hat' Crosland, so nicknamed because of his habitual black woollen hat.

At 2.00 am, HMS *Arrow*'s main armament jammed and remained inactive for the next two hours. Captain Bob Ash RA was the B Company Forward Observation Officer and had just repaired a malfunctioning radio:

It was totally black, and you couldn't even make out the horizon. I started using the ship for adjustment with their star shell. After a few rounds it jammed – and that was the end of it . . . So, I didn't even get one 'in the parish' where I could try and pick up any positions.

2 Para were now reliant upon 8 (Alma) Commando Battery, and three Mortar Platoon 81mm mortars and the limited amount of ammunition they had. On the right, D Company, in reserve, advanced. Major Neame:

Unfortunately, we had somehow got ahead of 'H'. He suddenly came stomping down the track from behind. 'What the hell are you doing here?' were his opening words. My response of 'Waiting for the battle to start' did not placate him; he didn't take kindly to his reserve company being closer to the battle than he was. (Adkin, *Goose Green*)

Lieutenant Colonel Jones disappeared and when he came under fire from Coronation Hill, he instructed Neame to deal with the enemy. Neame, like most of 2 Para that morning, had no idea where they were in relation to the enemy or their own forces, nevertheless D Company advanced and clashed with Manresa's men on Coronation Hill. Lieutenant Chris Webster commanded 11 Platoon on the left flank:

> Corporal Staddon's Section and Platoon Headquarters were best placed to move close toward the enemy, so we crawled up in more or less a straight line. Suddenly a heavy calibre opened up and I think that was when Lance Corporal Cork was hit in the stomach. Private Fletcher went to assist and at about the same time some mortars started falling around us. Luckily the ground was soft and absorbed most of the blast, but I remember thinking that command and control is all very well but what can you do when you and everyone around you is deaf. (Adkin, *Goose Green*)

Cork and Fletcher were the Battalion's first fatalities. When 10 Platoon, on the right, attacked trenches on his right flank and a few rounds impacted near B Company, Neame resolved the matter with Crosland. The fighting was tough and D Company lost three dead and two wounded. One problem quickly emerged – the casualty evacuation plan was weak and some soldiers would wait twelve hours waiting to be collected. Once again, 2 Para was delayed as D Company reorganized. Phase Three was complete.

A Company had been waiting in heavy drizzle west of Burntside House and when Jones ordered the Company to advance in Phase Four it was about 4.30 am, half an hour behind schedule. HMS *Arrow* was still non-operational and Major Rice was switching the Light Guns between the companies. Support Company, apart from the Medium Machine Gun Platoon, was directed by Jones to find a fire support base. By the time that A Company reached Coronation Point the timetable had slipped by about an hour and twenty minutes. Major Farrar-Hockley, with A Company well ahead of B and D Companies, wanted to press on and take advantage of the darkness. Adkin: 'When Farrar-Hockley went forward to verify his position, he was aware that if he ignored his Phase 4 orders to remain in reserve (to B Company attacking Boca House) and advanced on Darwin Hill he could catch up on lost time. He radioed Tac HQ for authority to continue the advance.' (Adkin, *Goose Green*)

However, Lieutenant Colonel Jones, whose command style was restrictive, told him to wait so that he could personally assess the situation. Jones had difficulty finding A Company in the dark and when he eventually instructed it to seize Darwin Hill, Farrar-Hockley moved 3 Platoon (Second Lieutenant Guy Wallis) to a fire support position north-east of Darwin Pond near the bridge. A Company then advanced with 2 Platoon (Second Lieutenant Mark Coe) leading, taking as his axis a gorse-filled gully leading onto Darwin Ridge.

Ahead was a thin fence. Time was short, dawn was peeping over the horizon and it was still drizzling.

Lieutenant Colonel Piaggi was confident that if his main defence line across the isthmus held, he stood a good chance of victory. Pushing 7th Platoon, 8th Infantry Regiment (Lieutenant Second Guillermo Aliaga) on to Boca Hill, he instructed 1st Platoon, C Company, 25th Infantry Regiment (Second Lieutenant Nestor Estevez) to reinforce the composite Headquarters Company platoon (Second Lieutenant Peluffo) on Darwin Ridge and told both officers that defence was more important than attack. The survivors of Manresa's shattered company trickled back and were slotted into defensive positions. About 200 defenders occupied at least twenty-five trenches, bunkers and shell scrapes. A brief break in the weather gave Air Commodore Pedrozo the opportunity to evacuate several Bell-212 helicopters from Goose Green. The CH-47s had left three days before.

In the grey gloom of a wet dawn, Estevez's men thought that figures approaching the ridge were more A Company survivors. Corporal Camp's section reached the gorse when three figures appeared on the spur to the right. One para thought it was a civilian walking a dog, but Lance Corporal Spencer believed them to be paras and shouted. The three figures waved amicably and one shouted back in Spanish. There was a momentary pause before Camp's section opened fire and dived for cover in the gorse. The defenders of Darwin Ridge then opened fire at A Company strung out in file in the open below them.

While 2 Section (Corporal Dave Hardman) and Platoon Headquarters joined Camp, Corporal Steve Adams's section skirmished to the right of the spur but was forced to withdraw under heavy fire which wounded Adams and Private Tuffen. The latter could not be rescued but Adams was able to join Camp. Company Tac HQ made it to the gorse, as did most of 1 Platoon (Sergeant Terence Barratt). As those caught in the open withdrew under accurate fire onto the small beach of Darwin Pond, the Company medic, Lance Corporal Shorrock, was shot in the spine. Private Martin was a member of Corporal David Abols's Section in 1 Platoon:

> I was at the back of the Platoon with Company Headquarters. When the firing started, we doubled forward a bit, went to ground and opened fire on the hill. We were soon under mortar fire as well but saved by the soft ground. One man was killed going forward. It was all chaos with no orders as the Section Commander had gone into the gully. Gradually we made our way down the beach. Shorrock crawled back and we put a dressing on him. We met a signaller who told us that 2 Platoon had been wiped out. (Adkin, *Goose Green*)

The soldier killed was Corporal Michael Melia, of 59 Independent Commando Squadron RE. At about the same time, when 7th Platoon, 8th Infantry Regiment, on Boca Hill opened fire on B Company advancing down

Middle Hill, 4 and 6 Platoons found cover in the gorse; 5 Platoon, however, was caught in the open by artillery and struggled back up the bare slopes. Private Jimmy Street opened up with his 2-inch mortar and then Private Curtis heard him shout to Private 'Taff' Hall that he had been hit in the legs. Hall then screamed, 'My back, my back!' As Curtis reached Street, Privates Steve Illingworth and 'Pooley' Poole were with Hall when a shell burst nearby, bowling Curtis over. Dazed, he got to his feet and sheltered in the smoking crater. After Illingworth and Poole had dragged Hall into shelter, Illingworth then ran back to where Hall had been wounded, stripped off his webbing and was sprinting back, shouting 'We need the ammo!' covered by Curtis with his GPMG, when he was killed 15-feet from the crater.

Farrar-Hockley's immediate problem, several trenches on the eastern slopes of the spur, were attacked by ad hoc groups of officers and soldiers from the Royal Artillery, Royal Engineers and Parachute Regiment working together to nibble at the defences. Corporal Camp and Private Day, who was Second Lieutenant Coe's radio operator, used Private Robert Pain's back as a GPMG firing platform. A left-flanking attack up the gully by Coe and 2 Section stalled at the cost of Private Worrall seriously wounded on the wrong side of a bank alight with burning gorse. Corporal Abols was awarded the Distinguished Conduct Medal for his conduct during the battle:

> I returned to Corporal Prior and Worrall but we couldn't coordinate the covering fire because of the noise of the battle, so I skirmished forward and dived over the bank again to discover that Corporal Russell had been hit by shrapnel from an anti-tank weapon. Then Sergeant Hasting, Lieutenant Coe and a few privates assisted us with covering fire, so I returned to Corporal Prior and we decided to throw a smoke grenade, which would be the signal for the covering fire . . . I threw the smoke grenade, then we grabbed Worrall but couldn't move him as his webbing had caught on some gorse roots. By the time he was ready to be moved, the smoke had disappeared, so we decided to take a chance and go over the bank with him. Just as we were about to move, a sniper shot Corporal Prior in the back of the head . . . Then Corporal Hardman and Lance Corporal Gilbert came over and we managed to get Corporal Prior over the bank and returned for Worrall . . . I then rested and had a few fags and returned to the battle on the hill. (Adkin, *Goose Green*)

Corporal Underwood, the Company Mortar Fire Controller (MFC), was directing fire but the Mortar Platoon was running short of ammunition. Deciding that concentrated fire was essential, Farrar-Hockley grouped six GPMGs under Sergeant Barratt on the spur as a fire base to dominate Darwin Ridge, but it had only enough ammunition for about an hour. North of Darwin Pond, 3 Platoon gave support at extreme range and was then shelled. Fog at sea prevented a Harrier strike.

The battle was at a critical stage. The Argentine platoon commanders had inspired their conscripts and at 6.00 am, when Piaggi informed Menendez that the British had been halted, optimism prevailed in Stanley. In anticipation of Skyhawk support, Company Sergeant Major Coelho laid out strips of white sheets as markers. Before 2 Para had attacked, the three Argentine Pack Howitzers were well forward, however as the Argentines withdrew, the parachute gunners changed position several times, although always into unprepared sites. Nevertheless throughout the battle, they kept up the pressure. The one jeep that First Lieutenant Chanampa had was invaluable for towing and moving ammunition. When Estevez was killed on Darwin Ridge, while adjusting artillery fire, his radio operator, Private Fabrizio Carrascul, continued directing the guns until he too was killed. Thereafter Chanampa's targets tended to be either speculative, based on local knowledge or from the map. Estevez was posthumously awarded Argentina's highest gallantry award.

At Camilla Creek House, the demand on 8 (Alma) Commando Battery was high; the guns became unstable and were being resighted about every fifteen minutes. The lack of meteorological information, the inability of Forward Observation Officers to see fall of shot and a gusting wind was making accurate shelling difficult. One gun developed a buffer oil leak, which was cured with rifle-cleaning oil. Empty shell cases littering the gun pits were removed by the gunners, contributing to their fatigue – most had not rested for thirty-six hours. In spite of the weather, three Pucaras appeared over Camilla Creek House at about 8.00 am, and as Lieutenants Cimbra and Arganaraz lined up for a low-level rocket attack on the gun line, a Blowpipe fired by 43 Battery, 32nd Guided Weapons Regiment Blowpipe detachment, commanded by Battery Sergeant Major Wilson, deflected Cimbra. Another missile launched at Arganaraz exploded on the ground, flinging the Pucara upside down for a short time. All three aircraft returned to Stanley.

Although A Company had been halted in front of the strongest part of the defence of Darwin Ridge and although he had reserves, Lieutenant Colonel Jones rejected several suggestions. Neame, well placed in the centre to support both flanks, suggested to Farrar-Hockley on the Battalion radio net that D Company could outflank the Argentine defences, but was told by Jones, 'Stop clogging the air; I am trying to conduct a battle.' Major Crosland suggested that B Company could seize Boca Hill and roll up the enemy from the west. Captain John Young suggested placing Milan Platoon on Middle Hill to shoot at the main defence line. Lieutenant Peter Kennedy, C Company's Second-in-Command, assembled twelve GPMGs on the eastern slopes of Coronation Ridge and when he asked A Company for targets was told, 'Get off the radio. I'm trying to run a battle.'

Trapped at Darwin Pond for an hour and unable to influence the fighting, Lieutenant Colonel Jones was impatient. His radio operator, Sergeant Norman: 'The CO got on the radio and told them to get a grip, speed up and continue the movement, which they couldn't. So he said "I'm not having anymore of this" and decided to go and join up with A Company. To say he

107

got a little pear-shaped would be an understatement.' (Adkin, *Goose Green*)

Crawling, running, sprinting and diving, the radio operators that make up Tactical HQ, weighed down with radios, batteries and bergens, found it difficult to emulate the fast pace set by Jones. It was about 8.30 am. According to Wilsey: 'H effectively ended up running the battle in the gully.' (Wilsey, *H Jones VC*)

Jones urged Major Rice and Captain Worsley-Tonks to get the guns and mortars going respectively, however the British and Argentines were too close. When Jones instructed Farrar-Hockley that he should seize a ledge at the top of the spur, Farrar-Hockley assembled about fifteen men. Wolsey-Tonks arranged for smoke but the wind dissipated this quickly. Lance Corporal Gilbert:

> I can't remember anybody organising anything; we just went. We were walking initially, then crawling to the top. As we went forward round the slope, I was in time to see Captain Dent killed. He was hit in the chest, fell back on his radio and was then hit again. I crawled past the Adjutant, who was on his hands and knees, encouraging us saying 'That's it, lads, Airborne all the way. Remember Arnhem!' After ten minutes I looked back and he was dead too. Myself and Corporal Hardman worked our way to the left while the position was being smoked. Then it dispersed and I saw Hardman fall. He didn't move. I crawled over to him and checked. He was obviously dead. I had to take up a fire position behind him, using his body as a rest. I felt his body twitch as it was hit again. I took his ammo and crawled back. (Adkin, *Goose Green*)

Further attacks would have been suicidal and the survivors found cover. Sergeant Blackburn then heard Jones mutter, 'We've got to do something about this.' Wilsey:

> He took command of the situation locally and with the resources immediately available deliberately set out to regenerate the lost momentum. He sensed how to rejuvenate the assault on the ridge. His whole life had been in preparation for this moment. He did not tumble into it; it was coolly calculated. He deliberately led an out flanking movement to set an example, to show the way, to tip the balance at a critical moment and to determine the outcome. This, in the final analysis, is the commander's job. (Wilsey, *H Jones VC*).

Without telling anyone or looking back, he ran up the gully that Corporal Adams had attacked when A Company was first fired upon, past the seriously wounded Private Tuffen. Sergeant Barry Norman, his close escort, was the first to move, followed by Lance Corporal Beresford, who was part of his escort and had been Jones's driver, Major Rice and his two signallers. Jones advanced up a small re-entrant toward a trench, which Corporal Osvaldo Olmos, from Estevez's platoon, later claimed was held by his group. Norman shouted, 'Watch out! There's a trench to the left!' and dived for cover. Jones evidently heard the warning and briefly paused to change his Sterling SMG magazine. Norman, while under heavy fire from the left, then fired a complete SLR magazine into the trench and also changed magazines, although this took longer than he expected because the magazines had become jammed in his pouch. When he popped up, seeing Jones check his magazine and advance up the slope, he shouted for him to watch his back. However, Jones continued and then fell. It was 6.30 am. Major Chris Keeble was at Battalion HQ to the north of Darwin Pond. 'And in this confusion over the radio came "Sunray is down". I couldn't believe it and actually asked for verification. Colour Sergeant Blackburn, his signaller shouted again, "Sunray is down for Christ's sake". Then a surge of apprehension and fear ran through me.' (Adkin, *Goose Green*)

Then, at 6.31 am, when Brigade Headquarters heard the message 'Sunray injured. Sunray Minor taking over. Over', there was also disbelief. Brigadier Thompson, assured by Keeble that he could win the battle and with the Mount Kent operation postponed, ordered ammunition to be flown to 2 Para. Soon afterwards, the Argentine defence began to wither, largely because the Argentines were short of ammunition and with little prospect of resupply. Company Sergeant Major Colin Price fired a 66mm at a bunker but missed, however Corporal Abols was successful and the paras seeped on to Darwin Ridge. Second Lieutenant Peluffo was lying in a trench after being wounded in the head and leg:

> I told a soldier to tie a napkin to his rifle and wave it. He was shot at. He got back into the trench very frightened. I told him to wave it again, so he came out of the position and then we saw the British coming out into the open. I was still at the bottom of the trench. I couldn't move . . . A British soldier arrived and asked me in English if I was all right. I didn't understand him. I saw him standing there with a sub machine gun and thought to myself: Well, this is it. Then he asked me again 'Are you OK?' and I realised that he was not going to shoot me after all. He told me the war was over for me and that I would be going home. (Bilton and Kominsky, *Speaking Out*)

By about 9.30 am, the fight for Darwin Hill was over at the cost of three officers and three other ranks killed and eleven wounded. Of the ninety-two defenders, eighteen were killed and thirty-nine wounded. Collecting 3 Platoon, C Company moved through A Company.

For fifteen minutes, Sergeant Norman waited. When the firing died down, he reached Jones and, turning him on his back, assessed that from the lack of blood, he had internal wounds and not long to live. Other paras placed Jones on a corrugated sheet to take him to a helicopter landing site but he rolled off. A second attempt succeeded. A post mortem suggested that he had been mortally wounded by a single bullet entering his shoulder and exiting midriff. Controversy will surround Lieutenant Colonel Jones and whether his action unlocked the defences. His bodyguard, Sergeant Blackburn summarized: 'It was a death before dishonour; but it wouldn't have passed junior Brecon.' Infantry training took place at the training area at Brecon.

Following frequent requests by Major Farrar-Hockley to evacuate his wounded, at about 10.30 am, two 3 Commando Brigade Air Squadron Scouts, which had been flying ammo forward and returning to Ajax Bay with casualties collected from the RAP, were briefed at Camilla Creek House to collect A Company wounded. Captain Jeff Nisbett RM led the flight. Meanwhile, in response to two aircraft detected leaving Stanley to support Task Force Mercedes, at 10.58 am, an air raid warning 'Red' was passed to 2 Para. Shortly before midday, Lieutenant Miguel Gimenez, on his second mission of the day, singled out the Scout piloted by Lieutenant Richard Nunn RM. Sergeant Belcher was his crewman:

> Suddenly two Pucaras appeared, approaching head on. They split up, so did we. Nunn turned about and we were hit by a burst of cannon fire from directly behind. I was hit in the right leg above the ankle, which took me out. I lay across the back and started to pull out the aircraft's first aid kit . . . while at the same time trying to watch the Pucara and tell Nunn where it was, what it was doing, when it fired, talk him through the situation so he could take evasive action. It flew past our starboard side, turned on its wing and came at us head on, firing its 7.62mm machine gun. Nunn was struck in the face, dying instantly, and I was hit again, this time above my left ankle. We crashed, bounced, turned through 180 degrees, the doors burst open and I was flung clear. (Adkin, *Goose Green*)

Returning to Stanley, the two Pucaras separated in the mist and Gimenez vanished. His wrecked aircraft was found in 1986. Nunn's brother, Chris, had commanded M Company, 42 Commando in the recapture of South Georgia. There was still a battle to be fought. After hearing that Jones had been killed, Major Keeble spent twenty minutes trying to get a clear picture of what was actually happening 800 yards to the south. He had D Company in reserve and the question was whether to reinforce A Company or sort out B Company who were pinned down by machine-gun fire from the Argentine defensive position at Boca House.

Assessing that the best opportunity lay with B Company, Keeble, whose style of command allowed for initiative, passed command to Major Crosland and then led his Tac HQ, laden with extra ammunition, toward the fighting, scrambling for cover as the two Pucaras roared overhead. In the meantime, Keeble: 'In the time it took for me to get up to B Company, Phil Neame – the canny Phil Neame – had realized that he could outflank Boca House by slipping his Company down onto the beach; there was a small wall between the grassland and the beach.

Sending 10 Platoon to join Support Company on Middle Hill firebase, Neame led 11 and 12 Platoons along the wall. Though under fire from Milans, the Argentines mortared the firebase until two Milans struck Second Lieutenant Aliaga's position and then, at about 11.10 am, white flags appeared. 12 Platoon, dangerously exposed, advanced across open ground against the enemy position showing white flags, but ran into a minefield. When the Middle Hill firebase then opened fire, Neame radioed for everyone to stop firing until 12 Platoon reached Boca Hill where they found twelve dead Argentines and fifteen wounded, including Aliaga, most terribly injured by the Milans.

At about the same time, at Stanley Racecourse, First Lieutenant Esteban with a combat team of 3rd Platoon, A Company, 25th Infantry Regiment, and survivors of Combat Team Eagle, were squeezed into an Army Puma and six Iroquois, and were escorted by two Hirundo gunships to a landing site several hundred yards south of Goose Green. Although Piaggi's most experienced officer, Esteban handed over 3 Platoon to Second Lieutenant Vasquez and was instructed to organize the defence of Goose Green with Air Force personnel. Esteban took no further part in the fighting. All that now stood between the British and Goose Green was Vasquez's platoon at the Schoolhouse and 3rd Platoon, C Company, 25th Infantry Regiment (Second Lieutenant Gomez Centurion) holding the high ground around the airstrip windsock, and plugging the gap with the School of Military Aviation security companies. Brigadier General Parada was still encouraging Piaggi to counter-attack.

Meanwhile on the left, C Company and 3 Platoon had pushed through A Company, who had set up a firebase on Darwin Hill, however as they descended, Air Force Rh-202 gunners and Army mortar and machine-gun crews opened fire, killing one man and wounding eleven, including Major Hugh Jenner, the Company Commander. Support Company suppressed the Argentine fire, but the range was long. It was about 2.30 pm. On the right, B Company had halted. Private Curtis:

Crosland called B Company together and said we were going to attack Goose Green from the south-west. It meant that we'd be effectively isolated from the rest of the Battalion, but it was a chance he was willing to take. We started tabbing off the hill in arrowhead formation. Again, it was like the First World War stuff, as howitzer rounds whistled and landed randomly around us. But the fear of the night had gone and I was far happier fighting in the day, knowing everyone's position. I also felt more secure to be moving forward as a company again. It was also re-assuring to see JC [John Crosland] wearing his black bobble hat, looking around nonchalantly. He had an aura of invincibility about him. (Curtis, CQB)

In the centre, D Company was approaching the airstrip. With 10 Platoon weakened by injuries and therefore detached, shortly after examining a suspected command bunker on the edge of the airfield, and assembling some prisoners, they came under fire from Darwin Hill. Waving their red berets, the paras managed to get the fire lifted. Neame had hoped to bypass the Schoolhouse, which was a known strongpoint, but it threatened his left flank. D Company was widely dispersed: 10 Platoon were at the airfield; 12 Platoon had run into more mines and, after their experience at Boca Hill, were nervous. He was about to order 11 Platoon to attack when he learnt that Lieutenant Barry and two soldiers had been killed arranging a surrender near the windsock – the 'white flag' incident.

12 Platoon had been advancing towards Goose Green when a white cloth was seen being waved near the windsock. Believing the Argentines from Centurion's Platoon wanted to surrender, Lieutenant Barry told Sergeant Meredith, his Platoon Sergeant, that he was going forward. When this was reported to Company HQ, Major Neame instructed him to wait, however Barry had set off. With his medic/runner, Private Godfrey, and his radio operator, Private 'Geordie' Knight, Barry collected Corporal Paul Sullivan's section; Sullivan uttered prophetically 'He's going to get me killed.' Godfrey:

> There was a group of three or four Argies with a white cloth wanting to surrender. I've no doubt about this group. They were less than 100 metres from us, but the ground was open like a football field. They were up this slope by a fence with a gap in it. Mr Barry and his radio operator, Geordie Knight, were in the lead with myself a short distance behind, then came Corporal Sullivan's section in support. When we got to the top, I saw that there more Argies in trenches nearby. The first group still seemed to want to give up, but I was worried about the others as they were not leaving their trenches. Mr Barry went right up to the fence, only a few feet from the Argies. I was about 200 feet behind him. He started to demonstrate to the Argies that they were to surrender by putting down their weapons. He went through the motions of putting down his own. (Adkins, *Goose Green*)

Godfrey recalled that a long burst of automatic fire cracked overhead from behind, most likely from a Machine Gun Platoon gunner seeing Argentines in the open. There was a furious exchange of fire. Godfrey:

> Suddenly there were bullets everywhere. All the Argies opened up. Mr Barry was hit at point blank. I fell flat. There was fire from everywhere. I could see rounds striking the ground all round; a lot was coming from the trenches. I was in a bit of a state as the strap of my medical bag was wrapped around my neck. A bullet went through my sling and another through the heel of my boot. (Adkins, *Goose Green*)

112

Godfrey dived into a tractor tyre rut. Knight shot two skirmishing Argentines and Carter dominated another trench with rifle fire. When Corporal Kinchin advanced with his section, Corporal Jeremy Smith was killed instantly when a bullet struck his 66mm as he squeezed its trigger. Corporal Sullivan was also killed and Private Sherrill badly wounded. When Knight reported that Barry was down, Meredith opened fire on the Argentine trenches with a GPMG with deadly accuracy, not so much because his Platoon Commander was down, but because his frustration at 'Barry for being so stupid'. The newspapers inevitably made much of this scrap, however both sides agreed that this was a tragic misunderstanding. The Argentines later claimed that when Second Lieutenant Centurion was offered terms by Barry, he replied, 'Son of a bitch! You have got two minutes to return to your lines before I open fire. Get out!'

At the same time, Vasquez's platoon was vigorously defending the Schoolhouse. 11 Platoon had opened the attack by firing four 66mm at an outhouse and then Second Lieutenant Waddington was leading a small group along the southern foreshore of the inlet when he met the Patrol Platoon Commander, Captain Paul Farrar, crossing the bridge. Thereafter C and D Companies intermingled. Vasquez eventually abandoned the building when it was set on fire and withdrew covered by Braghini's two 35mm Oerlikons, preventing British exploitation. With Goose Green surrounded, Major Keeble ordered 2 Para to go firm. It was about 2.30 pm.

After three Pucaras had flown from Argentina during the afternoon, two of them and two Navy MB-339 Aermacchis were prepared for a sortie against British mortar positions at Goose Green. Shortly after 4.00 pm, when the Aermacchis attacked D Company, Marine Strange, of 3 Commando Brigade Air Defence Troop, shot down Sub Lieutenant Daniel Miguel, who died as his aircraft crashed near B Company. The Pucaras approached from the north-west and attacked D Company with napalm, however, the paras were alert and Lieutenant Cruzado ran into massive ground fire which smashed his controls. Bailing out at low level, he was captured. Three Harriers then damaged the Oerlikons with 2-inch rockets. The gunners abandoned them, leaving the Argentines without artillery and air defence.

By late afternoon, the Argentine situation at Goose Green was serious and Brigadier General Menendez released Combat Team Solari from the Reserve to reinforce Task Force Mercedes. When a flight of Army UH-1H Iroquois arrived on Mount Kent to collect them, First Lieutenant Ignacio Gorriti, the B Company Commander, received a message from Brigadier General Parada cancelling the move but it was too late. Shortly before dusk at 6.30pm, the helicopters landed south of Goose Green. To Major Crosland, they posed a threat. Private Curtis:

It was getting dark as Crosland called his herd together. Bedraggled bodies emerged from enemy trenches and sangars that we now occupied; we had been in battle for the best part of thirty-six hours,

113

with hardly any food, drink or sleep. The OC decided to take us to a knoll just behind our position – the highest feature around Goose Green – and to form all-round defence. As we made our way wearily up the hill, the cold breeze stiffened and I suddenly became aware of my senses again. I was knackered, cold and hungry. With no digging tools, we had to use bayonets to carve our shallow trenches in the frozen mud. Something told me it was going to be a long, hard night. (Curtis, *CQB*)

The artillery fire mission requested by Lieutenant Weighall, Private Curtis's Platoon Commander, was so accurate that the first shells exploded on the landing site. Two NCOs sent by Piaggi to guide the Combat Team appeared out of the gloom and explained that the British had surrounded Goose Green; nevertheless the reinforcements reached the settlement.

Except for the clatter of British helicopters and the occasional firing, a dark silence crept across the battlefield. Although Piaggi believed he could withstand a siege but recognized that relief was slim, Army Group, Malvinas encouraged him to abandon Goose Green, make for Lafonia, cross the Bodi Creek bridge and wait for B Company, 6th Infantry Regiment (Major Oscar Jaimet) from the Reserve. Menendez then authorized Pedrozo and Piaggi to decide the best course of action and at 7.30 pm Parada told Piaggi, 'It's up to you.' There is some evidence that the Argentines believed they were facing a brigade and were hopelessly outnumbered. Piaggi later recalled:

The battle had turned into a sniping contest. They could sit well out of range of our soldiers' fire and, if they wanted to, raze the settlement. I knew that there was no longer any chance of reinforcements from 6th Regiment's B Company and so I suggested to Wing Commander Wilson Pedrozo that he talk to the British. He agreed reluctantly.

Shortly after midnight, one of Piaggi's officers used Eric Goss's CB to contact Alan Miller at Port San Carlos to arrange a ceasefire. Major Keeble sent in two officer prisoners with terms for Piaggi with the ultimatum that if they returned by 8.30 am, surrender had been accepted. He then arranged an all-arms firepower demonstration on call from HQ 3 Commando Brigade, if needed. Thompson placed J Company, 42 Commando (Major Mike Norman) on immediate stand-by to reinforce 2 Para. Company Headquarters and 9 Troop (Lieutenant Trollope) was established from former NP 8901, which had surrendered to the Argentines in April and then been repatriated without giving parole. 42 Commando Defence Troop formed 10 Troop (Lieutenant Tony Hornby). Hornby was the Assistant Training Officer and was in the Chinook crash which killed key intelligence personnel from Northern Ireland. 11 Troop (Lieutenant Colin Beadon) was raised from Milan Troop. When the two Argentines arrived back at Keeble's

Contemporary air photograph showing Yorke Beaches and Stanley Airport where the Argentine 2nd Marine Infantry Battalion landed.

One of the two 2nd Naval Air Squadron Sea Kings on the *Almirante Irizar* that landed troops at Stanley. *(Captured photo)*

3. 601 Combat Aviation Battalion Puma AE504. This aircraft was shot down by Lt Mill's detachment at South Georgia. *(Captured photo)*

4. Her Majesty's Hospital Ship *Uganda* after being requisitioned in early April. Over 500 operations on 730 patients were performed, 20 per cent of whom were Argentine.

(Author's Collection)

5. Mid-April. A Royal Marine 81mm mortar detachment practices on Ascension Island.

(Author's Collection)

6. HMS *Fearless* off Ascension Island. Like its sister ship, HMS *Intrepid*, this LPD was designed to accommodate a battalion landing group of about 750 men. During the campaign, it carried about 900 men and housed a brigade and then divisional HQ.

(Author's Collection)

7. Two Sea Harriers on board HMS *Hermes*. The naval Sea Harriers dominated the air war, while the RAF GR3s supported the ground forces. *(Author's Collection)*

8. 1 May. Piloted by Flt Lt Withers, Vulcan XM607 lands at Wideawake Island after its epic flight 'Black Buck 1' to bomb Stanley Airport to open the British offensive.

(Author's Collection

9. 5 May. English Bay, Ascension. Troops board an HMS *Fearless* LCVP. On the right is a LCU. *(Author's Collection)*

10. An 845 Naval Air Squadron Sea King drops an underslung load at Wideawake Airport Ascension Island. *(Author's Collection)*

11. HMS *Ardent*. Sunk on 21 May. (Author's Collection)

12. 17 May. HMS *Fearless* refuelling at sea. (Author's Collection)

13. 20 May. 40 Commando in the main galley of HMS *Fearless* after being transferred from Canberra. (Author's Collection)

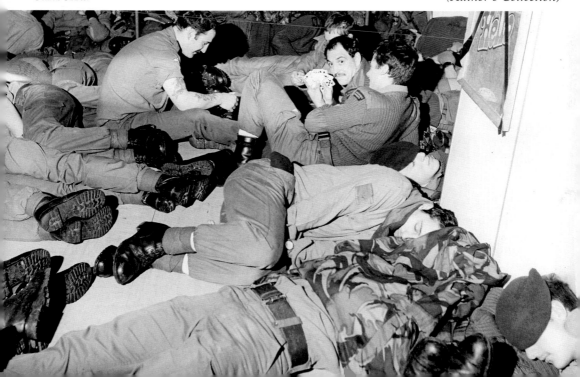

14. 20 May. A Royal Marine of the *Fearless* Embarked Forces receives his ration of Action Messing – stew and a roll in an explosives canister. *(Author's Collection)*

15. 22 May. SSgt Nick van der Bijl (Intelligence Corps) HQ 3 Commando Brigade has a meal in the Intelligence Section bunker at San Carlos. *(Author's Collection)*

16. 24 May. Spiralling smoke from HMS *Antelope* after being abandoned during the
    night.   *(Author's Collection)*

17. 25 May. The Skyhawk of Lt Ricardo Lucero is shot down in San Carlos Water.
    Lucero's parachute can be seen over the bow of RFA *Sir Galahad*. He was picked
    up, badly wounded, by Marine Geoff Nordass.   *(1st Raiding Squadron RM)*

18. 29 May at San Carlos. Goose Green garrison commander, Vice Comodoro Perdroza, is welcomed by Brigadier Thompson. Taking the briefcase in Major Richard Dixon. Behind him is Corporal Dean (Royal Military Police), who was Thompson's close escort. In the background is a Type 12 destroyer. *(Author's Collection)*

19. Royal Marine LCpl 'Smudge' Smith at the entrance of the San Carlos interrogation centre – Hotel Galtieri – a complex of several stables. The gap in the corrugated iron leads to air-raid trenches. *(Author's Collection)*

20. 4 June. A 45 Commando mortar detachment leaves Teal Inlet. *(Author's Collection)*

21. 7 June. LCU F4 at Bluff Clove. Next morning it was sunk in Choiseul Sound.
(1st Raiding Squadron RM)

22. 8 June. Troops abandoning *Sir Galahad*. The 847 Naval Air Squadron AS Wessex piloted by Lt Hughes uses its rotor downwash to shepherd a life raft from the ship. (*1st Raiding Squadron*)

23. 9 June. HQ 3 Commando Brigade prepares to leave Teal Inlet in its BV202 Snocats.
(Author's Collection)

24. About 9 June. Two members of 81 Intelligence Section, Sergeant Steve Massey and Corporal Barry Lovell. Both wear rubber boots to prevent trench foot and other infections caused by wet and cold feet. *(Author's Collection)*

25. Major General Moore wearing his distinctive desert cap.
(Author's Collection)

26. 12 June. A Royal Marine sergeant helps an Argentine medic with a wounded Argentine soldier after the battle for Mt Harriet. He wears nuclear, biological and chemical overboots in order to protect his feet. *(Author's Collection)*

27. 12 June. 45 Commando escorts prisoners from Two Sisters to the rear. *(Author's Collection)*

28. 16 June. A waterlogged Argentine M56 pack howitzer gun position on Stanley Common. *(Author's Collection)*

9. 17 June. The Argentine icebreaker *Almirante Irizar* at Stanely collecting Argentine wounded.
(Author's Collection)

30. A convoy of ships near the Falklands after the surrender. *(Author's Collection)*

31. The logistic dump at Ajax Bay (Red Beach). *(1st Raiding Squadron)*

32. Argentine Skyhawk
Part of a collection
of photos donated
to the Task Force.
(Author's Collection)

33. 245 armoured car
several years after
the war.
(Author's Collection)

34. Argentine prisoners collect food from an Argentine field kitchen at Stanley Airfield.
(Author's Collection)

35. The Type 42 destroyer HMS *Exeter* (Capt Hugo Balfour LVO). On 7 June, a clear day, she shot down with a Sea Dart a 1st Air Photo Group Learjet flying at 40,000ft over San Carlos.

(Author's Collection)

36. HMS *Hermes* (Capt Lindley Middleton DSO). With HMS *Invinsible*, she was a vital factor in competing for air superiority. For the San Carlos landings, she carried 15 naval Sea Harriers, 6 RAF GR3s, 6 Sea Kings, 2 Lynx and 1 Wessex.   *(Author's Collection)*

headquarters with the news that Pedrozo and Piaggi wanted unconditional surrender, Keeble agreed. It was the Argentine Army's National Day, usually a time for celebration. Keeble:

> Eventually about 150 people in three ranks marched up and formed a hollow square. An officer in an Argentine Air Force uniform walked up to me and saluted. I asked for his pistol and took it. When we looked closely we saw that these people weren't soldiers at all. They were airmen. We reckoned there must have been 150 of them. I said 'Where are the soldiers?' He indicated the settlement and said 'They're coming.' Three or four of us moved forward to look down into the settlement. There, to our amazement, must have been 1,000 men, marching up in three ranks. We just held our breath. Somebody murmured 'I hope they don't change their mind.'

For the Argentine 12th Infantry Regiment, 29 May would always be remembered as the day it capitulated. Piaggi burnt his regimental flag. It was also the day when snow first fell across the bleak islands. Broadcasting to the Argentine people and referring to the catastrophe, President Galtieri had this to say:

> At this time of supreme sacrifice before the altar of the country, with all the humility that a man of the armed forces may have deep in his heart, I kneel before God, because only before Him do the knees of an Argentine soldier bend. The Country's arms will continue fighting the enemy for every Argentine portion of land, sea and sky, with growing courage and efficiency, because the soldier's bravery is nourished by the blood and sacrifice of his fallen brothers.

The battle cost 2 Para sixteen killed, half of them from D Company, and thirty-three wounded. A Royal Marine helicopter pilot and a commando sapper were also killed. Of about 300 who took part in the fighting, Task Force Mercedes lost 45 killed and 90 wounded, with 12th Infantry Regiment losing 31 killed, 25th Infantry 12 killed, 5 from 8th Infantry, 2 from 1st AA Group, 4 Air Force and 1 Navy pilot; 1,007 were taken prisoner. That evening Air Commodore Pedrozo and Lieutenant Colonel Piaggi were helicoptered to San Carlos and were met by Brigadier Thompson. Piaggi, bitter and angry, said that Task Force Mercedes 'would have fought until the last man if Parada had demanded it'. Nevertheless, his men had forced 2 Para to fight a long and confusing battle, longer than any other Argentine commander would do. He had confounded Jones's theory, 'Hit them really hard and they will fold.'

3 Commando Brigade was suddenly faced with dealing with the largest number of prisoners captured since the Second World War, an event made worse by the loss of the prisoner-of-war camp on the *Atlantic Conveyor* and the need to support the breakout. Eventually the prisoners were flown to San

Carlos where about 200 were interrogated at Hotel 'Galtieri' before being transferred to the prison camp at Ajax Bay. Most were quickly ferried to *Norland* for repatriation.

Great Britain had demonstrated resolve and the US encouraged Argentina to consider a solution to the war. For Brigadier Thompson, now that the tricky and pointless battle of Goose Green was over, he could concentrate on attacking Stanley.

Chapter Nine

The Left Flank –
3 Commando Brigade
27 May to 11 June

While 2 Para were preparing to attack Goose Green, 3 Commando Brigade broke out of the San Carlos beachhead on 27 May. At dawn, 45 Commando filed down Sussex Mountain and were ferried by LCU to Port San Carlos. With each man carrying about 100lb, it then 'yomped' 13 miles to New House that night and early next day reached Douglas Settlement, a small hamlet at the north-west corner of Port Salvador Bay. Recce Troop provided the advance guard while Surveillance Troop protected the flanks, with the leading company deployed tactically, two troops up. Three BV202s carried Commando HQ radios and four were used for ammunition. The column stretched for about 3 miles. The Commando arrived at Teal Inlet on 30 May just after 3 Para had left. It had advanced 25 miles in 36 hours over wet and rough terrain and had suffered twenty-six leg and foot injuries, with six men being evacuated. Tractors and trailers helped move bergens and heavy equipment from Douglas. After a rest, the Commando pressed on to Mount Kent.

At 1.00 am, 3 Para reached Teal Inlet, a small hamlet on Port Salvador Bay, during the night of 29 May. Next day, it 'tabbed' to the few farm buildings of Estancia House and then occupied Mounts Estancia and Vernet on 1 June. The Battalion had marched about 50 miles in six days, on tracks and cross country, and had encountered no opposition.

During the night of 29 May, HMS *Fearless* (Captain Jeremy Larken) left San Carlos Water taking Commodore Clapp to meet Major General Moore and Brigadier Wilson, who had cross-decked from *Queen Elizabeth II* to HMS *Antrim* at South Georgia. Both ships then lurched through mountainous seas and met with HMS *Hermes* for an afternoon conference between Moore, Wilson, Clapp and Rear Admiral Woodward. Amphibious warfare doctrine suggests that the land force commander, in Moore's case a major general, and the amphibious commander, in Clapp's case equivalent to a brigadier, ought to be of equal rank and so Clapp suggested that to ease inter-Service command

and control, he should be appointed Chief-of-Staff (Navy) to Moore. This was rejected by Woodward, who said that he should remain as Commander CTG 317.0 in case he needed to command ships. Technically, it was Northwood's decision. Clapp was then designated Commodore Inshore Naval Operations and Logistic Support, as opposed to Commodore Amphibious Task Force. As the most junior of the triumvirate, Clapp was in an invidious position and hoped that his contribution would not be affected by his status. With more and diverse command and control assets joining the Task Force, and secure communications becoming an issue, Moore moved his HQ to HMS *Fearless* but, like HQ 3 Commando Brigade, found its Amphibious Operations Room inadequate – it was designed for a battalion HQ, however needs must. Next day, Moore landed at San Carlos. A member of HQ 3 Commando Brigade observed his arrival:

Major General Moore, who was wearing a desert kepi, strode up the path from San Carlos followed by a gaggle of officers. When everyone was sat down, Major General Moore said he would wear his cap in order not to patronise the green beret of the Commando Brigade and offend the red beret tradition of 5th Infantry Brigade. Major Chester, Thompson's Chief-of-Staff, briefed on the current situation. The Commando Brigade had split two ways, with 2nd Parachute Battalion down at Goose Green and 45 Commando and 3rd Parachute Battalion marching for Douglas and Teal Inlet respectively. 40 Commando, the Commando Logistic Regiment and Brigade HQ were still confined to the beachhead. The enemy had not yet reacted to their defeat at Goose Green . . . Moore concluded by ordering the two Brigade HQs to plan the defeat of the enemy on the basis that 3rd Commando Brigade was to continue its northerly axis while 5th Infantry Brigade took the southerly route. For us who had been ashore for the seven days, talk of the approach to Port Stanley was exciting and we looked forward to leaving San Carlos.

I noticed a scruffy, unkempt individual, whom I recognised to be the journalist Robert Fox, pushing himself forward to speak to Brigadier Thompson. He had been at Goose Green and I recognised the nervousness of a man recently exposed to unusual danger . . . He analysed the Argentine surrender to be a matter of honour, which did not seem to add up considering the tactical situation. He expressed some concern for the civilians at Port Stanley who could be held hostage; they were anyway. Fox was then introduced to Major-General Moore, who seemed a little impatient with him. Moore said he had landed to take the political pressure off Brigadier Thompson and allow him to advance on Port Stanley. This statement was a relief for the political pressures imposed on our Commander had begun to seep through to some members of the HQ Staff. Every time we saw Brigadier Thompson going on board HMS Fearless to use the satellite communication link, we

118

sympathised – another reprimand from someone 8,000 miles away with very little concept of our difficulties.

Moore was aware that Woodward's ships and crews were taking a pounding from the South Atlantic and it would be only a matter of time before their combat efficiency would decrease. Using Thompson's strategy, Moore intended to breach the Stanley defences in a three-phase operation on consecutive nights:

Phase One

A punch by 3 Commando Brigade from the west attacking the Outer Defence Zone.

Phase Two

An uppercut by 5 Infantry Brigade attacking Tumbledown and Mount William from the south.

A straight left on Wireless Ridge by 3 Commando Brigade.

Phase Three

The *coup de grâce* by 3 Commando Brigade supported by 5 Infantry Brigade.

The momentum of the attack must be kept in all phases and the Argentines must be given no time to regroup. Moore planned to attack after dark on 6 June. Although there was an opportunity to reform both brigades with their original units, Moore elected not to do so. 40 Commando, much to Lieutenant Colonel Malcolm Hunt's disappointment, was Force Reserve and then rearguard defending the beachhead. Although resented by the Commando, the Argentines had a plan to use 5th and 8th Infantry Regiments to counter-attack from West Falkland and the Royal Marines were suitably trained in amphibious and helicopter work to deal with any interdiction. G Squadron inserted patrols to watch both garrisons. The SAS and SBS were to be tasked by HQ LFFI. The Royal Navy had command of the sea. Pilots harassing Stanley found that they were now up against anti-aircraft gunners more practised after each sortie.

Thompson was still keen to seize Mount Kent, however the plan for D Squadron to reinforce the SAS patrol inserted on 24/25 May within twenty-four hours foundered when helicopters were needed to rescue survivors from HMS *Coventry*. Next night, 26/27 June, D Squadron piled into four Sea Kings. Sergeant Ratcliffe:

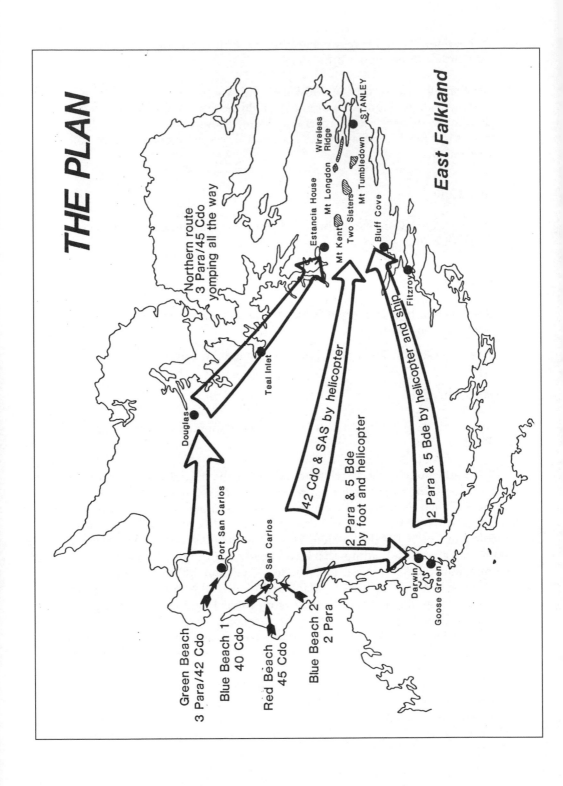

THE PLAN

East Falkland

Northern route
3 Para/45 Cdo
yomping all the way

STANLEY

Wireless
Ridge
Mt Longdon
Mt Tumbledown

Estancia House

Two Sisters

Mt Kent

Bluff Cove

Fitzroy

Teal Inlet

42 Cdo & SAS by helicopter

2 Para & 5 Bde
by foot and helicopter

2 Para & 5 Bde by helicopter and ship

Douglas

Port San Carlos

San Carlos

Darwin

Goose Green

Green Beach
3 Para/42 Cdo

Blue Beach 1
40 Cdo

Red Beach
45 Cdo

Blue Beach 2
2 Para

We had been dropped in the middle of bloody nowhere . . . We had not the least idea where we were, and whatever the lead pilot might have thought he had seen, it certainly wasn't the signal we had agreed. Almost the entire squadron was there on the ground, completely lost. The night was getting more and more misty and we could not see a thing . . . We sent people out on different compass points to try and get a fix while I stayed on the (Clansman) 320 radio, desperately trying to establish Morse-code communications with the ship. The four compass-point parties returned just as I eventually established contact. We had a meeting to decide where we were, and the men we'd sent out said that they thought that we were in an area marked 'Obscured by cloud'. I got through to Intrepid and told them where we were, or at least thought, we were. About four miserable, damp hours later the helicopters came back to collect us. It turned out we were miles away from Mount Kent, and about twenty kilometres from where we should have been dropped off. (Ratcliffe, *Eye of the Storm*)

Next night, while the British waited for the Goose Green garrison to surrender, D Squadron successfully landed east of Mount Kent with instructions to secure a landing zone for the 42 Commando fly-in the following night. The Argentines were also planning to seize Mount Kent.

When Fidel Castro's 1959 invasion of Cuba inspired Communist subversion through Central and South America, in Argentina, US advisers ran counter-insurgency and Ranger courses at the Airborne Infantry School at Cordoba. In preparation for the 1978 World Football Championships, Major Seineldin formed Special Team Halcon (Hawk) 8. Consisting of a cadre of an OC, six subalterns and eight warrant officers and SNCOs, it developed unconventional warfare techniques and ran three-month Special Forces courses at the Commando Wing of the School of Infantry at Campo de Mayo. Those who passed were awarded the prestigious green beret and were either posted to an operational commando unit or back to their parent arm, with the liability of being recalled for Special Forces duty. Inherent weaknesses were limited bonding and selections based on political affiliation leading to poor mutual understanding and fragile team spirit. Three Special Forces units were on the Falklands, the Army 601 Commando Company, 601 Border Guard Special Forces Squadron and the Air Force Special Operations Group pathfinders.

The two 601 Commando Company assault sections sent to West Falkland to follow up reports of British Special Forces were cut off from Stanley by the landings. An attempt to recover them by 601 Combat Aviation Battalion on 23 May resulted in the destruction of three helicopters, the second disaster to the Battalion in three days. The surviving Puma returned to Stanley with 2nd Assault Section. 1st Section remained on West Falkland and, four days from the end of the war, intercepted a Mountain Troop patrol directing naval gunfire on to Port Howard, killing Captain Hamilton and capturing his radio operator, Sergeant Fosenka. After the San Carlos landings, Major Castagneto, who commanded 601 Commando Company, and Brigadier General Daher devised Operation Cameleon, a Special Forces operations to neutralize a suspected British air defence position north of Mount Usborne, however he cancelled the operation because, with two commando sections stranded on West Falkland, success could not be guaranteed. Meanwhile, Major Aldo Rico, Second-in-Command, 22nd Mountain Infantry Regiment and confidant of Lieutenant Colonel Seinelden, had reasoned that with 601 Commando Company committed to the defence of the Falklands, another should be raised to defend the Atlantic Littoral. This was accepted by Army Headquarters and on 21 May, Rico was instructed to raise 602 Commando Company. Brought up to a strength of 50 all ranks by 4 cavalry warrant officer Blowpipe instructors and 2 medics, few were physically fit for active service after several years in line units.

With the return of 2nd Assault Section, Daher resurrected Operation Cameleon and shortly after dark on the 23rd a four-man patrol cached supplies on Mount Simon. Next day, Daher warned the patrols that because of the helicopter attrition rate, extraction might be difficult. The commandos found the going tough and one patrol covered just 2 miles in daylight. When the weather turned nasty on 25 May, the weary patrols were extracted by a CH-47. All reported considerable evidence of enemy helicopter activity but no ground troops. When the Argentines planned for a Special Forces operation to re-occupy Mount Kent during the night of 29 May, Brigadier General Menendez requested 602 Commando Company. On 27 May, after their training was cut short, it joined 601 Commando Company. Some SNCOs, in particular, later perceived the Company to be an ad hoc unit flown to the Falklands because Menendez had greater faith in Special Forces than infantry. Some questioned the quality of the leadership, views that may have influenced tactical decisions. The same day, Brigadier General Menendez assembled all the Special Forces into the Special Forces Group and instructed Brigadier General Daher, in Operation Autoimpuesta, to establish a north-south screen, gather intelligence on 3 Commando Brigade and take 'prompt and decisive action as necessary to deal with the British incursion into Stanley'. Mount Kent was to be seized at the earliest opportunity. The Special Forces Group set about planning the operation:

Mount Estancia – 601 Army Commando Company to establish an observation post once Mount Kent had been captured.

Mount Simon – To be occupied by 1st Assault Section, 602 Army Commando Company.

Mount Kent. Three-phase operation:
2nd and 3rd Assault Section, 602 Commando Company to gain a foothold on 29 May.

The 65-strong Border Guard Special Forces Squadron to seize the summit. Major Jaimet's B Company, 6th Infantry Regiment, to provide the defence.

Smoko Mount – To be seized by the Air Force Special Operations Group.

Lieutenant Horacio Losito, of 1st Assault Section, 602 Commando Company later recalled the preparations:

At 21.00 Captain Jose Verseci returned with the Orders for the mission. Normally we followed a strict planning sequence but this was aborted for several reasons and had to be adapted to the reality of the situation and not the text-book style. First, the very short period between drawing up the plan and the start of the operation, at 06.00 the following day. Secondly, the nature of the mission, our speciality being combat missions rather than the recce we were now being asked to do. This confused us. Thirdly, the great quantity of equipment we had to prepare, some of which had only recently arrived in Stanley. One fundamental observation is that in peacetime one should practise planning, in detail, so that in hostilities when the enemy creates the unknown factor and when the physical and psychological conditions are different, the sequence can be greatly reduced. Nevertheless the operation was detailed, in particular the first phase of getting close to the objective and subsequent operation on Mount Simon. The later phases were badly planned. In all commando operations, withdrawal is fundamental but generally less attention is paid to it than the offensive phase. It should also be remembered we had been in Stanley for just three days, had done some short recces of the defences and were still familiarizing ourselves with the situation. We knew nothing about the area to the west and had no knowledge of the threat or the enemy's ability to intercept or jam our radios. Intelligence was scarce but no one was at fault; it simply wasn't available.

Shortly after dawn on 28 May, when the Special Forces Group linked up with B Assault Company, 601 Combat Aviation Battalion, at Moody Brook and the Racecourse, 602 Commando Company were flown out. However, rain and thick wet mist then blanketed Stanley and Lieutenant Colonel Juan Scarpa, the senior Army helicopter pilot, cancelled the remainder of the fly-out until 8.00 am the next day. Thus, the newest Special Forces unit found itself in the field, isolated, in unfamiliar territory and reinforcements unlikely until the next day. On Mount Kent, D Squadron were unprepared for the sound of a Puma and four Huey helicopters bringing in twenty-nine commandos consisting of five-strong HQ Section (Captain Eduarado Villaruel) and 2nd (Captain Tomas Fernandez) and 3rd Assault Sections (Captain Ferrero), both twelve-strong. In the grey gloom, the helicopters became separated and Fernandez's landing near Bluff Cove Peak was detected by Sergeant Stone's Mountain and Arctic Warfare Cadre patrol on Bull Hill.

Ferrero's Section landed on the eastern slopes of Mount Kent and were soon engaged in a confusing close-quarter battle with Air Troop. Ratcliffe:

> Mountain Troop had been allocated a location to the south of Mount Kent . . . We lay up all day and into the night. Away on our flank, Air Troop made contact with an Argentinian patrol. Then we heard our Troop Commander (Captain Hamilton) scream 'Contact!' I wondered what was happening, because there had been no sounds of firing from his position. We grabbed our belt kits and weapons and ran down the mountainside to meet him. We found him running towards the landing site. (Ratcliffe, *Eye of the Storm*)

Three Argentines managed to infiltrate the SAS positions and force the British, with two wounded, higher up Mount Kent. Meanwhile, Villaruel had also landed on Mount Kent and, avoiding contact, withdrew to high ground.

When 42 Commando was formally ordered to reinforce the SAS by Brigadier Thompson on 28 May. Lieutenant Colonel Vaux's plan was for K Company (Captain Peter Babbington) to seize the summit and then for L Company (Captain David Wheen), a 7 (Sphinx) Commando Battery section, Mortar Platoon and a Blowpipe section to follow in the second lift. After dark, K Company set off for Mount Kent in four 846 NAS Sea Kings but heavy snow showers induced 'white-out' and extremely poor visibility prevented landing, forcing the pilots to grope their way back to San Carlos by frequently landing to pinpoint their location. Skirmishes on Mount Kent continued for most of the night. It seemed to HQ 3 Commando Brigade that D Squadron was under pressure but information was scarce. Abandoning Mount Kent and regrouping at Estancia were discussed but Brigadier Thompson, keen to seize the feature, told Lieutenant Colonel Rose that he must hang on. Help was on its way.

Throughout the next morning, which was bitterly cold and overcast with ominous snow clouds, 42 Commando waited. At midday, a passing Wessex was talked down, but the pilot said that he had been tasked for the morning only. When the surviving Chinook and a Sea King appeared, the Chinook pilot, Squadron Leader Dick Langworthy, clearly exhausted after forty-eight hours, offered to fly in the guns if the Sea Kings would take the troops, but the Royal Navy pilot said he could fly only two sorties when three were needed. Vaux was furious:

> There followed an arid and acrimonious conversation between John Chester, the Brigade Major, and myself. I was furious that we appeared to have been let down by the Staff, he was adamant that they had done all they could. Eventually we agreed an uneasy compromise. K Company, Tac HQ and the four 81mm mortars would fly in that night. The remainder would have to wait until the following evening. (Vaux, *March to the South Atlantic*)

At the time, Vaux did not appreciate the tension in Brigade HQ with limited resources being pulled in three directions: to the south by Goose Green, to the east on Mount Kent and to the north by the departure of 45 Commando and 3 Para. A Royal Navy Mobile Air Operations Team then arrived with 42 Commando to organize its deployment to Mount Kent. Matters were considerably eased when 846 NAS came ashore from HMS *Intrepid* to a forward operating base near Ajax Bay. Taking advantage of a window of favourable weather, three Sea Kings carrying K Company headed for Mount Kent. At about the same time, believing that Ferrero and Villaruel were still in the area, Fernandez and 2nd Assault Section set off for Mount Kent but clashed with the SAS losing two men killed. Sergeant Ratcliffe:

> We climbed on to the ridge overlooking open ground to the south of Mount Kent. We could see for miles, and almost at once spotted a four-man Argentinian patrol working its way toward us. I was leading our own four man group and signalled that we crawl forward to our OP among the rocks and wait for the enemy to approach. None of us said a word. All communication between us was by hand signals. Apart from the buffeting of the wind, there was complete silence. Through my binoculars, I watched as the Argentines came steadily towards us. Wearing green uniforms and carrying packs on their backs, they were in single file at normal patrol speed, holding their weapons at the ready. When they were 100 metres away, we opened fire with our M-16 rifles, a far better weapon than the heavy and cumbersome 7.62mm SLR with which the rest of the British forces were armed. They immediately took cover behind a big boulder, although we knew we had hit two for certain, because we saw them go down and could hear screaming. (Ratcliffe, *Eye of the Storm*)

Breaking contact, the Argentines scrambled downhill, however Sergeant Alfredo Flores, the signaller, was knocked out when he fell and was captured.

Taken aback by the fighting, the Royal Marines headed for the summit. Squadron Leader Langworthy flew in three Light Guns, however when he landed he found their weight was pressing the rear undercarriage into the mud, so he kept the Chinook at low hover while the twenty-two commando gunners dragged the two guns down the ramp and lowered the third from its underslung hook. When Lieutenant Colonel Vaux learnt of the fighting, he halted the fly-in, asked the pilots to keep their engines running until he had a better idea of what was happening. Langworthy left Mount Kent but a fierce snowstorm played havoc with his navigation and the Chinook splashed into a stream midway between Mount Kent and Teal Inlet, causing slight damage. Meeting Vaux, he mentioned that the SAS had the situation under control, which did not seem to be the case to everyone else engaged in the operation.

Since the delay had eroded the helicopter fuel margins, Vaux revised the schedule to a single lift to take L Company, palleted artillery ammunition and other essential personnel. Lieutenant Colonel Rose's Tac HQ piled in on top of ammunition and spare radios batteries – such is the luxury, in war, of breaking the rulebook. The ubiquitous correspondent Max Hastings claimed that Brigadier Thompson had personally given him a seat, although he could hardly claim to be essential – as it turned out to be untrue, he was given a Blowpipe missile to carry as a punishment for his dishonesty. Fifteen minutes later the helicopters lurched to the ground; the battle with Fernandez was still being fought. When Major Delves told him that he did not know if the summit was secure, Vaux decided that: 'It seemed best not to appear surprised, although back in Brigade HQ they certainly believed the summit had been scouted.' (Vaux, *March to the South Atlantic*)

Concerned that K Company might encounter a strong enemy force turned to relief when Captain Peter Babbington radioed that he had found evidence of a rapid Argentine pull-out. A secondary position covering the path to the Murrell Bridge was also found. By first light, 42 Commando was firm on Mount Kent. About 18 kilometres to the east they could see Stanley. Over the next two nights, the rest of the Commando, 2 Troop, 59 Independent Commando Squadron RE and all of 7 (Sphinx) Commando Battery, joined K Company. L Company and the sappers were immediately advanced to Mount Challenger and established an OP on Mount Wall, which was named Tara after one of Vaux's daughters.

Captain Ferrero, without any sign of Major Spadaro, abandoned Mount Kent and in mid-morning linked up with one of four Army helicopters seen collecting troops from Mount Wall. The pilot said that they were supporting the redeployment of 4th Infantry Regiment to Two Sisters and Mount Harriet, and was then asked to pass a map reference for Major Rico when he deployed into the field. Shortly afterwards, two Harriers screamed overhead and attacked the helicopters, which managed to avoid destruction. The fly-out of the Border Guards was delayed because of Harrier patrols and it was not until about 11.00 am that their Puma took off but then crashed near Murrell Bridge, killing six and injuring eight. It is possible the Puma was brought down by Argentine ground fire, however it is more likely that it hit the ground avoiding rockets from the two Harriers which had passed over Villaruel's position. During the afternoon Villaruel was joined by Ferrero. With no sign of the Border Guards or 601 Army Commando Company, Captain Villaruel assembled the surviving 602 Army Commandos and set off for Stanley at midday on 31 May and reached 7th Infantry Regiment on Mount Longdon. After two days intermittent fighting, Mount Kent was in British hands and Brigadier Thompson now had a springboard from which to launch the assault on Stanley. But the entire operation had taken up virtually all the support helicopters and had delayed the arrival of 5 Infantry Brigade.

Operation Autoimpuesta had not gone well and with the British now occupying Mount Kent, Stanley was under direct threat. This and the defeat at Goose

Green demoralized the soldiers and several officers, critical of the performances of Brigadier Generals Menendez, Parada and Jofre planned a mutiny, however they had insufficient support. Major Rico, one of the conspirators, was given command of the Special Forces Group. Of some concern to him was that nothing had been heard from 1st Assault Section, 602 Commando Company. Cancelling the deployment of 601 Commando Company, he instructed Major Mario Castagneto to rescue 602 Commando Company, who had been told to assemble on Mount Estancia. Castagneto was leading a column of motorcycles and Land Rovers when it was mortared by 42 Commando. Abandoning the Land Rovers, he and seven men reached the northern slopes of Mount Kent where they were mortared again and eventually they returned to Stanley.

On 28 May, 1st Assault Section had been dropped near Top Malo House, which is about 7 kilometres from Mount Simon. Believing that it would give his mission a better chance of success, Captain Verseci split his section into two groups. Shortly after midday they met and established an OP near the summit. In deteriorating weather, they saw British helicopters with underslung loads, including the surviving Chinook, and probably witnessed the insertion of K Company onto Mount Kent. Attempts were made to contact HQ Special Forces Group, however their radio had a fault which prevented them transmitting. The fighting on Mount Kent worried them, because the intelligence was that there were no enemy between Mount Simon and Stanley. Anxious about being cut off, Verseci decided to link up with the 601 Combat Engineer Battalion company known to be at Fitzroy Bridge. Shortly before midday on 30 May, the Section headed south, however the freezing drizzle, heavy loads and fatigue took its toll. By 3.00 pm, it was on the banks of the swollen Arroyo Malo and had no choice but plunge to waist deep into the icy water. Emerging the other side, Verseci accepted the advice of two Antarctic veterans to shelter at Top Malo House. It was nearly dark when the Argentines arrived at the abandoned two-storey timber building, an outhouse and a privy overlooking a small corral sloping down to Mullow Stream. A patrol checked the area and, finding no signs of the British, the Argentines moved into the welcome shelter of the house.

However, a Mountain and Arctic Warfare Cadre patrol, commanded by Lieutenant Fraser Haddow, was in the area. The 3 Commando Brigade Recce Troop, the Cadre was skilled in mountain and winter warfare. When the war broke out, its strength was larger than normal because a Mountain Leader course was nearing its end. With the urgent need for specialist troops, its final exercise was the war. Captain Rod Boswell, who commanded the Cadre, had spread patrols across 3 Commando Brigade's frontage when Haddow's report was received. Believing that the Argentines had been sent to neutralize him, Haddow waited until it dawned on him that he had not been spotted. Air support was not available because the Harriers were engaged in other operations and night was approaching. Boswell tried to direct other patrols to meet Haddow, but atmospheric conditions made high frequency radio transmissions impossible, although he did manage to assemble nineteen men from his reserves, Stone's patrol, which had just returned, and his own HQ and split them into a seven-man fire support group and a twelve-man assault group. At about 8.30 am on 31 May, Boswell's men were flown to a position about 1,200m from Top Malo House. Inside the house, the Argentine commandos were preparing breakfast when the helicopter was heard. Lieutenant Ernesto Espinosa, on watch on the upper floor, then reported that it did not have the Argentine yellow recognition stripe and must therefore be British.

On high ground above Mullow Stream, when Boswell fired a green mini flare, three 66mm smashed into the timber house and Corporal Groves, armed with a L42 sniper rifle, shot an Argentine who appeared at an upper window. Another 66mm volley ripped into the building. The impact of the rockets stunned the Argentines, but they quickly recovered and returned fire. Soon the house was burning. Verseci was assembling his men by the front door ready to rush out, when a grenade exploded, wounding Lieutenant Losito. The Argentines flung open the door and took up positions to return fire. Expecting his assault group to skirmish forward, with the two sections leapfrogging through each other, Boswell ordered the assault. However, the eleven Royal Marines charged down the slope. Keen to lead from the front, Boswell sprinted after them. One section angled toward the burning house and the dazed Lieutenant Luis Brun, using a pistol, was wounded a second time. He tried to throw a grenade but was weak from loss of blood. The wounded Horacio Losito recalled:

The enemy were now about fifteen metres away. They were without any protection, as they thought they were not going to meet any resistance, believing us to be dead or wounded, but they had not reckoned with the covering fire from inside the house. I made for the stream, as did almost everyone else. The ground was totally devoid of cover and our only protection was our own tactics. So we ran a few yards, threw ourselves on the ground and returned fire. Sergeant Sbert joined Captain Verseci and First Lieutenant Gatti giving covering fire from the fence but he was killed rescuing the wounded Lieutenant Helguero, hit yet again by a grenade splinter.

The momentum of the charge was lost when it seemed that no one knew where the enemy were, except for short outbursts of firing as the Argentines scuttled from cover to cover. The Cadre skirmished toward the fence. Losito:

The British passed the house and came toward us in a classic assault, straight out of the schoolbooks, shouting and firing according to their tactical philosophy. I crossed a fence between the house and stream and tumbled into the stream, dazed and bleeding badly. My intention was to cross, but there was total confusion, shots, explosions, shouting and

128

I was then hit in the thigh and fell into the ditch. My head wound was bleeding profusely and I wondered if an artery had been cut. I could hardly see, but remained calm amidst the firing and shouting. I tried to tie a tourniquet around my leg, but since the enemy were close, I did not have the time and, wriggling on my back, returned fire but with little success.

Reaching the corral, one of Sergeant Doyle's ammunition pouches was hit by tracer, which detonated some rounds, severely wounding him in the arm and shoulder. A third group moved to the back of the houses to deal with Argentines in dead ground exchanging shots with the fire support team, wounding Groves in the chest. In the bed of the stream the Argentines were reasonably well organized. Black timber smoke was swirling across the battle-field. One Argentine was hit five times by 5.56mm Armalite rounds, and Sergeant Stone was wounded in the stomach by a single 7.62mm FAL round when he broke cover to draw fire. The British forced the Argentines into dead ground and prepared to roll them up. On the right, when Royal Marines had occupied a small knoll and called on the Argentines to surrender, some did, while others fought on. Losito:

It is not easy to surrender when one carried the responsibility of my commando beret and the success of the mission. The outcome for a commando is victory or death and I continued firing. To my right two British came towards me and because I was drowsy, I didn't realize at first they were shooting; it sounded like rain on sand. I swung round to fire but having no strength slowly collapsed into the ditch, oblivious of the water. One of them pointed his rifle at me and thinking he was going to shoot, I entrusted myself to God. However, he lowered his weapon, dragged me out of the ditch, took away my FAL and said, 'No problem; it's war.' He then tied a tourniquet on my leg with his scarf. He asked if I had any medicine and, when I told him my kit was in the house, he took out a morphine capsule from his inside pocket and injected my leg. One or two Argentines were still resisting further down the stream and we were in danger of being caught in crossfire.

The calls to surrender becoming urgent, 1st Assault Section realized the hopelessness of the situation. The fight had lasted about fifteen minutes. In one of those moments of camaraderie between enemies, Boswell mentioned to Captain Verseci, 'Never in a house!' The destruction of 602 Commando Company signalled the end of Operation Autoimpuesta and Army Group Stanley was now virtually blind to the British advance. Of the 170 commandos earmarked for the operation, about 50 made it into the field and of these, 32 men had been killed, wounded or were missing.

Now that the Argentines had been cleared from the Brigade axis, during the night of 31 May HQ 3 Commando Brigade left San Carlos for Teal Inlet in BV202s, escorted by a Blues and Royals Troop. The principal activity was patrols to gather information for the attacks on Stanley scheduled for 6 June. The Royal Engineers would be vital to recce minefields and bring back mines. Ahead, G Squadron and the Mountain and Arctic Warfare Cadre provided a light screen. One SAS patrol ambushed a SBS patrol in British uniforms on 1 June, killing Sergeant 'Kiwi' Hunter. The SBS had been dropped in the wrong area. A patrol on the desolate Beagle Ridge had an excellent view of Stanley and when joined by Captain Hugh McManners and his NGFO 1 provided excellent naval gunfire support.

On the left flank, 3 Para reached Estancia House on 31 May and then began to prepare to attack Mount Longdon and indeed, during the morning of 2 June, began an advance to contact until Lieutenant Colonel Pike was reminded by Brigadier Thompson during the later afternoon that the attack on the Outer Defence Zone was a Brigade attack. Thereafter the Battalion began an intensive patrol programme from a defensive position west of Murrell Bridge. The ambushing of an Argentine patrol early on 6 June resulted in six enemy being killed, although the paras were forced to withdraw under heavy mortar and machine-gun fire.

In the centre, 45 Commando probed at the positions held by 4th Infantry Regiment. During the night of 8/9 June, two strong patrols managed to establish themselves on the lower slopes of Two Sisters but were then forced to withdraw. The following night, a Recce Troop patrol ambushed an Argentine infantry patrol escorting marine engineers near Murrell Bridge, killing three engineers and four infantry. A local truce was arranged so the Argentines could recover their dead. However poor communications and poor weather led to a friendly fire incident when a patrol attacked the Mortar Platoon, resulting in four Royal Marines killed and four wounded. These patrols did at least find a track leading east from Mount Kent to Two Sisters.

On the right, 42 Commando had several tussles with 4th Infantry Regiment. On 3 June, in thick fog, a Recce Troop patrol were driven from Mount Wall and lost almost all its equipment and a laser rangefinder. Thompson instructed Lieutenant Colonel Vaux, 'I should like you to get back as soon as J Company is established.' Next day, 10 Troop found the OP empty. Vaux decided to attack Mount Harriet from the south although several patrols from K and L Companies suffered casualties when they encountered minefields. The explosions risked compromising his approach while casualty evacuation proved extremely hazardous.

Nevertheless, the amount of intelligence collected concerned only the first hundred yards of the Argentine defences. Poor weather had prevented air photo recces of Argentine positions in depth and no prisoners, who could describe the Argentine positions and plans, were captured.

For two weeks, 3 Commando Brigade were exposed to stinging curtains of rain and snow sweeping across the bleak high moors driven by chaotic kabatic winds which whipped up from the Antarctic ripping shelters aside. Sometimes a harsh overnight frost would herald a few hours of precious warmth from a weak morning sun. Brigadier Thompson offered to bring 42 Commando, in the most exposed positions, out of the line to recuperate but, such was their enthusiasm, the idea was rejected. He was keen to bring the combat-fit 40 Commando back from the drudgery of guarding the divisional supplies dump at San Carlos Water. On 2 June, the hybrid J Company rejoined the Commando from Goose Green. Major Rod MacDonald, who commanded 59 Independent Commando Squadron RE, later wrote: 'It was at this stage we started to compete with 5 Brigade for the limited helicopter assets to bring up guns and ammunition for our advance forward as well as resupply for our forward troops who were living in the worst conditions I have ever experienced, and that includes Norway.'

The priority being the flying forward of ammunition and other essentials meant that bergens, the precious sleeping bags and water took second place. When rations arrived, they were often the dehydrated Arctic type, which requires at least nine pints of water for a decent meal. The brackish water in pools was unfit even when boiled and consequently diarrhoea and dehydration was not uncommon. The cold and constant damp of wet clothing, sodden sleeping bags and soaking ground weakened those who were suffering even more. Keeping feet healthy in these inhospitable conditions became a top priority. Lieutenant Colonel Vaux:

But no matter the footwear, we all had soaking feet almost all the time. On the move blisters and abrasions usually followed from wet boots. But protracted immobility on sentry, or in an ambush, reduced circulation and could cause cold weather injuries, which became so painful that in extreme cases an individual could not walk. The antidote was to dry and powder the feet whenever possible, before cherishing them in a dry pair of socks inside a warm sleeping bag. These last critical conditions became increasingly hard to sustain, although everyone appreciated their importance. That precious pair of dry socks was only worn at rest, and then carefully protected from getting wet until the next time. (Vaux, *March to the South Atlantic*)

Chapter Ten

The Right Flank –
5 Infantry Brigade

On 2 June, forty Argentine sappers from 2 Section, 601 Combat Engineer Company (Lieutenant Horacio Blanco) blew up Fitzroy Bridge with 80lb of Trotyl. When the smoke cleared, about 40 per cent of the 150-foot bridge had collapsed into Fitzroy Inlet. Destroying the bridge meant a 14-mile march around its head at River Camp.

Reverted back to 5 Infantry Brigade after Goose Green, 2 Para had not been idle. Major Crosland had hatched a plan to telephone Bluff Cove settlement to find out what was happening in the Fitzroy/Bluff Cove area by advancing to Swan Inlet House by helicopter.

Following the briefing at San Carlos, Brigadier Wilson arrived at 2 Para to brief them about his plans to advance along the southern flank. Things did not go well. During an exercise in February, the Battalion had lost confidence in his methods of handling parachute troops and this was further eroded when Wilson arrived wearing a red beret and green Wellington boots, a dress code that offended Parachute Regiment sensitivities. Wilson rejected the Swan Inlet plan and explained that he wanted the Battalion to secure his left flank by picketing the snow-covered Mount Usborne and Wickham Heights. Etiquette cast aside, his proposal drew the response from one company commander, 'Brigadier, are you pissed?' When the briefing broke up, Wilson and 2 Para were both angry.

Assured by Major General Moore that his Brigade would have parity with 3 Commando Brigade, Wilson lobbied hard without much success. While 3 Commando Brigade had BV 202s for transporting heavy equipment and for Brigade Headquarters, Wilson's request for some was rejected. Throughout the campaign, his HQ was either man-packed or relied upon the Royal Navy or helicopters to move its Land Rovers. The Royal Navy had the ability to move 5 Infantry Brigade, however Commodore Clapp's preference was that the Army brigade should march. With two LCUs supporting the 3 Commando BMA at Teal Inlet, the remaining six were under his command unloading men, equipment and stores at San Carlos. Clapp did not assign any landing craft to Wilson because, quite naturally, he felt that 5 Infantry Brigade lacked amphibious experience and would not use them 'sensibly'. A Royal Marine officer was attached to the Brigade but he was not supported by an amphibious warfare liaison team.

Determined not to miss the opportunity of attacking Stanley and with everything conspiring against a simple move, Brigadier Wilson reappeared at 2 Para and told Major Keeble to 'Do it', referring to the Swan Inlet scheme. Major Crosland alerted 6 Platoon and Colour Sergeant Alan Morris from the Intelligence Section. Captain Greenhalgh arrived with five Scouts, two fitted with SS-11 wire-guided anti-tank missiles. At about 11.00 am, the SS-11 Scouts softened up Swan Inlet. Covered by a para armed with a Sterling sub-machine gun in both helicopters, the assault helicopters then landed with four men in each. The paras found the settlement uninhabited. Crosland and Morris found a telephone and when Crosland cranked it, twelve-year-old Michelle Binney answered and summoned her father, Ron, the Fitzroy settlement manager. Frost:

> Explaining who they were, they asked if there were any enemy in Fitzroy or Bluff Cove; the answer was negative, although the bridge at Fitzroy had been tampered with. 'We'll be seeing you shortly,' said John and rang off. The news was radioed to Major Keeble back at Goose Green: 'Fleet and Balham are clear.' (The choice of nickname was fairly typical. John Crosland lived in Fleet, Hampshire and Balham, according to a famous comic monologue is 'gateway to the south'! (Frost, *2 Para in the Falklands*)

When Keeble advised Brigadier Wilson, he abandoned his plan of marching to Fitzroy in preference for a *coup de grâce*.

Meanwhile, 2 Para greeted a new Commanding Officer, Lieutenant Colonel David Chaundler. Posted to the Ministry of Defence, he was earmarked to take over from Jones, anyway. With little time to prepare and after a long flight from the UK, he parachuted from a C-130 Hercules into the sea near the Carrier Battle Group and was picked up by HMS *Penelope*. He knew Brigadier Wilson and told him that any difficulties he encountered were his problem. Scrounging a lift in a Sea King to Darwin, he then walked across the Goose Green battlefield to Battalion HQ. Since most had expected Keeble to command for the duration, his arrival was greeted with something of a shock. After being briefed on the Fitzroy and Bluff Cove operation, Chaundler told Keeble to execute it. He would assume command next day.

Helicopters were much in demand. Pressures from the International Committee of the Red Cross meant the surviving Chinook was being used to ferry Goose Green prisoners of war to San Carlos and for most, repatriation. The move of an artillery battery, 100 rounds per gun and gunners required at least forty-five lifts. 'Cadging lifts' and 'informal retasking' were not unknown and part of the 'can do, must do' culture on which the military thrives. With the fear that the telephone conversation with Binney and her father might have been intercepted, the Chinook was 'retasked' at Goose Green by A Company HQ and two platoons, B Company HQ and a platoon and Mortar and Anti-Tank Platoons detachments. Two 656 Squadron Scouts took two Patrols Platoon sections to mark out landing sites between Fitzroy and Bluff Cove.

ZA 718 (Flight Lieutenant NJ Grose and Flying officer C Miller) was used to advance men from 2 Para forward from Goose Green. With seats folded against the side, 81 fully-armed paratroops were crammed into the helicopter for its first mission. That was well above the manufacturer's advertised troop-carrying capability (of forty). The second mission involved 74 fully-armed paratroops and both were conducted in poor visibility with a low cloud base over an area that had not been fully confirmed as clear of enemy troops. (Burden et al., *Falklands: The Air War*)

However, no one had advised 3 Commando Brigade, or indeed HQ LFFI. Lance Corporal Steve Nicholls was with Lieutenant Murray's Mountain and Arctic Warfare Cadre patrol:

Our team was due to be tasked again and we were ready and impatient to be deployed this time watching the area of Fitzroy. The outline tasking was deliberately vague – 'Watch the road/track for any evidence of troop movement and activity. In particular a large wooden bridge which would be vital to any flanking movement by friendly forces if they were to advance towards Stanley. On arrival, we positioned ourselves on Smoko Mount in a fairly bleak, windswept position but it was the only possible vantage point that offered cover from view and an escape route. Near us was a flagpole, complete with slapping halyards, which helped to confirm where we were in the low and poor visibility on the walk-in. It was also used to elevate the radio antenna. Our main focus of attention was the wooden bridge and the immediate area either side of it. Whenever the mist cleared, we could see the Argentineans scrambling over the struts. It had all the hallmarks of being prepared for demolition and this we reported. By now our routine was much smoother and we continued to work radio schedules, reporting at fixed time but always with the ability to report in if needed. Visibility proved difficult with a wet clinging mist frequently enveloping the position for several hours at a time obscuring the bridge and approaches. We could hear vehicles and voices but it was all routine. As at Teal Inlet, the Argentineans were not alert, no sign of sentries being posted or any attempts to position a fire team on high ground. They did not have the appearance of being particularly well disciplined or tactically aware, nor were they bivvying in the immediate area. Our pattern of life in the OP was dull, damp and uneventful.

The sound of helicopters on 2nd June was unusual, as none had been previously sighted. Mist and low cloud cover prevented us from seeing anything. It then became apparent that there were several helicopters, including the distinctive deep 'swish, swish' of the twin rotors of a Chinook. Our intelligence suggested that only one had survived the loss of the Atlantic Conveyor. The activity below us suggested a fairly large troop deployment but without a clear view, we could only guess at their identity. Occasionally the mist lifted for a few seconds and we were able to identify heavily laden troops moving around but never long enough for a positive identification. Calculating co-ordinates for a fire mission on the troops, who were bunched and in the open, I opened up communications in clear seeking confirmation of friendly forces movement to prevent any loss of reporting time. Cadre HQ at Teal Inlet, who were co-located with HQ 3rd Commando Brigade, confirmed there should be no friendly troops to our front. After several questions and answers to confirm details, the fire mission was accepted. We originally planned for a small-scale fire mission but as the size of the target grew, we requested that more guns be made available. The cloud cover continued to mask most of the area to our front but the helicopter activity continued and increasing numbers of troops could be seen out in the open. We received confirmation that the guns were prepared.

29 Commando Regiment accepted Murray's report and gave the fire mission to 7 (Sphinx) Commando Battery, just 8 miles to the north of the target. In his command post, the Battery Commander, Major David Brown, completed his fire orders and soon everything was ready – guns loaded, range and bearing calculated, Number Ones waiting. Fire mission confirmation was then sought. Nicholls continues:

We were waiting for the executive order of 'Three rounds fire for effect,' which would initiate a salvo of three rounds from each gun to target the area. These were zeroing rounds that would be adjusted by us to hit the target. Once the guns were 'on' they would commence the full fire mission. The gap between final confirmation and opening fire is usually a very short one. Our checks and controls were complete and delays could allow the target to escape. Precisely at this point the cloud cover opened a 'window' and we saw the easily recognized figure of a Scout helicopter with British markings. We knew the Argentines were not equipped with them. It all unfolded in a few very brief seconds, the radio handset was already poised and the command 'Check, check, check, confirmed sighting of a Scout helicopter'. This was repeated back from the gun lines and the net went instantly silent. It still wasn't clear if all the activity could be attributed to the British but it was apparent that we had been very close to bringing down fire on our own side.

With Fitzroy Bridge now under British control, Murray's patrol was extracted. This was essentially the end of Nicholls' war. Rejoining 45 Commando as a section commander, he returned to the Cadre, in 1984, to complete the Senior Mountain Leader when the BBC filmed the Cadre in *Behind the Lines*.

A fundamental principle of warfare is always to keep neighbouring units informed of strategies that may affect them. On this occasion, a potentially damaging 'blue on blue' had been avoided by a fortunate break in the clammy clouds. Knowing that Major General Moore intended to attack the Outer Defence Zone on 6 June, and under huge pressure to advance, Wilson had taken a huge risk and, so far, his judgement had paid off. It was a bold, if controversial, move. As he later said on television: 'I've grabbed my land in this great jump forward. Now I want to consolidate it.'

Communications between Fitzroy and Goose Green were poor and when the two Scouts returned from dropping the two Patrols Platoon sections, they had exhausted their flying hours. Wilson stepped into the breach and shortly before dark, Corporal Banks and a Signals Platoon rebroadcast team were inserted midway on Wickham Heights in his helicopter. At about the same time, Lieutenant Colonel Chaundler, Major Keeble and B Company were approaching Fitzroy in the Chinook. Chaundler remembers that the RAF loadmaster drew a laugh when he invited everyone to sit down. Frost:

> Connor had switched on the strobe light to bring in the helicopter. Once landed, Major Keeble, assuming A Company to have landed correctly at Bluff Cove, ordered the recce party to move to higher ground to establish communications, and this they did. But already the darkness had led to a loss of contact with the B Company group below and Keeble therefore decided that the best course would be to move forward to Fitzroy. Only then did the magnitude of the helicopter pilot's error become apparent, as the paras realised that they were full 4 kilometres short of the proposed landing site. (Frost, *2 Para in the Falklands*)

Connor was Lieutenant Chris Connor, the Recce Platoon Commander. Covered by B Company on the ridge, Connor checked the settlement for enemy. Learning that there were none, Chaundler recalled: 'We walked forward and had tea with Ron Binney.'

While Mrs Binney was producing tea and cakes, her husband reported that Fitzroy Bridge was damaged. Connor and a patrol were taken by Land Rover and when they estimated that the damage could be repaired, this was passed to Major Chris Davies at 9 Parachute Squadron RE. He and three Signals Section hitched a lift in a Sea King and were taken to the bridge by Tim Dobyn of Bluff Cove:

The Argies had indeed had a reasonably successful attempt at rupturing the one hundred and fifty metre (or so) bridge, which spanned the cold black water of the western neck of Port Fitzroy inlet. There was a gap of sixty-six feet in the eastern end of the bridge. The wooden decking had gone and of the three wooden loadbearers, one had gone completely and one was broken, although it had dropped only a couple of feet onto the rocky abutment. The third was pitted by the explosion but still spanned the gap providing the precarious tight rope connecting the bridge to the bank. The pair of piles nearest the eastern bank had gone too. I could see that the nearest four pairs of piles had demolition charges attached to them and that an apparently intact detonation cord ring main connected these together and led away to a firing point. In addition, there were a number of mines of a type unknown to me lying amongst the rubble. (Davies, 'A Memoir of 9 Parachute Squadron RE')

Alert to booby traps, Davies prodded the ground with his bayonet, cut detonation cables and dragged out mines with cord. The Argentine camp was littered with boxed explosive, mines and loose ammunition. Using 2 Para's Assault Engineers and several civilians, he dismantled explosive charges and jury-rigged a wobbly footbridge across the gap. Davies then sent a list of material that he needed to 61 Field Support Squadron (Major 'Taffy' Morgan) at San Carlos.

When late in the afternoon, Squadron Leader Langworthy strolled into the HMS *Fearless* Amphibious Operations Room and reported that 2 Para had seized Fitzroy and Bluff Cove, this was received with astonishment because no one was aware that Brigadier Wilson was planning such a *coup de main*. Wilson then convinced Moore that his initiative should be supported quickly.

Brigadier Wilson ignored advice from Chaundler that an air defence and logistic envelope should be developed around Fitzroy and issued orders that: the Welsh Guards were to defend Bluff Cove; the Scots Guards were to take over from D Company, 2 Para east of Bluff Cove Inlet; and 2 Para was to pull back to Fitzroy as Brigade Reserve. The Brigade would then be ready to move through 3 Commando Brigade in the attack on Stanley on 6 June. The remaining troops would be landed at Fitzroy.

When Major Smith, of T (Shah Shujah's Troop) Air Defence Battery, was then instructed to send Rapiers to Fitzroy, he had a tactical problem – too few Rapiers. The beachhead still required air defence because of the risk of raids on clear days. I Troop was at Teal Inlet protecting the 3 Commando Brigade Forward Maintenance Area. This left two Troops at San Carlos, however he knew that the Rapier-equipped 63 Squadron, Royal Air Force Regiment, was due to land. Smith therefore instructed Lieutenant Adrian Waddell, who commanded H Troop, to take a composite Troop from firing units, whose loss could be afforded. Bombardier Stewart McMartin's Rapier positioned above Port San Carlos had experienced a command transmitter fault. The transmitter is the nerve centre into which variables of weather conditions and environment are fed to help the operator align the missile launch pads – without a functioning transmitter, the Rapier cannot be fired. Sergeant Bob Pearson's unit had also developed a problem. Smith and Waddell agreed to send two fully operational and two malfunctioning Rapiers, in the hope that they could be repaired by a REME technician to accompany the faulty Rapiers. Until the weather cleared, none could be moved anyway.

Next morning, 3 June, the fly-in of the remainder of 2 Para proved to be interesting. C (Patrol) Company was delivered to Fitzroy instead of Bluff Cove and D Company was flown to their position on the eastern shores of Bluff Cove creek in full view of Mount Harriet and 2 miles from their intended position. Eventually, the Battalion sorted themselves with: A Company defending Bluff Cove; B Company on Fitzroy Ridge to the north of the settlement; C Company covering the approaches from the north-east; and D Company across Bluff Cove Inlet to deal with any approaches directly from the east. Battalion HQ was at Fitzroy. Bergens and supplies would not arrive for two days because of bad weather.

The Kilmartins at Bluff Cove did much to rejuvenate the weary paras with hot meals, somewhere to dry socks and transport to move equipment. Nine Polish seamen, who had defected from their ship in February and had made their way to Fitzroy, were conscripted as labourers. Those British who came into contact with the civilians in the 'camp' are unlikely to forget their loyalty to the Crown and generosity in raising spirits. Their contribution to the campaign was significant.

Meanwhile, 5 Infantry Brigade was approaching San Carlos Water. Stopping briefly at Sierra Leone, the *Queen Elizabeth II* had circled Ascension on 21 May taking on stores and then rendezvoused with HMS *Antrim* to transfer Major General Moore and Brigadier Wilson and their staff before anchoring off Grytviken on 27 May. There followed a lengthy process to cross-deck the Brigade onto the *Canberra* and *Norland*. Staff Sergeant Andy Peck, of 81 Intelligence Section, wrote:

The actual cross decking was very confusing; chaotic, boring and proved the old adage 'Hurry up and wait'. Corporal Ramsey and myself spent nearly three hours sitting on the deck of a trawler getting very cold, as Canberra could not load troops fast enough. Once aboard, it was with a real sense of urgency that we practised air attack and abandon ship drills. Sipping soup in the dining room while one's waiters cheerfully regaled you with tales of Mirages swooping in below bridge height not only gave one indigestion but also dispelled the cruise atmosphere quickly. The weather also decided to let us know what the South Atlantic could produce in the way of waves. Conscious of the fact that I had been booked that week for a cruise to Cherbourg on Gladeye, I took to my bed feeling exceptionally seasick.

Accompanied by *Baltic Ferry*, the ships anchored not far from the Blue Beaches. Anxiety about air raids meant that within thirteen minutes an LCU was alongside. Supported by four ships' boats, it was hoped to unload the 3,000 men by the end of the day, which seemed optimistic by any imagination, considering it had taken over twenty-four hours to cross-deck the Brigade at Grytviken. This was an administrative landing, in which troops are landed tactically on secure beaches, nevertheless it took twenty-four hours to empty the two passenger ships. An additional complication was that while some vehicles and stores were being unloaded from the *Baltic Ferry*, *Nordic Ferry* was not scheduled to arrive for another day. Some stores never reached their units. 97 (Lawson's Company) Field Battery was reliant upon quadrants and prismatic compasses for several days until the gun sights turned up.

1st Welsh Guards dug in around the general area of Old Horse Paddock, which is about 3 miles south of San Carlos, and found mortar ammunition and rations dumped by 2 Para. The Scots Guards took over positions around San Carlos and 1/7th Gurkha Rifles, less D Company, were flown to Goose Green, releasing J Company to rejoin 42 Commando. D Company (Major Mike Kefford) deployed on to Sussex Mountain. Father Alfred Hayes, Roman Catholic chaplain to 5 Infantry Brigade:

> Once ashore, the order came from RSM Bill Hunt 'Gentlemen, dig in or else you will die.' This spurred us into digging shell scrapes above Blue Beach. I cooked some soup, then went over to the place I thought it best to be, the Field Ambulance. There I encountered difficulties with the CO, who told me that he didn't want a Chaplain since, in his experience, the sight of a priest at a dying man's side made the man give up. I said that in my four years as hospital chaplain in a large general hospital before joining the Army, I never had that experience, and had usually found that patients got genuine comfort from the priest.

The Field Ambulance had already upset the 3 Commando Brigade rear echelon by demanding that Hotel Galtieri be handed over, a suggestion which was rejected with two-word soldierly robustness.

2 Para needed to be reinforced, and quickly. The Royal Navy had the experience, organization and resources to execute a sea move, but the will was not always evident. Commodore Clapp: 'Although anxious to help the soldiers out, I never liked the idea of such a move forward by sea for the men and hoped that it could be avoided. (Clapp and Southby-Tailyour, *Amphibious Assault Falklands*)

He does acknowledge that warfare 'requires dash and initiative', nevertheless amphibious operations require coordinated planning. Aware that Fitzroy Bridge had been damaged, he preferred that 5 Infantry Brigade should be ferried to Brenton Cove and then march to Fitzroy and to his great credit, he set about solving the problem. Each time Clapp gave his staff the problem,

139

they came back with the same solution – an assault ship was needed. Clapp signalled Rear Admiral Woodward outlining his intention:

At first light on 6 June, land the Scots Guards and half the Welsh Guards from HMS *Intrepid* in the Bluff Cove area using her landing craft. The ship had to be back in San Carlos by first light on the 7th.

RFA *Sir Tristram* to ferry the remainder of the Welsh Guards, the Rapier detachment, the Brigade War Maintenance Reserve and a Mexeflote for the Brigade Forward Maintenance Area to Fitzroy. She would return when empty.

Major Southby-Tailyour offered his expertise:

I had asked if there was anything I could do, to be warned by a member of COMAW's staff that the two LSLs might be tasked to take the Guards battalions direct to Bluff Cove. This worried me for I knew there were no suitable LSL beaches in the area and so we would have to use LCUs, but with their maximum speed, even when empty, of under ten knots, I was not sure how we would get them forward. If the LCUs went in their mother ships then so could the men, but an LPD could not get close enough to either anchorage due to shallow water. We could load LCVPs as deck cargo and un-ship them at the destination, but whatever we did the whole enterprise would need sea and air protection. (Southby-Tailyour, *Reasons in Writing*)

Southby-Tailyour suggested that Mexeflotes would be needed. A Mexeflote is a three-part (bow, centre and stern), multi-purpose pontoon specifically designed for salt-water operations and can be used as rafts or joined together to form jetties, causeways and breakwaters. Each Mexeflote has its own specialized diesel engine. During the campaign, 17 Port Regiment, Royal Corps of Transport, operated them. Landing craft could either be taken in an assault ship or sail independently, which over a long distance was out of the question.

Although the flank had not been cleared of enemy, Clapp viewed the operation as a sea move. He asked Woodward for two escorts, naval gunfire support and combat air patrols, and wanted to take advantage of the bad weather that was prevailing at the time. There was also good intelligence that the Argentines had a land-based Exocet at Stanley. After the sinking of HMS *Sheffield* and the *Atlantic Conveyor*, the Royal Navy had become pre-occupied with Exocet almost to the exclusion of everything else. Clapp himself was not particularly concerned about the threat.

Soon after the attacks on 1 May, the Argentine Navy had decided that an Exocet at Stanley would deter the Royal Navy from bombarding military positions. Since converting a shipboard system would take at least forty-four days and consequently a simple design was needed, a naval engineering officer, Commander Julio Perez, and two civilians were asked to design a solution within ten days. Named the 'Do-It-Yourself Firing Installation', their system consisted of a generator and two Exocet launcher ramps removed from two of Argentina's A-69 corvettes, all mounted on two old wheeled trailers. The manual firing sequence was operated from a box with four telephone switchboard switches, each of which had to be thrown in specific order timed by a stopwatch. Ready in mid-May, an attempt to fly the system to Stanley on 24 May was thwarted by British air activity. Eventually, in early June, the system was landed. With the risk of the Firing Installation becoming bogged in mud, a short stretch of the tarmac road between the town and airport was selected as the firing point. Each night at 6.00 pm, the system was dragged from beneath camouflage netting and placed behind a 16-foot high bunker, ready to be fired from 8.30 pm when British ships tended to begin their bombardments. Air Force Westinghouse radars with the 2nd Air Surveillance and Control Group swept a 60-degree arc to the south of Stanley Common and the Army provided fire control with its AN-TPS 43 system. So far, three Exocets had been launched. The first one proved to be defective and the second was wasted when the transformer was incorrectly fitted and the missile veered to the right, as opposed to the left. The third was more successful when on the night of 27/28 May, a large projectile hurtled across the flight deck of HMS *Avenger* while she was on the gun line south of Harriet Cove, and out of range of conventional artillery. Suspecting an Exocet system on the Falklands, Rear Admiral Woodward created a 25-mile sanitized zone south of Stanley that no ship was to enter. Four more missiles arrived by C-130 during the night of 5 June.

Rear Admiral Woodward wanted a second Harrier forward operating base at Goose Green so that he could withdraw the Carrier Battle Group further to the east, so concerned was he about the Exocet threat. When the Argentine counter-attack threats against the beachhead emerged, he suggested that San Carlos be emptied of ships, but did not explain how the two Brigades should be supplied. Fortunately, Clapp rejected these suggestions but agreed that as the conventional forces closed on Stanley, Special Forces patrols should monitor Port Howard and Fox Bay.

The most pressing issue for HQ LFFI was to organize logistics to support both brigades. 3 Commando Brigade, in the rugged mountains to the north, were probing Argentine defences, however the urgency to reinforce 2 Para resulted in its helicopter support being diverted to 5 Infantry Brigade. The Brigade suddenly found itself starved of warm clothing, regular rations and fresh water. Some troops were without their bergens for nearly five days in temperatures that dropped to -11 degrees. Combat effectiveness decreased as sickness rates from exposure and hypothermia crept up, even among those familiar with the cold of Norway.

Even though 5 Infantry Brigade was ashore, it still needed to sort itself out for the first time after leaving UK. A Light Gun from 29 (Corunna) Battery, the Command Post and seventy gunners was flown to Bluff Cove, but when the only Chinook was diverted to another task, the gun was left without ammunition for two days. The Command Post could do absolutely nothing about several fire missions it received. On 5 June, the rest of the Battery arrived and was soon registering targets identified by D Company.

Assured that his Brigade would be ferried to Bluff Cove, Brigadier Wilson issued instructions on 3 June that the Scots Guards were to embark on HMS *Fearless* on 4 June. Lieutenant Colonel Rickett:

We were all extremely frustrated being in San Carlos. I remember meeting Tony Wilson, our Brigade Commander, with Mike Scott and one or two members of the Brigade HQ staff the morning after we had landed. There were no available 'assets' to be given to the Brigade as the Commando Brigade were on their positions in the mountains and were preparing for the build-up for the next phase the taking of the Mount Harriet/Two Sisters line. The only way we could get anything was by 'pirating' the odd passing helicopter to give us a lift. I suggested to Tony Wilson that the best way for us to get out of San Carlos was by walking and I volunteered to get things going by leading off with my battalion towards Darwin where Brigade HQ Tactical now was; thence we would march on from there towards Bluff Cove or 'to the front' wherever we were required. Tony Wilson agreed instantly and I asked if my Recce Platoon could be lifted forward ahead of us to be my eyes and ears; this was also agreed and helicopters would lift them forward but short of Darwin/Goose Green at last light. He also said that he would do his best to get us some Snocats, which was all he had at his disposal, to take our mortars, Browning machine-guns, ammunition and bergens. Notwithstanding this I tasked my 2ic to beg, borrow or steal some sort of tractor lift from the settlement at San Carlos, as I was not sanguine that we would get any Snocat lift.

At last light our Scout helicopters arrived and took off with Recce Platoon. We waited, in vain, for the promised Snocat and then set off with our 81mm mortars, Milans and ammo loaded on a light tractor and farm trailer. We carried our heavy Browning Medium Machine Guns. About an hour after our departure the Snocats appeared from the direction of Darwin, empty of fuel and unclear of what they were meant to be doing. It was immediately apparent that these vehicles would 'bulk out' in any case – there simply wasn't space for our equipment. So I decided to press on. Morale was high and, providing the tractor kept going, I was confident we could get across the Sussex Mountains and marry up with the Recce Platoon. The tractor, which was a small wheel based one, immediately bogged down piling the mortars and ammo into the mud. We dug it out once, twice, three times but by this time I realized that to carry on in this way was hopeless. We waited in vain for the sound of any returning Snocats but to no avail. I had two choices – either we could continue on light scales, but bearing in mind we were to march to the Bluff Cove area, not just to Darwin, or we could return to San Carlos and wait for some other means to get us forward. I wasn't prepared to fight a war without my mortars and other heavy weapons and with the chaos reigning around us I wasn't prepared to be separated from our equipment. After all it had been my idea to move under our own steam self-contained, now it was the turn of somebody else to give us the support we required to get us forward.

So, extremely tired with morale now on the low side, we returned to our foul area in San Carlos ready to start again the next day but this time with proper support. At first light somehow I managed to 'pirate' a helicopter to take me to Brigade HQ at Darwin where I reported our position and demanded some means of support to get the battalion into line. After a while I was told that the battalion would be taken round by ship.

By this time I was getting extremely anxious about my Recce Platoon as we had heard nothing from them and I asked for a helicopter to search for them and make contact. Sharing a helicopter with Captain Tim Spicer, Operations Officer of the Scots Guards, who wanted to go forward to recce Bluff Cove as 2 Para had made their great leap forward by then, we set off. We searched in vain for the Recce Platoon but had to go on to Bluff Cove, as fuel was getting tight, which was highly frustrating for me as I was extremely worried about them. Eventually returning to San Carlos I learnt with great relief that the Recce Platoon had made contact with Brigade HQ and was safe.

So far, there had been no reaction from the Argentines. The Special Forces Group had been defeated on Mount Kent and with Army Group, Malvinas still expecting 5 Infantry Brigade to land at or near Stanley, the strong 10 Infantry Brigade was waiting for something that would not happen. To prepare for the move, Commodore Clapp instructed the SBS and a diving team from 1 Troop, 9 Parachute Squadron (Captain Richard Willet) to select Yellow Beaches at Fitzroy and Bluff Cove. While the SBS would check gradients and beach composition, the Royal Engineers would check for mines and assess the suitability of the beachhead to support a military force. Lieutenant Commander Chris Meatyard, a mine clearance diving officer, joined the recce. Until they reported, Clapp could not advise ships' captains where to anchor. When the team flew to Port Pleasant during the night of 4/5 June, Major Davies met Willet and instructed him to assemble his Troop and repair Fitzroy Bridge. Meanwhile, Major Morgan had received Davies's request for supplies and his sappers were scavenging ships and supply dumps for welding gear, bags of nails, timber and rolled steel joints, all of which were loaded on LSL *Sir Tristram*.

5 Infantry Brigade was still marrying equipment to units and concerns

emerged about the time it was taking to sort itself out. While Rear Admiral Woodward worried about the seaworthiness of his ships after two months at sea, Major General Moore wanted to attack Stanley by the 6th, and 3 Commando Brigade was ready. Commodore Clapp admitted that he failed to appreciate the lack of amphibious operations understanding by the Army Brigade, and some naval officers did not appreciate that in land warfare supplies need to be stockpiled before an attack. When the Welsh Guards aborted their march and Woodward suggested that they try again, it shows just how isolated those on board the ships were from reality. The Royal Navy had forgotten that their traditional role is to support the ground forces and were slow to react to Wilson's initiative, taking four days before the first ship left San Carlos. Half the problem was that the Royal Navy was inexperienced in amphibious warfare, a far cry from the Second World War. Several suggestions also hindered implementing the plan. Clapp received a signal from Woodward suggesting 'more robust plan might be to move the troops forward by foot/helo and provide logistic support by one/two relatively inconspicuous LSLs at Teal.'

Clapp put the suggestion down to a communication problem between colleagues separated by miles of turbulent ocean. Admiral Fieldhouse, co-incidentally, then suggested that the Guards be landed at Teal Inlet and not Bluff Cove, citing the risks from the Argentine 155mm artillery, the air threat and sea-mines outweighing the likelihood of success. This still did not solve the isolation of 2 Para. Major General Moore and Commodore Clapp jointly signalled Northwood emphasizing that the sea move from San Carlos to the Port Pleasant sector was the only option and then tasked their staffs to plan that: '*Intrepid* should sail east at dusk, launch her LCUs in two waves with a battalion in each wave, straight into Fitzroy. This would ensure that she would only be at sea and away from San Carlos in the dark' (Clapp and Southby-Tailyour, *Amphibious Assault Falklands*).

On 5 June, Brigadier Wilson selected D Company, 1/7th Gurkha Rifles (Major Mike Kefford) to be his Brigade Patrol Company and instructed Kefford to seek out an artillery and radar unit thought to be somewhere in the Port Harriet area. Instructed to march to Darwin to be ferried to Fitzroy, the Gurkhas shouldered their loads. Twenty miles and thirty hours later, after an extremely difficult march, D Company was dug in north of Goose Green when they received orders to be ferried to Fitzroy on the *Monsunen*.

The Argentine forces had seized the 230-ton Falkland Islands Company coaster MV *Monsunen*, after finding it abandoned off Lively Island, and used her to ferry supplies. Beached near Goose Green after being attacked by HMS *Yarmouth* on 23 May, she was refloated by a HMS *Fearless* party with the help of 23-year-old Janet MacLeod, a local diver. Although Major Robert Satchell, Wilson's senior Engineer Staff Officer, was placed in charge of her, Commodore Clapp did not relish the Brigade operating its own fleet. He therefore appointed Lieutenant Ian McLaren and three ratings from HMS

Fearless to crew it as Naval Party 2160, with instructions that it was to sail only at night and requests from 5 Infantry Brigade were to be confirmed with his staff. While 3 Commando Brigade had the 1st Royal Marine Raiding Squadron, 5 Infantry Brigade was denied dedicated maritime resources. As a member of 97 (Lawson's Company) Field Battery commented: 'It seemed that nobody was really concerned with helping blue berets. After all, we were trespassing on an operation to maintain the mobility of the Red and Green berets' ('4th Field Regiment in the Falkland Islands').

During the afternoon, the SBS/Royal Engineer beach recce reported to Commodore Clapp and Brigadier Wilson that they had not found any obstacles at Bluff Cove and that two beaches, Yellow Beach One and Two, were suitable for landing craft operations. Major Davies disagreed:

> Quite apart from it being clearly in view of the Argentine high ground, there was insufficient cover and the meagre freshwater supply would never have supported the large number of men associated with such a set up. I pointed all this out to the SBS Patrol commander but, clearly, his horizons were limited to swimming and beach gradients and he had no comprehension of the basic needs of a 'campsite'. I told him he must not recommend Bluff Cove as the BMA but he went ahead. I put the facts to the Brigadier and managed to convince him that Fitzroy was a much better location. It had more water and there were larger sheep sheds and other buildings that could provide some shelter. The weather, and its effect upon the troops, was of increasing concern. It was cold and windy all of the time. For the most part, it was wet too. (Davies, 'A Memoir of 9 Parachute Squadron RE')

Wilson agreed. Commodore Clapp then instructed Colonel Ian Baxter, Moore's senior logistics officer, to order the two Guards battalions to embark on HMS *Intrepid*. Captain Robin Green, captain of *Sir Tristram*, was given confirmatory orders to load Lieutenant Waddell's Rapier Troop, however it was trapped by fog. Major Forge had improved communications with Port Pleasant by installing a signals detachment and a defence section, commanded by Corporals Daughtrey and Corporal 'Dizzy' Wicken respectively, on to Pleasant Peak.

The final plans were being firmed up when, late in the afternoon, Admiral Fieldhouse instructed that the two LPDs were not to be risked out of San Carlos in daylight, in case their loss would force the Government to negotiate for a ceasefire. The cynic might suggest that since Fieldhouse and Woodward had been unable to persuade Moore and Clapp to land 5 Infantry Brigade at Teal Inlet, the two assault ships, which are designed to deliver troops to enemy beaches, were now politically sensitive. They had not been so at San Carlos. The recipients were nonplussed. It seems that the War Cabinet were again meddling in military affairs and someone was remarkably defeatist. The British had seized the initiative from Argentine forces simply waiting to be attacked. And now, Britain's resolve was being tested by risking an assault ship in a landing. Clapp:

> At 16.45 that afternoon I signalled back that while I recognised the political views over the LPDs, the less-than-satisfactory and more time-expensive alternatives would be to use at least one, and preferably, two 'expendable' LSLs to which Admiral Fieldhouse replied that that would not be vetoed by politicians. He ended his signal with the words, 'The man on the spot must decide.' As 'that man', I decided to send two LPDs totally in the dark and over two nights, but an LSL would be needed and it would have to stay in daylight. (Clapp and Southby-Tailyour, *Amphibious Assault Falklands*)

The plan:

> HMS *Intrepid* (Captain Peter Dingemans) to land the Scots Guards at Bluff Cove during the night 6/7 June.

> Leave the LCUs at a forward operating base at Bluff Cove.

> The Rapiers and other essential stores and equipment to be delivered to Fitzroy by LSL and unload, even if that meant in daylight.

> Landing craft to meet HMS *Fearless* during the night of 7/8 June and land the Welsh Guards at Fitzroy.

Sending a frigate to protect the beachhead was rejected in case it provoked the Argentines, even though its absence would give less firepower and warning of air attack. Until the Rapiers landed, the ground forces would be vulnerable to air attack. While San Carlos Water had been heavily protected since 21 May, the same resources were again not being made available to 5 Infantry Brigade. Clapp:

> I knew that Peter Dingemans held the view that the LPD was a major war vessel and, as such, carried the same political weight as an aircraft carrier. During my briefing for his night's task he had challenged me with the opinion that an LPD was too high risk to lose. I had gone through all the arguments many times with Jeremy's and my own staff and the only risks I knew of were two enemy patrol craft (one was beached and the other holed up in Stanley), mines (which would affect the LCUs and LSLs not the Lids, which could stand offshore) and the weather suddenly changing for the better (not the forecast), if he was still at sea in daylight (unlikely). (Clapp and Southby-Tailyour, *Amphibious Assault Falklands*)

Brigadier Wilson's plans were again thrown into disarray. For a commander under continual pressure to 'get on with it', here was yet another

146

obstacle not of his making. For the Welsh Guards, it was order, counter order, disorder! Orders were sent to them to return to their soggy trenches. Commodore Clapp continued to receive several conflicting signals from Rear Admiral Woodward and Northwood, most of which he filed in the wastepaper basket. Woodward suggested that all six LSLs be filled with troops to land in Stanley Harbour; this was sent on a low classification. When its content became known, LSL morale wavered.

Major Southby-Tailyour, still under the impression that landing craft would take the two Guards battalions from San Carlos to Canberra Beach for their march to Fitzroy, was summoned to HMS *Fearless*:

> I was anxious to be involved in any operation that took me away from San Carlos, which was fast becoming a mere maintenance and stores area. I was not the only one interested who wanted to put San Carlos behind them. 5 Brigade, for rather more relevant reasons, was anxious to get on the move, and any distance that I could take them by landing craft would be a bonus. I braced myself for the inevitable teasing as I entered the Staff Planning Office (The Chapel), after which the officers warned me that they were now looking again at the Canberra Beach option. (Southby-Tailyour, *Reasons in Writing*)

He was instructed to transfer to HMS *Intrepid* and, using the warship's four LCUs, to take the Scots Guards from a drop-off point near Elephant Island to Bluff Cove. Elephant Island was just outside the 'Exocet' perimeter. He was then to wait until the next night, 6/7 June, when he was to rendezvous with HMS *Fearless* and land the Welsh Guards at Fitzroy. Southby-Tailyour commented that since the landing craft were not designed for long open sea voyages, he would still prefer to take the infantry to the upper reaches of Brenton Loch, from where they could march to Fitzroy. Southby-Tailyour returned to his headquarters. Captain Dingemans was placed in command of the operation and given the destroyer HMS *Penelope*.

Woodward was still expecting 3 Commando Brigade to attack Stanley during the night 5/6 June and assigned the destroyers HMS *Cardiff* (Captain Michael Harris) and HMS *Yarmouth* (Captain Tony Morton) and two frigates, HMS *Active* and HMS *Arrow* to support the assault. However, when it became clear that 5 Infantry Brigade was not ready and Major General Moore had postponed the attack until the 9th , Woodward, recalling the two frigates, left the two destroyers to ambush aircraft blockade-runners using Wickham Heights as a way finder to Stanley. He also assured Clapp that he would not have any ships operating in the area where HMS *Intrepid* would be operating. Clapp:

> One snippet I did learn from Sandy that day was that he was with-drawing HMS *Hermes* further to the east for a routine boiler clean. While it was not my place to comment, I did think it was a strange time

to remove the largest 'airfield' we had in the war at such a critical time. He must have appreciated how badly we would need close air support and CAP over the next few days if the cloud-base lifted. He was possibly, quite simply, taking no chances on a longer term view. (Clapp and Southby-Tailyour, *Amphibious Assault Falklands*)

Clapp is too generous. He was equal in authority to Woodward and was entitled to challenge such a critical decision. If the weather cleared, there would now be less combat air patrols during the move, except for the Harriers using 'Sid's Strip'. During the day, Captain Greenhalgh flew over the many islands east of Bluff Cove, searching for Exocet traps without success, while a Gurkha patrol checked Lively Island. HMS *Avenger* was ordered to bombard Fox Bay and then investigate the steep-sided and narrow Albemarle Harbour as a suitable bolthole for ships caught in the open in daylight. Clapp:

This caused a small eruption. Sandy signalled that ships should not use it. This was the first and only occasion when he countermanded my orders. I did not agree with him and he had not consulted with me. It was clearly better for the LSLs to know that I was concerned for them and if they had to use it, then I would probably have the time to place a frigate to cork the bottle and provide some protection. I decided to quietly ignore Sandy's signal. I was in control of this area and would accept the consequences.

Chapter Eleven

The Bold Move
5 to 8 June

Although Captain Dingemans wanted to drop the LCUs as close to Elephant Island as he dared, in direct command of 540 sailors he had to consider predicted sea states and the tactical situation, in particular the land-based Exocet threat. When retracting the LCUs, the tank deck was flooded with 7,000 tons of sea water, which dropped the stern from 23 feet to 30 feet and decreased speed to 4 knots. Launching the LCUs in open sea in a swell is dangerous, with the landing craft crashing against each other as the ship pitches and yaws as water, flung from side to side, collides with seawater rushing in. Dingemans felt he had two choices:

Carry on to east of Lively Island and retract the LCUs in open water and no cover.

Launch to the leeward side of Lively Island and retract in calmer waters.

He chose the latter option in the full knowledge that he was committing 600 soldiers to a long and cold voyage in four open landing craft along a coast not cleared of enemy and through seas in which vessels must be assumed to be hostile. Clear of Fanning Head, Captain Dingemans told Major Southby-Tailyour that '*Intrepid* is not, politically, allowed further east than Lively Island. The risk to an LPD is too great.' Dingemans's comments were contrary to the orders by Clapp but Southby-Tailyour was unable to seek clarification and could not persuade Dingemans to drop the LCUs off Elephant Island, as agreed. He told Southby-Tailyour that the only ships he would see would be enemy but was unable to provide the Carrier Battle Group recognition signal as he'd been told there would not be one. Having previously exercised with Southby-Tailyour, Dingemans was confident that he would successfully execute the passage to Bluff Cove.

As the LPD neared Lively Island, it experienced a noticeable increase in the height and motion of the swell. Worsening weather was predicted. At about

10.30 pm, HMS *Intrepid* retracted the LCUs 2 miles west of Lively Island with about 150 men to each landing craft. Visibility was poor. According to Lance Sergeant McDermid, of Right Flank, the troops were briefed that the passage would not last long and each man was equipped with a life jacket but not a survival suit. HMS *Intrepid* then left the scene, leaving the LCUs bobbing around on the ocean. Since Dingemans had not shared his position with Southby-Tailyour, Southby-Tailyour, on Tango One (Colour-Sergeant Barry Davies) made landfall on Lively Island for a fix. Estimating that the passage would take at least six hours, Southby-Tailyour: 'I asked Major Ian Mackay-Dick [Second-in-Command] and Major John Kiszely, who commanded Left Flank, to join me in the navigation compartment. It was tiny but at least we could discuss our problems in private and I was close to the cox'n to give orders.'

At about 11.30 am, the landing craft were rounding the southerly point of Lively Island when there were several unexplained flashes to the north.

At about the same time as the troops were filing into the landing craft, Corporal Daughtrey reported that he needed technical support for his Clansman PRC 352 radio. Since he had dropped the rebroadcast team during the evening, Staff Sergeant Christopher Griffin, of 656 Squadron, was tasked by Major Lambe to fly Major Forge and the A Troop Staff Sergeant, Joe Baker, to Pleasant Peak. Unfortunately, HQ 5 Infantry Brigade did not advise anyone of this mission so that when HMS *Cardiff* detected a contact approaching from the west to east across Wickham Heights inside the 'killing zone' box at about 11.50 pm, Captain Harris ordered a Sea Dart to be fired, in the belief that it was a C-130 en route to Stanley. This connected at a range of 11 miles near Pleasant Peak and the blip disappeared. Very soon after Daughtrey had signalled the Gazelle with a strobe light, the hillside was engulfed in a violent orange light and an explosion. Brigade HQ then asked him to search for the Gazelle because communications had been lost, however with poor weather closing in, this was abandoned.

East of Lively Island, Tango One's radar failed, possibly because Southby-Tailyour was necessarily flicking it off and on to get fixes, without giving away his position. Mysterious high-explosive fountaining into the sea highlighted the vulnerability of the LCUs. Soon after Southby-Tailyour had checked his navigation with Colour Sergeant Garwood on Tango 3, two radar contacts appeared about 4 miles astern. Assuming them to be enemy ships, Southby-Tailyour led the landing craft, in rising seas, toward the craggy shelter of Dangerous Point and then, taking advantage of tide and current, altered course toward the shallow entrance of Choiseul Sound where survivors had a reasonable chance of reaching land. Agreeing with Mackay-Dick that the speed of the landing craft was no match for the ships, Southby-Tailyour then set course for East Island, his original heading. It seemed to him that when the Royal Navy was most wanted, it was absent.

HMS *Cardiff*, keyed up after its kill, and HMS *Yarmouth* picked up the four contacts about an hour after launching the Sea Dart. Unaware that there were British inshore naval operations planned for the night, Harris assumed they were Argentine vessels. Through their binoculars, Southby-Tailyour and his Scots Guards command team could see the bow waves of fast warships evidently pursuing their slow, blunt-nosed LCUs thrashing into rough seas. Suddenly, six star shells burst in quick succession over the landing craft. Lance Sergeant McDermid: 'There was mayhem as everyone grabbed their SLRs and pointed them in the general direction of the ships, although we couldn't see any of them. When it was all over, there was little else to do but keep dry as possible as water slopped all over the place.'

A signal light flickered in Morse, 'Heave to'. Southby-Tailyour ordered his flotilla to stop. At least the message was in English. The next signal sparkled: 'Friend'. Southby-Tailyour replied, 'To which side?' No reply and then the mysterious ships disappeared into the darkness of the south-east. Southby-Tailyour was furious – no counter identification from the ships, his presence compromised and no offer of assistance. Although Rear Admiral Woodward knew about the Fitzroy operation, it seems that Captains Harris and Morton did not. He would later claim that the landing craft were late and in the wrong position. Absolutely correct, the LCUs should not have been in the area – they had been dropped off Lively Island against orders. The political consequences of 600 soldiers drowned in a 'blue on blue' would have been far more disastrous than the loss of a LPD. It was fortunate that Captain Harris, already concerned about the validity of the air contact, had fired starshell. According to Woodward, the next morning Harris expressed concern that his air contact just might be the missing Army Gazelle. The wind had risen. Lieutenant Alastair Mitchell was 14 Platoon Commander with Left Flank:

It was appalling from the word go. We were running in a heavy swell and these with their flat bottoms and a bevel edge at the front just smack into the waves. The spray came over and everyone was drenched with ten minutes from setting off. We had to endure nine hours of this. After an hour people were entirely numb. The bottom half of our bodies went to sleep because we were cramped so tight. We were absolutely freezing cold. People had been joking to start with but they shut up after half an hour. There was complete silence, just the crackling of the radios and the awful drumming of the waves on this craft. (Bilton and Kominsky, *Speaking Out*)

There was nowhere to sit and making a brew was out of the question. Southby-Tailyour resumed his course for East Island and led the landing craft into the 'Exocet Box'. In the early period of a northerly gale, the LCUs crept along the coast and reached the maelstrom of 'Z Bend' just as another murky dawn cracked the eastern horizon. Selecting the longer but safer course around East Island into Fitzroy Sound, at about 7.00 am, the LCUs nosed through the narrow neck of Bluff Cove Inlet. Ashore, Bombardier Marsh of 29 (Corunna) Field Battery saw the landing craft and shouted, 'There are enemy landing craft in the bay!' Sergeant Morgan, in a frantic radio conversation with the Battery Commander, Major Tony Rice, established that they contained the Scots Guards. When they came alongside the jetty and were met by 2 Para, Lieutenant Mitchell recalled:

> Getting people off was incredible. We had to pick people up, straighten their legs, put their bergens on their backs and throw them off the front end. We hadn't had anything to eat, you couldn't do anything. So we staggered on to this beach and tried to get people sorted. There were dazed specimens coming ashore. I remember seeing one particular character who stormed on to the beach and then absolutely stood stock-still, facing the landing craft. (Bilton and Kominsky, *Speaking Out*)

Mitchell was just about to push the soldier into a column of Guardsmen when he recognised him to be Major Kiszely, his Company Commander. MacKay-Dick and Captain Tim Spicer, the Operations Officer, were then told by Lieutenant Colonel Chaundler that they should move north and dig in. Chaundler:

> The weather was dreadful and after about an hour, some Scots Guardsmen, who were the worst cases of exposure I have ever seen, started coming into the shed and my medics were working on them to keep them alive. I went outside to find hundreds of Scots Guardsmen standing in the lee of the few buildings with rain pouring off their helmets. I was not amused and went to find the Second-in-Command and Operations Officer. I found them in a shelter and I asked them, 'What the hell do you think you are doing? If you don't get this Battalion moving and digging in, you will write them off.' The Second-in-Command replied, 'I can't do anything until the Commanding Officer arrives.'

Phase One of the 5 Infantry Brigade move was complete and Brigadier Wilson flew to Fitzroy, taking with him his Tac HQ under the command of Major Barney Rolfe-Smith, a Parachute Regiment staff officer, and Lieutenant Colonel Scott, who commented several years later: 'We could have the lost the whole battalion in the LCUs.'

Brigade HQ was set up in the sheep-shearing shed. Wilson and Scott then flew to Bluff Cove where they met Chaundler:

> I suggested to them that the Scots Guards, rather than moving into open country and taking up a defensive position, would be better off in Bluff Cove, where at least they had some shelter to sort themselves out and we (including D Company) would take the LCUs that had delivered them and return to Fitzroy. My motives were not entirely altruistic. I

suspected the Battalion would once again be committed and I was concerned about its general state. By getting them together in one place – Fitzroy – we could get ourselves properly prepared for battle. Wilson agreed to this.

When approached with this proposal, Major Southby-Tailyour agreed that the LCUs could be used to ferry the companies across Bluff Cove Inlet. After ordering his four coxswains to wait for instructions, he then hitched a Sea King lift back to San Carlos and debriefed Major General Moore and Commodore Clapp on the night. However, by the time a runner reached the jetty, the landing craft had disappeared and 2 Para did not have their radio frequencies. Frost:

> It was thought that the LCUs were still waiting at the mouth of the cove just over the ridge from the settlement, but with their radios switched off so this could not be confirmed immediately. Major Keeble took off in a light helicopter to persuade the LCU crews to help the battalion move by the shortest route – by sea to Fitzroy . . . Chris Keeble was a past master at such negotiations. His style of bluff and rhetoric, matched by the occasional wave of a pistol in the direction of the coxswain's direction, soon left no doubt as to the urgency of the need. (Frost, *2 Para in the Falklands*)

The four coxswains had no alternative but disobey Southby-Tailyour's explicit orders and ferry 2 Para to Fitzroy. Without charts, hindered by poor visibility and a faulty radar, and needing to avoid the lengthy entrails of kelp, navigation was very difficult and within two hours the landing craft were back in Bluff Cove Inlet. Chaundler:

> The visibility was bad and, as a sailor myself, to end up without apparently knowing was incomprehensible. Besides I wanted to deploy at Fitzroy in daylight. Instead of which we arrived in the dark on an extremely unpleasant wet and windy night. However, on the jetty was [Captain] Banks Middleton, the TQM, with a line of hayboxes full of stew and tea. It was having soldiers like that who use their initiative and anticipate what is needed that makes soldiering so worthwhile.

Another weather front steamed in and the LCUs became stormbound, unable to beat against the prevailing wind to Bluff Cove and wait for Southby-Tailyour, as planned. Their inability was a catalyst in the rot that would end in disastrous circumstances.

On Pleasant Peak, a patrol sent by Corporal Daughtrey found the wreckage of Griffin's Gazelle but no survivors. When it was thought that it been shot down by Argentine patrols operating on Wickham Heights, Brigadier Wilson instructed 1/7th Gurkha Rifles to destroy them. Issuing orders to Lieutenant

153

(Queen's Gurkha Officer) Rai Belbahadur to find the Argentines responsible, Lieutenant Colonel Morgan told him 'to take out anyone up there'. Combing Pleasant Peak, the higher that the Gurkhas climbed, the mistier it became, however as they were about to search the lower slopes, they heard voices above them, which turned to be Corporal Daughtrey. Post mortems on the bodies at Ajax Bay confirmed, beyond doubt, that their injuries were consistent with an explosion beneath them. Ministry of Defence air crash investigators reported in a confidential document that there was no evidence that the Gazelle had been shot down by a Sea Dart. However, the families, in particular that of Lance Corporal Cockton, Griffin's aircrewman, forced the Ministry to hold an independent inquiry, which confirmed that the wreckage included parts of a Sea Dart. The Ministry then accepted that the Gazelle had been downed by HMS *Cardiff*.

Meanwhile, the Gurkhas, supported by 656 Squadron, were searching the soggy mass of Lafonia for Argentines thought to be targeting helicopter routes and rounding up Goose Green stragglers. At about 1.00 pm, a heliborne Recce Platoon patrol requested helicopter support at Egg Harbour House. Sergeant Ian Roy, flying from Darwin, skipping over a ridge, saw four Argentines run from a building into a gully. Captain Philip Piper then arrived and Roy returned to Goose Green to refuel. Piper, and his air gunner, Lance Corporal Les Beresford, circled the gully keeping the enemy pinned down until Roy returned, bringing Captain Sam Drennan in his Scout. At Goose Green, Gurkha reinforcements were loaded into an 825 NAS Sea King. Meanwhile, the three pilots decided to winkle the Argentines from the gully and when Sergeant Roy's aircrew, Corporal Johns, fired a SS-11 missile at an enemy position, it turned out to be a crop of rocks! Flying over another part of the gully, eight Argentine soldiers ran into the open and surrendered. Drennan landed, however as his air gunner, Lance Corporal John Gammon, jumped out, his belt buckle broke, condemning him to marshal the Argentines holding his sub-machine gun in one hand and his trousers with the other. When the Gurkhas arrived, none were fluent in English and none of the Argentines spoke English, let alone Nepalese. The Army Air Corps only spoke English. It was all a little muddled. When an Argentine officer refused to lie down, as instructed, because it was undignified and wet, a Gurkha NCO fingered his kukri. Among the captured weapons was a Soviet SA-7 Strella ground-to-air missile, one of 130 delivered from Peru on 24 May.

After being briefed by Major Southby-Tailyour, Clapp's staff set about finalizing Phase Two:

Load and despatch RFA *Sir Tristram* with sufficient ammunition and other stores that could be unloaded in one day, in line with Commodore Clapp's policy.

Move the Welsh Guards, Rapiers, 4 Field Troop RE, 16 Field Ambulance and others to Fitzroy in either *HMS Fearless* or *HMS Intrepid*.

However, 16 Field Ambulance was not ready for loading. When Captain Larken heard about the political sensitivity of the LPDs, he offered HMS *Fearless,* even though it was carrying Moore's Headquarters, which was accepted. He had shown considerable leadership during the fighting after the 21 May landings. The plan was to:

Rendezvous south of Elephant Island with Major Southby-Tailyour and the four HMS *Intrepid* LCUs coming from Bluff Cove.

Cross-deck the troops into two of them and two HMS *Fearless* landing craft, Foxtrots One and Four, for the return trip to Fitzroy.

Return to San Carlos with the two remaining HMS *Intrepid* landing craft to help unload ships in the beachhead Transport Area.

When Major Southby-Tailyour returned to Bluff Cove in the late afternoon, storm force winds were whipping up the sea and freezing rain blasted across the moorland. Looking for the LCUs, he found only one sheltering under White Point. Before being dropped at Bluff Cove, he wrote a message to be given to Commodore Clapp that the bad weather was expected to moderate. Southby-Tailyour did not mention, and had no reason to do so, that he had found only one LCU. He sheltered with the Scots Guards, confident that the missing three LCUs would appear once the weather moderated. Later, he radioed HMS *Fearless* that the weather was still bad and that the operation might have to be cancelled. Both messages arrived with Clapp after the LPD had left San Carlos and caused some puzzlement because, at sea, conditions were fair. As the hours passed, Southby-Tailyour was forced to concede that with three landing craft still missing, he would not make the rendezvous. True to style, he described it as an 'embarrassment'.

At 7.30 pm, HMS *Fearless*, accompanied by *HMS Penelope* and HMS *Avenger*, entered Falkland Sound. HMS *Avenger* dropped a SBS patrol to search Sea Lion Island for a suspected radar station. Two hours later, RFA *Sir Tristram* left San Carlos. By 10.00 pm, Captain Larken was off Elephant Island but there was no sign of Southby-Tailyour. Risking compromise, he launched his Lynx helicopter to search for them, without success. At 11.00 pm, with his departure time near, Larken had Major Guy Yeoman, Clapp's Army movements' staff officer, wake up Major Tony Todd, also a Royal Corps of Transport officer with maritime experience, and also serving on Clapp's staff. Yeoman told Todd that the four *Intrepid* LCUs had missed the rendezvous and he was to take half the Welsh Guards and 1 Troop, 9 Parachute Squadron in the two *Fearless* landing craft to Bluff Cove. Yeoman was apparently not aware of the Phase Two plan that the troops should be landed at Fitzroy.

Lieutenant Colonel Rickett was again faced with the prospect of splitting 1st Welsh Guards. He sought out Major General Moore and when he said that Brigadier Wilson's orders were that he should dig in north-east of Bluff Cove astride the track from Stanley, Moore assured him that the rest of the Battalion would arrive the following night. Rickett, more confident, instructed Battalion and Tac HQs, Number 2 Company and Recce, Anti Tank Platoon and the Machine Gun Platoon to embark on the two landing craft, along with 1 Troop, 9 Parachute Squadron, which was tasked to repair Fitzroy Bridge, and Major Jordan, the Battery Commander of 97 (Lawson's Company) Field Battery, which was supporting the Welsh Guards. This left the Prince of Wales Company (Major Guy Sayle) and 3 Company (Major Charles Bremner), 4 Field Troop RE, and several small units, including a 3 Commando Brigade Royal Signals rear link detachment, on HMS *Fearless*. At about 00.15 am, under clear skies, HMS *Fearless* left for San Carlos. In less bumpy seas than experienced by the Scots Guards, and escorted part of the 19-mile passage by HMS *Avenger*, Todd guided the landing craft to Bluff Cove jetty, coming alongside four hours later. It was raining.

The first that Major Southby-Tailyour knew about their arrival was the appearance of two Welsh Guards Provost staff on motorcycles. Recce Platoon (Lieutenant Symes) led the Guards through the settlement to positions north-east astride the road to Stanley. Rickett established his command post in several caravans abandoned by workers constructing the new road to Stanley. Symes's patrols fanned out and within hours were in contact with Argentine activity south and east of Mount Harriet. Still concerned at the missing LCUs, Major Southby-Tailyour, in preparation for the swift unloading of LSL *Sir Tristram*, led the two HMS *Fearless* and one HMS *Intrepid* LCUs through the now tranquil 'Z' Bend to Fitzroy, where, to his relief, he found the three missing landing craft. When briefed by the coxswains why they had missed the rendezvous, their account did nothing for Southby-Tailyour's humour.

So far, fortune had favoured the British. Over two nights, they had landed the Scots Guards and half the Welsh Guards at Bluff Cove, without inter-ference. The unloading of *Sir Tristram* at Port Pleasant was underway using LCUs and Mexeflotes. But the cost had been high – a 656 Squadron Gazelle, its crew of two and two Royal Signals confirmed killed. Southby-Tailyour:

> I was later told that neither CLIFFI nor COMAW were aware that 5 Brigade could not talk to their forward troops. The continual lack of communications was the cause of so much that occurred during those few days. The loss of the relay station was a prime contributory factor, but the lack of understanding of the third dimension, the sea flank (with its command and control peculiarities) added to this non-amphibious Brigade Headquarters' loss of tight control. (Southby-Tailyour, *Reasons in Writing*)

While Southby-Tailyour is correct, it was the lack of communication between Rear Admiral Woodward and two of his captains that weakened communications.

1 Troop, 9 Parachute Squadron, were ferried by landing craft to Fitzroy Bridge with the equipment that had arrived on RFA *Sir Tristram*. Working in appalling conditions for two days, the sappers rebuilt the damaged bridge. By the time the bridge was finished, although originally built for 4-ton farm vehicles, it could now handle 10 tons and thus the Scorpions and Scimitars were sent around the head of the creek when they were moved to Bluff Cove. Davies later reflected that the bridge was completed with methods 'that Alexander the Great would have recognised. In all, I was quite proud of our efforts there.'

Commodore Clapp's Phase Two was still incomplete and, despite his reservations of more sea moves, he was persuaded by Colonel Baxter to organize a third trip to Port Pleasant so that 5 Infantry Brigade would be at full strength for the 9 June offensive. The complication of the embargo on HMS *Fearless* and *Intrepid* being unable to leave San Carlos during the day remained. With all but one LSL on other tasks, the only ship available was the *Sir Galahad* (Captain Philip Roberts), which had just arrived, fortuitously empty, from Teal Inlet. Roberts was placed on immediate notice to take troops to Fitzroy. So far, the LSL had led a charmed existence. On 24 May, a 1,000lb bomb hit her on the port side when she was packed with 300 men of the Commando Logistic Regiment.

Clapp had another problem. The naval logistic organization in San Carlos Water was near collapse because there were not enough LCUs to unload ships, some of which had sailed direct from Ascension. The anchorage was becoming crowded and, with better weather predicted, there was greater risk of air raids. Two HMS *Fearless* LCUs were at Teal Inlet and the remaining six, Foxtrots One and Four and the four from HMS *Intrepid* were at Fitzroy. Clapp issued orders to Captain Larken to recover his two landing craft from Teal Inlet.

During the day, the balance of the Welsh Guards, 16 Field Ambulance, at last, 4 Field Troop, which was urgently required by Major Davies to support the Brigade Forward Maintenance Area – latrines to be dug, tracks to be repaired and water points to be erected – and several other small units embarked. When the Rapier Troop embarked, some Welsh Guards took pity on their bedraggled state and gave up their cabins so that the gunners could shower, clean up and rest in some comfort. This was in sharp contrast to the rifling of personal property and equipment left behind on the ships by soldiers and on mess decks loaned to the troops. An 825 NAS Sea King was embarked to land the Rapiers. The Embarked Force totalled 470 men. It had been intended that she would leave with HMS *Intrepid* at 5.50 pm but cross-decking was slow and the LPD left to meet its LCUs, which had sailed to Low Bay from Fitzroy in another long, unprotected voyage.

The two Guards companies embarked in the belief that they would be landed at Bluff Cove, as had been assured by Major General Moore the previous night. One scheme was to beach *Sir Galahad*, another to cross-deck the troops to two landing craft south of Elephant Island and another for the ship to disembark the troops into two landing craft at Fitzroy to be ferried to Bluff Cove. Much depended on the weather, which, after days of foul wind, rain and snow, promised near clear skies.

Meanwhile, the Argentine 1st Air Photographic Group Learjets had been photographing San Carlos Water in support of the plans being developed to attack the anchorage. At about 12.00 pm, in near blue skies, four Learjets, led by Wing Commander Rodolfo de la Colina, the squadron commander, were over San Carlos, line abreast flying at 40,000 in the belief they were safe from interdiction. HMS *Exeter,* which was in Falkland Sound, identified them as Canberra bombers and fired two Sea Darts. Those who witnessed the incident are unlikely to forget the missile spearing upwards into de la Colina's aircraft in a small blinding flash and a faint thump. Minus its tail but with the pressurized cabin intact, the doomed Learjet slowly cartwheeled to earth, the crew coherent and unable to bale out, before it smashed onto Pebble Island. De la Colina was the most senior Argentine officer to die in the campaign.

At 8.30 pm, Captain Green on *Sir Tristram* at Fitzroy signalled Clapp that he was likely to be unloading next day, which led Clapp to believe that too much had been loaded than could be unloaded in one day. It also confirmed his suspicions that the Fitzroy beaches were unsuitable for amphibious operations. At 10.00 pm, Captain Roberts, reporting that *Sir Galahad* was ready to sail, appealed for a 24-hour delay so that he could sail to and from Fitzroy at night. Commodore Clapp rejected this on the grounds that covering 130 miles to Fitzroy, unloading in one day and returning to San Carlos was sufficient. The LSL slipped out of San Carlos Water. Most of the troops were accommodated in the cavernous tank deck.

Visiting 5 Infantry Brigade Tac HQ, Major Southby-Tailyour briefed Major Rolfe-Smith on issues emerging from the Port Pleasant anchorage. Southby-Tailyour:

> I was particularly keen that nothing prevented the speedy offload of *Sir Tristram* and to that end we had to devote every craft we then possessed, which were now two LCUs and a Mexeflote. We knew we could not complete the task that night, but if we worked fast, I suggested, she just might be ready to sail the following night. During this conversation, it was suggested that we send one of the two LCUs to Darwin to collect the Brigade radio vehicles so urgently needed. While the collection of the radios was vital for 5 Brigade, there were distinct disadvantages transporting them by LCU. On the other hand there were other ways of getting the vehicles to Fitzroy – overland or slung beneath a Sea King. (Southby-Tailyour, *Reasons in Writing*)

Southby-Tailyour explained there was no way to advise the Gurkhas guarding the approaches to Choiseul Sound, who had orders to shoot anything that moved. Convinced by Colour Sergeant Brian Johnston, coxswain of Foxtrot

Four, that the risk was not worth it, Southby-Tailyour rejected the request.

Within a day of their soaking passage from Lively Island, the Scots Guards were actively patrolling and acting on information provided by the SAS to Brigade intelligence searching for two suspected Pack Howitzer positions and a radar near Port Harriet. This was Operation Impunity. In spite of extensive searching, nothing was found; in fact, they never existed. Meanwhile 1/7th Gurkha Rifles, less C Company on rear security duties at Goose Green and D Company, the Brigade Recce Company, were flown forward to Little Wether Ground, a bleak area north of Fitzroy Ridge. Captain Matt Helm took command of the Headquarters and Signal Squadron on the death of Major Forge and worked hard at improving communications. Corporal Naylor and his Land Rover-borne radio rebroadcast crew reappeared, having been mistakenly stranded on Verde Mountains for three days. After a short rest, his vehicles replaced Corporal Daughtrey's manpack rebroadcast station. On 6 June, A (Radio) Troop (Lieutenant Mark Edwards) had tried to drive to Fitzroy but were beaten by the appalling state of the track; they covered just 15 miles in five hours at the expense of two Land Rovers broken down. Next day, Major Keith Butler took command of the Squadron. With only two days to go until 9 June, B Troop (Lieutenant Trevor Bradley) embarked on the *Monsunen* for a night passage to Fitzroy in order to set up Brigade HQ. Also on board were Kefford's Gurkhas and several dozen 2 Para left behind at Goose Green. The total Embarked Force was about 200 men, few with life-jackets or survival suits. At 10.00 pm, the *Monsunen* cast off for the four-hour voyage to Fitzroy. The remainder would follow in a landing craft, which was due in from Fitzroy during the night – LCU Foxtrot Four. Southby-Tailyour had relented to let it bring 5 Infantry Brigade assets to Fitzroy, provided it was escorted by the *Monsunen*. That evening Major Southby-Tailyour joined Captain Green and several of his officers for dinner on board *Sir Tristram*.

Chapter Twelve

Port Pleasant
8 June

Soon after 7.50 am on 8 June, Captain Green burst into Major Ewen Southby-Tailyour's cabin and told him that another LSL had arrived with troops on board. They both ran to the bridge and facing them inshore, about 200 yards from the shoreline, was *Sir Galahad*. Through their binoculars they could soldiers gathered on the sterngate waiting for transport ashore. Joined by Major Todd, they agreed that the ship and the men on board were in great danger. A key principle of amphibious warfare is to land the ground forces quickly.

HQ 5 Infantry Brigade was apparently unaware of what was happening and Lieutenant Colonel Ivor Hellberg, now commanding the enlarged Commando Logistic Regiment, including 81 Ordnance Field Park, which was part of the Brigade, had few resources to unload her. The day promised to be clear. Since there were no preparations for the arrival of the second ship, unloading *Sir Tristram* continued so that she could return to San Carlos Water that night.

Majors Todd and Southby-Tailyour motored to *Sir Galahad* in LCU Foxtrot One and were surprised to see soldiers. One of the two Army majors mentioned that the ship included the balance of the Welsh Guards and his instructions were to join the rest of his Battalion at Bluff Cove. Southby-Tailyour replied that with the probability of air raids, all troops should be landed immediately and after dark, landing craft would take his troops to Bluff Cove; soldiers milling around the confined space of the tank deck would hinder unloading vehicles and stores. When the two officers insisted that their companies be ferried to Bluff Cove, Southby-Tailyour said that the only way was on foot via Fitzroy Bridge, a distance of about 7 miles, and undertook to arrange for the heavy equipment to follow. The officers retorted that the bridge had not been repaired because 4 Field Troop RE, who they believed had been tasked to repair it, were on board and therefore the march would be 14 miles via Ridge Camp. In fact, the parachute sappers were already repairing the bridge. To Southby-Tailyour, the two officers seemed unable to grasp the vulnerability of the anchorage and reiterated despatching *Sir Galahad* in broad daylight to Bluff Cove under the noses of Argentine observers was out of the question. If they agreed, they could be ashore within twenty minutes and marching within half an hour. Southby-Tailyour:

> To be fair they had been messed around quite a lot back in San Carlos, marching and then coming back, and then setting off again and coming back. But they were in grave danger from enemy action and indeed ordinary accidents on board; there was no doubt in my mind. The landing craft and powered raft which I had to unload Sir Tristram had a load of ammunition on board. It was pointed out to me that men and ammunition do not travel in the same vehicles. I explained that this was war and we don't operate peacetime restrictions during war and that his men were in grave danger. (Southby-Tailyour, *Reasons in Writing*)

Nevertheless, about 100 men did go ashore on top of the ammunition from the LSL, although the state of the tide prevented beaching until 8.00 am. In the hope that the officers would acknowledge that Royal Marines majors are equivalent to Army lieutenant colonels, he issued a direct order to land. Guards officers are the first to acknowledge status, however the suggestion was rejected on the grounds that he and they were of the same rank. Southby-Tailyour persevered and warned them that they were staying on board against accepted practice. Returning ashore, when he told Major Rolfe-Smith that there were about 300 troops on board, including two Welsh Guards companies, Rolfe-Smith said that this was impossible because the Welsh Guards had landed the previous night at Bluff Cove. Southby-Tailyour explained that they had been returned to San Carlos and it was now up to Brigade HQ to get the two companies to Bluff Cove.

The top priority was to fly the Rapier Troop ashore. Lieutenant Waddell placed Sergeant Steve Brooks at Fitzroy. To his east and north of the settlement, not far from HQ Company, 2 Para, was Bombardier McMartin's malfunctioning firing unit. South-east of the settlement was Sergeant Pearson and on high ground in Fitzroy Park was Sergeant Morgan.

On board *Sir Galahad*, Captain Roberts, believing that the combat air patrol and Rapiers would cover the anchorage, rejected a Welsh Guards offer to defend the ship with machine-guns. At 'Sid's Strip' there had been another mishap when at about 9.30 am, a Harrier piloted by the No. 1 (Fighter) Squadron Commanding Officer, Wing Commander Peter Squires, careered through the panels after suffering a mechanical failure on take-off. While 11 Field Squadron RE fixed the mess, for the third time, combat air patrols reverted to Carrier Battle Group. However, HMS *Hermes* had retired to the east to maintain her boilers and thus loiter time over the Falklands was decreased.

Captain Drage of 4th Field Regiment, who commanded one of two Forward Observation Officer parties attached to the Welsh Guards, was on *Sir Galahad*:

At 11.00, seven minutes before first light, the two FOOs were looking at the coastline and dominating high features thinking what an ideal target an observer would have. Talking to the ship's officers, it was clear that there was no plan for unloading the Welsh Guards. We had no orders and it was not known if we were to disembark at Fitzroy or Bluff Cove. Shortly before midday members of the surgical teams were told to prepare to move. They went ashore probably at 10.30 on a half full Mexeflote. During lunch the Welsh Guards were hurried onto the tank deck to prepare to move. There was considerable waiting with all the men and equipment in company groups on the tank deck. We were preparing for the LCU to load the men and stores from the stern ramp. Once contact with the LCU had been made, it passed on the fact that the ramp would not lower and we would have to load over the port side. There was considerable effort required to prepare to load. All stores had to be moved and the top hatches opened. ('4 Field Regiment in the Falkland Islands')

The landing plan was for 16 Field Ambulance to land by Mexeflote and the Welsh Guards by LCU. However, when a LCU appeared at 11.30 am, Lieutenant Colonel Roberts insisted that his medics should land first.

Meanwhile Argentine intelligence had detected the activity around Port Pleasant on 6 June from observers, electronic warfare and air-photo recces. The Ministry of Defence later investigated a tape prepared by the journalist Michael Nicholson, filed 'in clear' with Independent Television News on a 48-hour embargo, referring to operations ('I can only describe as extraordinarily daring which, until completed, cannot be revealed'), may have alerted the Argentines to Wilson's bold move. It doesn't take much intelligence to deduce that with 3 Commando Brigade north of Wickham Heights, 5 Infantry Brigade was in the south and the 'operation' might well be somewhere in Port Pleasant. HQ Southern Air Force Command at Comodoro Rivadavia developed a plan for 5th and 6th Fighter Groups to attack Fitzroy and Bluff Cove while 8th Fighter Group diverted the British combat air patrol orbiting off West Falklands with a simulated attack on San Carlos Water. Normally based 300 miles inland, 5th Fighter Group had sunk HMS *Ardent* on 21 May, dropped the bomb on HMS *Antelope*, which then exploded so dramatically on the night of the 23rd, and then sank HMS *Coventry* and damaged HMS *Broadsword* two days later. It had also attacked 3 Commando Brigade at San Carlos and Ajax Bay on 27 May. The Daggers lacked in-flight refuelling capability and had weak electronic warfare countermeasures, while the Mirages had been outfought by the Sea Harriers. Times were organized so that the faster Daggers would arrive over the target area at the same time as the Skyhawks.

At about 10.50 am, eight 5th Group Skyhawk A-4Bs, armed with 500lb bombs, and eight 6th Group Daggers, each bombed up with two 1,000lb bombs, and a 1st Air Photographic Group Learjet guide, left Rio Grande. One Dagger returned to base after a bird strike. The Daggers, led by Captain Carlos Rohde, made landfall near Cape Meredith and banked north-east toward Falkland Sound, intending to cross Lafonia and then east to Port Pleasant. Three Skyhawks also returned to Argentina. A KC-130H tanker provided more in-flight fuelling. At about 12.35 pm, HMS *Exeter,* in the San Carlos area, issued Air Raid Red, however, by the time this reached the Port Pleasant sector, it was too late. Shortly before 12.45 pm, the four 4th Group Mirages, simulating an attack on San Carlos Water, were detected by two 801 Squadron Sea Harriers orbiting the southern end of Falkland Sound. Hopes to tempt them into a fight disappeared when the Mirages, as planned, broke away and were pursued by the Sea Harriers. The Daggers and Skyhawks streamed through the open door.

Aware of the raid, HMS *Plymouth* was steaming to Cancho Point to give naval gunfire for a Special Forces report of a suspected Argentine position on Mount Rosalie. At about 12.50 pm, a lookout reported five aircraft 2 miles to the south-west. Helm hard to starboard, the destroyer lurched around to the east and, at full speed, headed for the air defence umbrella of San Carlos Water. Believing that he had lost the element of surprise, Captain Rohde first flew over her and then in line astern, the Daggers attacked. In the face of 20mm fire from the ship's secondary armament and a Seacat missile, the Argentines opened up with cannon, damaging the hydraulic and electrical cables feeding the 4.5-inch main armament. Dropping four bombs, one careered through the funnel, two smashed the anti-submarine spigot mortar hoist and handling gear and the fourth caused a depth charge stowed aft to explode and start a fire in the Chief Petty Officers' Mess and galley. None exploded. As the Argentine pilots climbed, they saw the warship billowing smoke and limping back toward San Carlos where a helicopter delivered fire-fighting apparatus and evacuated five wounded to Ajax Bay. None of the Daggers were damaged and the pilots returned to Rio Grande in the belief they had sunk a ship.

The Skyhawks, now led by First Lieutenant Cachon, on his third combat sortie but first as mission leader, passed through rain showers, were briefly deflected by a Sea King near Choiseul Sound and surprised a Scout flown by Sergeant Dick Kalinski near Swan Inlet House. Hovering behind a hillock over MacPhee Pond, the drive shaft to the tail rotor failed as he started to climb and the helicopter dropped into 4 feet of water. At about 1.05 pm, in arrowhead formation, the Skyhawks flew over the western edge of Port Pleasant and encountered low-level air defence over Bluff Cove, which hit Lieutenant Galvez's aircraft. Seeing no ships, Cachon decided to return to base and with First Lieutenant Carlos Rinke, and Ensign Leonardo Carmona on his left, he heaved the flight to starboard through a 180-degree tight turn and climbed over East Island. As Ensigns Gomez and Galvez edged over to the left, Gomez reported two ships in Port Pleasant. The five Skyhawks split with Cachon, Rinke and Carmona aiming for *Sir Galahad* and Galvez and Gomez lining up on *Sir Tristram*. A Blowpipe missile whistled between Cachon's and Rinke's Skyhawks. The Rapier Troop had not completed the vital tests and adjustments, so necessary each time the firing unit was moved. Sergeant Pearson's gunner, Gunner Tony McNally, picked up the aircraft visually and pressed the firing button only to hear a systems fault message in his helmet. On Bombardier McMartin's Rapier, Lance Bombardier Tim Ward, knowing that the unit's command transmitter had not been repaired, lined up on the approaching aircraft and pressed the firing button, in the hope that the system would work, but the missile stubbornly remained on its ramp. As he later commented: 'Can you imagine how impotent we felt watching this disaster unfold before our very eyes? This feeling will remain with me for the rest of my life.'

Cachon released his bombs as he passed over the starboard side of the *Sir Galahad*. One hit the water, another pierced a diesel ready-use tank without exploding but the other two detonated. On Mount Challenger, Lieutenant Colonel Vaux was talking to a sapper when:

RSM Chisnall seized my arm in a vice-like grip. Such informality from him was so unusual that I knew something must be wrong, even before I heard his urgent direction, 'Look over there, Colonel – down the coast-line. Just look at those bastards!' Skimming down the shore were four A4 Skyhawks of the Argentine Air Force. Even as we watched, helpless with horror, they rose upwards, and then swooped down upon the unsuspecting ships. A myriad of malevolent flashes preceded the great booming explosions, with which we were all too familiar (from the days of Bomb Alley in San Carlos). We watched the aircraft make two passes. On the second, the left hand ship, *Sir Galahad*, erupted in flames and billowing smoke. Soon the scene was obscured by oily black smog, which hung like a shroud over the area in which 5 Brigade's troops had been landing. It was obvious they would not now be moving forward for a while, which must delay our advance as well. (Vaux, *March to the South Atlantic*)

Carmona opened up with his 20mm cannon peppering the upper works. When his bombs missed, his frustration was heard by Rinke, who thought that his bombs had been released. When Rinke realized his aircraft was still laden, it was too late to drop them. Galvez's stick hit *Sir Tristram* while those of Gomez fell short. The five Skyhawks banked to the south, climbed sharply to 35,000 feet and returned to Argentina, without refuelling, in the certain knowledge that they had caught two British ships undefended. It was all over in a few seconds.

On *Sir Galahad*, most of the troops were in the narrow confines of the tank deck waiting to disembark. Down the centre were Land Rovers and trailers, ammunition and equipment on pallets and packs, rifles and webbing, and soldiers killing time – playing cards, chatting, dozing. Captain Drage:

> Eventually at 12.45 the Prince of Wales Company began to load onto the LCU. The first group was Company HQ and FOO party. Some equipment, including bergens, was lowered into the LCU. At 13.00, as the first group were climbing down into the LCU, the attack came. There was a roar of jet engines very close and instantly two Skyhawk aircraft dropped their loads and flew over overhead. People in the LCU took cover. It was seconds later when the thick black toxic smoke appeared billowing out of the hold, then an enormous flash that shook the whole ship. Bombs were still landing around the ship; some looked like bomblets. One large bomb went through the stern of the ship just missing the LCUI. Two other bombs exploded. There was little time between the Captain giving 'Air Raid Warning Red' and 'Abandon Ship'. The wounded soon appeared and started to climb into the LCU. They were very shocked, many badly burnt and some with body wounds. ('4 Field Regiment in the Falkland Islands')

Most knew nothing until 'Air Raid Red!' was broadcast on the tannoy, shouts of 'Get down! Get down!' and then an explosion and a fireball charging through the cavernous deck. Swirling, thick smoke prevented breathing and ammunition exploded sending bullets and shrapnel blasting into the soldiers. Guardsman David Grimshaw was a GPMG gunner, carrying about 2,000 rounds of ammunition:

> The crew of *Sir Galahad* were mainly Chinese. As they slid open the door to the deck, there were these two Chinese men with these orange suits on. We were looking up at them at the time . . . they started shouting and screaming as they fell to the floor. As we turned round our company sergeant major shouted, 'Hit the deck!' So I turned over, face first, and hit the deck. Then there was a pause – five or six seconds, and then a big bang. I was unconscious for a couple of seconds. There was fire and smoke everywhere. I tried to stand up then and realised my leg had gone, so obviously I fell back down on the floor. When I came around, I was lying on the floor. All I could feel was the burning sensation in the lower part of my left leg. I remember looking at my left hand. It had melted. (Bilton and Kominsky, *Speaking Out*)

Captain Roberts knew his ship was fatally damaged and ordered 'Abandon ship'. Military discipline held. The ship's RCT Port Operator Detachment used their knowledge of the ship to send shocked soldiers to the upper deck. Second Engineer Officer Paul Henry was awarded a posthumous George

Medal when he gave his breathing apparatus to a junior officer who had returned to the Main Control Room, and told him to abandon ship. Company Sergeant Major Brian Neck of the Welsh Guards organized the evacuation from the wreckage of the tank deck. Rigid Raider coxswain Lance Corporal Bill Skinner and Sapper Leer, of 9 Parachute Squadron RE, were taking a short break on board. Skinner staggered from the 'heads' and, after assisting a dazed soldier to the upper deck, used his craft to ferry troops ashore. A Royal Marine, who was watching a film in a lounge, was leaving when he was punched by another Royal Marine, minus part of his leg. The Royal Marine tried to drag the wounded man to safety, but was overcome by smoke and told a rescue party where he could be found. When the order 'Abandon ship!' was given, he left in a helicopter in the belief that the wounded man was dead. Such was his guilt that during the night he attempted to commit suicide. Evacuated to SS *Uganda* as a psychiatric casualty, he tried to overdose using his own morphine. Although he was taken to see the wounded Royal Marine, the guilt remained, however he had a long recovery process. Fortunately, he had a supportive wife.

LCU Foxtrot One, skippered by Colour Sergeant 'Connie' Francis, took off men, as did Sergeant Boultby with his Mexeflote. He was awarded the Military Medal for his gallantry. The Sir Tristram RCT Port Operator Detachment motored to her sister ship and reinforced fire-fighting parties. Within thirty-five minutes, most able-bodied men had been evacuated.

The anti-submarine pilots of 825 NAS (Lieutenant Commander Hugh Clark) helped the stricken ships in very different conditions from their normal – billowing smoke and flames, explosions and men in the water. Most of those evacuated from the ship were assembled on the beach. Private Curtis, recently returned to 2 Para after nearly being evacuated to England because of the state of his feet, was from the Welsh Valleys:

> The Welsh Guards had always held a special place in my heart. Running to the cove, I looked across at the blazing hulks. Both transport ships had been hit; the *Sir Tristram* nearer the jetty, had been struck on the stern deck; from the *Sir Galahad*, thick, belching smoke was spiralling upwards and helicopters already buzzed around its hull. There were lift rafts in the water, trying to pull away from the ship. I never felt so helpless. I could see the boys piled into boats and hear their cries. Their accents were the same as mine and they were in distress and in pain. This, more than anything else, brought home the full horror of war. We waded into the cold, grey sea, dragging the boats to shore. There were lads in a terrible state – their hair gone and skin peeling off in charred strips; some had lost limbs. (Curtis, *CQB*)

Fortunately, 2 Para had a foresighted Medical Officer, Captain Steve Hughes RAMC, who had trained the paras in advanced first aid, including resuscitation and the treatment of specific wounds, including burns. Even for those who had fought at Goose Green, it was the first time that many soldiers had seen such wounds in such numbers – burns, lost limbs, the deafened, confused and blinded, and gunshot and shrapnel wounds. Corporal Kevin Moran was a 2 Para Regimental Medical Assistant on the beach:

> People were being pulled off by the choppers, which were working in pairs. One tried to get to the survivors, the other was trying to fan the smoke away so that the other helicopter could come underneath to lift anyone who was there. Without them fanning the smoke away, it would have been dangerous for the other pilot. He wouldn't have been able to see where he was flying.
>
> The scene on the beach was quite shocking. Your training takes over, that's how you get through it. You know what you've been taught, you know how to deal with certain things and you do your best. You can deal with a patient in different ways. I try to look at them as a lump of meat. You do all the 'There, there, kid,' and 'you're going to be all right, no problem.' Then you forget about it. Hopefully you've got someone else there who can maybe keep talking to the patient while you deal with the injury. (Bilton and Kominsky, *Speaking Out*)

Left on board were several ship's officers and 16 Field Ambulance medics. Sergeant Peter Naya was concussed by the explosion of the first bomb and had his head and back scorched. Establishing a first aid post on the forecastle, Naya organized triage, set up infusions and arranged evacuation of the wounded, some with fearful burns and others with lost limbs. Guardsman Grimshaw:

> Someone from the field surgical team who was on the ship with us put a tourniquet on my leg and injected me with morphine. He was very good. I think if he hadn't been there, I would have been a lot worse off. He acted so quickly, stopped the flow of blood and kept me calm. (Bilton and Kominsky, *Speaking Out*)

Three days later, Naya returned to his unit's Advance Surgical Centre in time for the attacks on Stanley. He was awarded a well-deserved Military Medal. Invited by Brigadier Wilson to film the build-up of his Brigade at Fitzroy were several journalists, including a television crew. Guardsman Grimwood:

> I was taken by helicopter to the beach. When it landed I was in the stretcher and was supporting my left leg in the air. There were bits hanging off it, so, I suppose, it look very horrific. I looked around and there was a film crew there. They seemed to jump at me. I was a bit annoyed at that. They were filming because of my leg. (Bilton and Kominsky, *Speaking Out*)

While visiting their para sappers erecting a water point in the BMA, Major Davies and Squadron Sergeant Major Pete Walker heard the bombing. By the time they reached their command post, a black pall of smoke was billowing from *Sir Galahad*. Davies:

I called the Defence Section to grab a stretcher, summoned the Second-in-Command and sent someone to warn the medical centre, which was close to our position. The first man we took off the helicopter was Chinese. He was crying with pain and burned flesh hung off him. I assumed the bomb must have hit the galley. Then another helicopter appeared with more suffering Chinese crewmen. The third helicopter brought blacked and singed men in Army uniforms. It was only after a couple of loads that the enormity of the tragedy began to dawn on me; there had been soldiers on the ships, after all. I lost count of the men we took from the helicopters to the medical centre, which rapidly filled to overflowing. We had to take screaming, bleeding, badly burned men off stretchers and put them on the floor to free more stretchers for yet more wounded. The sights, sounds and smell of burning flesh were horrific. Thankfully the brain can delay the realization of such horror and we ran with our smouldering loads, doused with water and fitted intravenous drips with a vague oblivion. Before long the medical centre overflowed. Those who had walked up from the shore stood around outside shocked and dazed. Many who had burns on the hands stood with them in drums of cold water; others walked around in silent pain with arms raised like prisoners. Some soldiers I took off the helicopters spoke to me as if they knew me. They were so blackened I did not recognize them. It was only when I saw their Royal Engineer stable belts that I realized 4 Troop must have been on board. Inevitably some people found it all too much. I found a medical officer in an agitated state just when the activity around the Medical Centre was at its height. He was saying how terrible it was, how the Second-in-Command had been killed and most of the medical stores lost. Since a RAMC staff sergeant was getting on with the task, I led the officer outside and told him to keep out of the way until he could do something useful. (Davies, 'A Memoir of 9 Parachute Squadron RE')

Lieutenant Colonel Rickett was visiting Number 2 Company (Major Christopher Drewry) with Regimental Sergeant Major Tony Davies when a radio operator told him that he was required urgently at Battalion HQ. His assumption that his two companies were on board the worst-hit ship was confirmed. Rickett:

I remember well seeing two ships in the distance coming into Fitzroy harbour but nobody thought very much about this, what the Navy did

168

was none of our business! Although it seemed somewhat strange to see them in the clear light of day. None of us had any idea that the balance of the battalion was on board one of these ships, certainly nobody at Brigade HQ told us anything . . . Together with the RSM and the Padre, Peter Brook, we set off for Fitzroy where a scene of indescribable chaos awaited us. We were still of course under constant air attack and there were groups of kit-less Welsh Guardsmen everywhere. I remember saying 'Stick close to me as I am lucky' and we took cover as best we could. Soon afterwards I can remember the Company Sergeant Majors calling the roll in a sheep shed, but it was impossible at that moment to ascertain who had been killed and who, amongst the wounded, had been taken off direct from the stricken RFA *Galahad* by helicopter. With a heavy heart I returned to Battalion HQ, assuring Guy Sayle and Charles Bremner that I would get back to see them all as soon as I was able. I remember clearly that neither of them wanted me to leave them but we had to get on with the war. From that moment I was determined that none of us would look backwards on these tragic events but instead concentrate our minds on the tasks before us.

At the Land Forces Main Dressing Station at Ajax Bay, Surgeon Commander Rick Jolly was treating other wounded when a helicopter crewman rushed in with the message: '*Galahad* hit before surgical teams unloaded. Many burn casualties'. The immediate priority was to triage those who needed immediate treatment from those who could be transferred to ships' sick bays for further treatment. He was struck by the Welsh Valley stoicism of the Welsh Guards as each man seemed to know someone who was worse off and should be treated first. The wounded were assembled in the Fitzroy Community Centre. Many would suffer years of painful treatment and permanent disabilities.

The Rapier Troop quickly came in for criticism. A Parachute Regiment major threatened to send Bombardier McMartin's detachment back to the United Kingdom. Told of the systems failure, he said he would have a replacement component within two hours. It never arrived. The Rapiers were not the only air defence – there were the 0.50-inch Brownings, a Blowpipe section from 43 Air Defence Battery and countless general purpose machine guns. *Sir Galahad* had a 40mm Bofors.

HQ Southern Air Force Command was elated with Cachon's attack and planned two more sorties before night fell, the first, an anti-shipping strike by 5th Fighter Group and an anti-personnel raid by 4th Fighter Group with top cover again provided by Mirages of 8th Fighter Group. So far, the war of 4th Fighter Group had been when, on 30 May, its pilots claimed to have sunk HMS *Invincible*. Using the pall of smoke over Port Pleasant as his beacon, First Lieutenant Bolzan, the 5th Fighter Group Mazo Flight commander, attacked from the south-west at about 2.30 pm. In spite of

Southern Air Force Command predictions, he found that the British were not demoralized. Sergeant Pearson's Rapier had been tested and the flight was met with a blistering barrage, nevertheless the Skyhawks escaped serious damage. The Scots Guards air defence profile fired over 18,000 rounds. Major C. Jordan of 97 (Lawson's Company) Field Battery: 'My second memory was of SSgt McLean's black mug filled with steaming tea in one hand and SMG crooked in his elbow in the other deliberately firing and drinking as the planes hurtled over our position' ('4th Field Regiment in the Falkland Islands').

Captain John Russell, the 4th Field Regiment Adjutant, was not so canny. Strolling to his trench with a cup of cocoa, as the Skyhawks screamed overhead, he dived into a trench occupied by Bombardier Nicholson, spilling most of his precious drink. 'What service, Bombardier, chocolate served in an air raid!' With stolid humour, Nicholson replied 'But, sir, you've drunk most of it!' Clearing Port Pleasant, Bolzan searched for other targets and saw, at the mouth of Choiseul Sound, a landing craft loaded with vehicles.

LCU Foxtrot Four had arrived at Goose Green at about 4.00 am and loaded nine soldiers and six Land Rovers of Brigade HQ and the Signal Squadron, commanded by Captain Carel Bouwens, a Royal Engineer staff officer; two of the vehicles were fitted with cryptographic equipment for secure communications. Aware of the importance of the load, Colour Sergeant Johnson ignored Southby-Tailyour's instructions not to sail in daylight. 'Bugger the orders. I've been frightened by a Royal Navy frigate when I was returning to Salvador Waters and I'm not going to risk that again in the dark. The Brigade needs these vehicles forward now. We'll sail.' At about 2.35 pm, about one mile south of Johnson Island, the alarm was raised as Bolzan and his wingman, Lieutenant Vasquez dived, leaving First Lieutenant Hector Sanchez and his wingman, Lieutenant Arraras, as top cover. Vasquez bracketed the landing craft with one 500lb bomb falling about 20 metres astern and his second landing on the stern, wrecking the wheelhouse and killing Colour Sergeant Johnson, three other Royal Marines and two Royal Navy engine room artificers, and fatally wounding Marine 'Griff' Griffiths. Marine Jim Quigley, on the wheel, climbed back on board after being blown into the sea. Marine 'Tich' Cruden, temporarily blinded, was crawling through a hole from the accommodation with his clothes and hair on fire: 'The Army put me out with a fire extinguisher.' On the tank deck, Airtrooper Mark Price, the Australian driver of the Commanding Officer of 656 Squadron, was also temporarily blinded when he was blown over a trailer.

The attack was spotted by two 800 Squadron Sea Harriers practising dusk deck-landing training conducted by Lieutenant Dave Smith for a recently arrived RAF pilot, Flight Lieutenant Dave Morgan. They shot down two of the Skyhawks and then watched Bolzan's Skyhawk career into sand dunes at Rain Cove. Sanchez escaped by ditching all his stores and spare fuel. He was fortunate to meet up with the KC-130H tanker.

Meanwhile, 4th Fighter Group's Yunque Flight left Military Air Base St

Julian at 3.00 pm for the third attack. With dusk approaching, Captain Mario Cafaratti was guided by the orange glows and spiral of black smoke, however the four Skyhawks were met with a hail of ground fire. Ensign Codrington, passing over Mount Kent, ran into fire from 42 Commando. The Harrier pilots reported the position of the LCU.

Near the mouth of Choiseul Sound, the crippled Foxtrot Four was wallowing in ocean currents with the soldiers tackling the fires. The Land Rovers and trailers were shuffled for'ard to lift the shattered stern. With one life raft damaged beyond repair, the second one was thrown over the side in case the landing craft had to be abandoned but this punctured on jagged metal. After Sergeant Alec Turner and Corporal Bob Taylor had disposed of the cryptographic material, Taylor improvised a raft from inflated lifejackets and a tarpaulin. Shortly before the attack, Colour Sergeant Johnson had fortuitously shown their position to Captain Bouwens and when Lance Corporals Mair and Davison persuaded a radio to work, a Mayday was sent to Brigade HQ. Two 656 Squadron helicopters failed to find the LCU, however a Sea King commanded by Lieutenant Miller, fresh from the rescues off Fitzroy, found it and everyone was winched on board.

During the late afternoon at Goose Green, a mixed bag of 180 Gurkhas and other soldiers, all under the command of Major Bill Dawson, the Gurkha Second-in-Command, embarked on the *Monsunen* to be ferried to Fitzroy. Concerned about the cryptographic material on aboard the LCU, Brigadier Wilson instructed Dawson to find it and tow it to Fitzroy. Lieutenant McLaren, in command of the *Monsunen*, arrived with a completely different set of orders from Commodore Clapp and confusion reigned until it was agreed that the landing craft must be found. After a several hours, she was found drifting south-east of Lively Island and a tow-rope was passed. However, a trailing rope snagged *Monsunen*'s propeller and when attempts by Gurkhas to untangle it failed, Dawson reported to HQ LFFI that he had found the LCU but that the *Monsunen* was immobilized; no one knew about the attempt to recover the cipher. HMS *Yarmouth* then found the two vessels and after her divers had freed the propeller, Dawson instructed McLean to return to Goose Green. The Gurkhas were flown to join their Battalion at Fitzroy by Chinook. LCU Foxtrot Four eventually sank, taking with her the valuable radio vehicles. For Brigadier Wilson, the loss of the radios was a serious setback – he was now reliant upon his lighter manpack Tac HQ.

Many of those who had dealt with the casualties from the two ships were strengthened by the quiet discipline of the survivors. The ability to equip those who had lost weapons, equipment and clothing was restricted by the loss of the *Atlantic Conveyor*. Davies took stock:

4 Troop had effectively been written off, with Corporal Andrew McIlvenna and Sapper Wayne Tarbard killed and eight wounded, Staff Sergeant Grant with shrapnel and Lance Corporal Thew and Sappers

Dodds, Ennis, Richards, Wallis and Williams, all with burns. As we reflected on the day's events, we recalled the horror, the excitement and, incredibly, the humour. For example the diminutive figure of Lieutenant John Mullins, who commanded Support Troop, came stomping up the track. He was shocked and could only speak in a whisper and kept saying 'It was terrible, terrible, David Foxley's dead, 4 Troop's gone . . .' I sat him down and asked someone to make him a brew. Shortly afterward Foxley appeared, a bit singed but otherwise unhurt. He had obviously been deafened for when he spoke, he yelled. He was all right and he was going to look after his Troop – and the whole world could hear him. (Davies, 'A Memoir of 9 Parachute Squadron RE')

4 Field Squadron joined HMS *Intrepid* as its embarked Sapper Troop and cleared West Falkland settlements of mines and booby traps. On 25 June, RFA *Sir Galahad* was torpedoed south-west of Stanley by the submarine HMS *Onyx*, the only diesel-electric British submarine to go south. RFA *Sir Tristram* was refloated and towed to Stanley where she was used for accommodation until 1984 when she was brought back to England and reconstructed.

The amphibious nature of the war presented both sides problems in the management of the wounded. The *Uganda* was a P&O liner that had been on an educational cruise in the Mediterranean, but was converted to a hospital ship and, in spite of the Junta's protests that she was delivering war stores, she collected wounded directly from Ajax Bay. Staff Nurse Marion Stock was a member of Queen Alexandra's Royal Naval Nursing Service:

We were told to go to the officers' mess, which had been turned into another ward to receive these casualties. Just before we got to the door, there was this awful stench of burning. We opened the doors and there were about forty beds of black faces. It was a feeling of horror. You wanted to close the doors and run. Then you thought; God, you've to hide this horror you have on your face because of the patients . . . Some had had nightmares about when they had been trapped. Others had seen their colleagues being badly burned and had tried to help or couldn't help. Their frustration came out and the only thing you could really do was sit and listen. You wanted to go back to your room and cry your eyes out because you felt desperately sorry for these people . . . Some of the patients wondered how their wives and girlfriends might react . . . How are my children going to react when they see me looking like this? But they never complained. They were very brave men – they were marvellous. (Bilton and Kominsky, *Speaking Out*)

HMS *Hydra*, *Hecla* and *Herald* and the logistic support ships, *British Test* and *British Trent*, were used as ambulance ships to take casualties from SS

Uganda to Montevideo from where they were flown to England in aeromedic VC-10s for treatment at the naval and military hospitals.

Argentina used naval transports for her wounded. When *Bahia Paraiso* arrived off the Falklands, painted white and displaying a large Red Cross on her flight deck hangar, the British, knowing she had been used at South Georgia in April, insisted on her being searched. She collected casualties, delivered medical supplies to Stanley and then met with the *Uganda*, in the 'Red Cross Box' to the north of Falkland Sound to collect prisoners wounded at Goose Green.

The attacks cost the Welsh Guards thirty-two non-commissioned officers and guardsmen; the REME, a corporal and a craftsman; and the Army Catering Corps, a lance corporal and three privates, all killed. 16 Field Ambulance lost much of their equipment and suffered three fatalities, including Major Roger Nutbeem, the Second-in-Command; it was fortunate that most of the unit had landed early. 4 Field Troop RE lost two killed and eight wounded. RFA *Sir Galahad* had three officers and three Chinese killed, and RFA *Sir Tristram*, two Chinese killed. Forty-six men were evacuated to Ajax Bay with serious wounds.

For the British public, reading the longest casualty list on a single day since the Korean War, and watching those dramatic pictures, was a shock. Wilson's bold move to Port Pleasant was full of risks, however it was significantly increased when 2 Para hijacked the landing craft meant to rendezvous with HMS *Fearless*. In a radio conversation next day, Admiral Fieldhouse and Rear Admiral Woodward distanced themselves from responsibility by agreeing that Major General Moore bore ultimate responsibility. Writing in his diary, Rear Admiral Woodward 'could strangle' Commodore Clapp after he'd been told not to put HMS *Intrepid* into Fitzroy, which Clapp had not. He wished that he had told Moore and Clapp not to land at Fitzroy and Bluff Cove; as the Carrier Battle Group commander, it was not his decision. A naval Board of Inquiry concluded that Commodore Clapp had taken a justifiable risk by sending the two LSLs to Port Pleasant – nevertheless, within a few years, he left the Royal Navy, still as a Commodore. He was never debriefed and has not been given sufficient credit for his major contribution to victory.

Menendez had sufficient troops to carry out a destabilizing attack on 5 Infantry Brigade. During the evening, Lieutenant Colonel Soria, whose 4th Infantry Regiment was defending Two Sisters and Mount Harriet, found Brigadier General Jofre in a fighting mood. 'New Commando units are waiting for the Air Force Chinooks and are ready for deployment to the British rear.' All he needed was for Menendez's Chief-of-Staff, Brigadier General Daher, to return from Argentina with confirmation that a general counter-attack was feasible. In an interview for the *New York Times* the following day, he said that the conscripts 'remained in excellent condition, physically and spiritually', and remained prepared to 'confront and rout the

173

colonial invaders'. He no doubt hoped that the word 'colonial' would strike a cord of sympathy for him with his American audience.

Military blunders usually follow personality weaknesses, technology and equipment failures, intelligence miscalculations and poor organization. There were mistakes and misjudgements during 'the bold move' and five Skyhawks were lost on that clear day.

Chapter Thirteen

The Outer Defence Zone
11 to 12 June

On 7 June, when Brigadier Thompson had informed Major General Moore that 3 Commando Brigade was in a position to attack Stanley during the night 8/9 June, differences in strategy began to emerge with Brigadier Wilson favouring a narrow front javelin strike along the Fitzroy to Stanley track south of Mount Harriet followed by a divisional breakout onto Stanley Common. This view was hardly surprising considering that his Brigade was being forced into a narrow frontage attack by Wickham Heights on his left and the sea on the right flank. Thompson, not unnaturally, favoured the broad front, including seizing the strategically important Mount Longdon, which dominated the ground north and south of Stanley Harbour. Both men were on board HMS *Fearless* at San Carlos when they learnt of the attack on the two LSLs and the conference broke up.

By 9 June, Major General Moore was confident that Brigadier Thompson could handle a three-battalion Brigade attack; however, with the attack on Port Pleasant, he was unsure about Brigadier Wilson's ability to fight any more than on a single-battalion frontage, particularly as the Welsh Guards had been decimated. Since 3 Commando Brigade had completed their recces and battle preparations, Thompson's option was adopted with the attack rescheduled for 10/11 June. There was some urgency because the health of 3 Commando Brigade was causing concerns. Moore issued his Operational Order for a three-phase attack on Stanley:

Phase One.

3 Commando Brigade to attack Two Sisters and Mount Harriet with the option of attacking Mount Longdon.

Phase Two.

5 Infantry Brigade to attack Tumbledown Mountain and Mount William.

Phase Three.

Secure Sapper Hill.

Next day, Brigadier Thompson summoned his commanding officers to Brigade HQ on Mount Kent and issued his orders for Phase One on the basis that if the Argentines folded, the momentum of the attack must be maintained:

3 Para to seize Mount Longdon and exploit to Wireless Ridge. Thompson had included Mount Longdon in May because he could not afford to be outflanked by a counter-attack or be subjected to enfilading fire. Mount Longdon was defended by 287 men from B Company, 7th Infantry Regiment, marine infantry and army engineers commanded by Major Carlos Carrizo-Salvadores, the 7th Infantry Regimental Operations Officer. The Argentines had been on Mount Longdon since April and had a defence based on a series of bunkers.

45 Commando to attack Two Sisters and exploit to Mount Tumbledown and Mount William. Two Sisters was held by about 200 men from C Company, 4th Infantry Regiment and two sections commanded by Major Ricardo Cordon, the Regimental Operations Officer. In support was B Company, 6th Infantry Regiment.

42 Commando, with the Welsh Guards in reserve, to attack Mount Harriet and be prepared to support 45 Commando on its drive to Mount Tumbledown. The feature was a formidable fortress defended by B Company, 4th Infantry Regiment and sections from the 1st Cavalry Regiment, 3 Infantry Brigade Defence Platoon and a platoon from Combat Team Solari. In command was Lieutenant Colonel Alejandro Soria. On Goat Ridge was a platoon from A Company, the rest of this company being with the reserve.

2 Para, having reverted to 3 Commando Brigade, was in reserve for the attacks on Mount Longdon and Two Sisters. Lieutenant Colonel Vaux was unhappy about the Welsh Guards securing his start line because he did not know them and they did not know the ground. This seems to have been a political decision imposed on Thompson by HQ LFFI and consequently Vaux had no alternative but to agree. He despatched Lieutenant Tony Allen RM to be his liaison officer. To replace the two companies shattered on *Sir Galahad*, the Welsh Guards were joined by A (Captain Sean Cusack) Company and C (Captain Andy Pillar) Company from 40 Commando. Lieutenant Colonel Rickett:

Their companies were very well trained. However I had to make sure that everything was carefully spelt out to avoid any unnecessary mis-understandings; I couldn't afford to take any short cuts in my orders or instructions which I could have done with my own Company Commanders who were totally in my mind.

The Battalion was also joined by 1 Troop, 59 Independent Commando Squadron RE (Lieutenant Robert Hendicott), who were impressed by the welcome – they were rationed, issued signals instructions and generally properly looked after. The arrival of the RFA *Engadine* at San Carlos on 9 June with four helicopters gave much-needed support helicopter reinforcement. When Murrell Bridge collapsed, 1 Troop, 9 Parachute Squadron RE at Fitzroy built an airportable bridge and Staff Sergeant 'Yorkie' Strickland, who had spent two years at the Joint Air Transport Establishment devising methods of delivering loads, convinced the Chinook pilot that it would be alright 'if you take it steady!' Precariously flown to the site, the bridge was gingerly guided into position by commando sappers. (When Major Davies tried the same trick in Scotland a year later, a strap broke, the Chinook nearly crashed and the bridge disappeared into the middle of a wood.)

Brigadier Wilson held his Orders Group at Fitzroy beginning, 'Well, we have suffered some setbacks . . . ' Major Davies:

> Brian Hanrahan and his team filmed the beginning for the BBC. The whole scene was a little unreal. In some ways the mechanics of what was happening were very much like those hundreds of exercises we had all done before. I suppose we were grateful for such mechanics. They do help to suppress the feeling of nausea which might otherwise prevent effective action in the fearful business of war. (Davies, 'A Memoir of 9 Parachute Squadron, Royal Engineers')

When the journalists left, Wilson emphasized that 5 Infantry Brigade must be ready to move through 3 Commando Brigade for Phase Two. By now, key officers in Brigade HQ agreed that 2nd Scots Guards were best prepared to lead the attack. It was unfortunate that the Welsh Guards had lost over half a Battalion and, although now reinforced, were not in a fit state to lead the attack. There was a feeling that 1/7th Gurkha Rifles was the strongest battalion and better placed to break out onto Stanley Common. The plan:

Phase One

> The Scots Guards, reinforced by D Company, 1/7th Gurkha Rifles, to provide right-flank protection for the 42 Commando assault on Mount Harriet.

Phase Two

> 1/7th Gurkha Rifles to patrol aggressively against Tumbledown and Mount William in the hope that the defenders, 5th Marine Infantry

Battalion, would surrender. If the features did not fall, the Scots Guards and the Gurkhas to attack Tumbledown and Mount William in a co-ordinated daylight operation by dawn on the 14th. This would involve a long uphill assault from the predicted direction through a minefield and across ground that had not been reconnoitred.

Phase Three

Once the two features were secure, the Welsh Guards would seize Sapper Hill to support the Gurkhas' breakout onto Stanley Common.

At a planning conference at his headquarters at Bluff Cove, when Lieutenant Colonel Scott asked Lieutenant Peter McManners RE, whose 3 Troop, 9 Parachute Squadron RE was supporting the Scots Guards, how long it would take to breach the minefield, McManners replied, 'All night'. Major Bethell suggested that if there was a delay, both battalions could hit their objectives piecemeal and in daylight. Scott then developed an alternative plan for Phase Two, to attack from Mount Harriet and Goat Ridge. This axis would not be expected by the Argentines and would allow the attack to be mounted from a secure base supported by 42 and 45 Commandos across ground that could be viewed. Brigadier Wilson agreed with Scott's proposals. Scott then terminated Operation Impunity, which was carried out under fire and resulted in several casualties.

Early next day, 10 June, when Brigadier Wilson pushed D Company, 1/7th Gurkha Rifles forward to Mount Challenger to establish a patrol base against Mount William, it was accurately shelled, causing four wounded. Meanwhile, the rest of the Battalion moved into positions ahead of 1st Welsh Guards, which nearly resulted in a clash because of poor radio communications and lack of unit co-ordination.

Meanwhile, the Argentines had drawn up plans to disrupt British operations in Operation Buzon (Mailbox). The idea was for 5th Infantry Regiment to land and seize San Carlos supported by 8th Infantry Regiment approaching from Goose Green. The 4th Airborne Infantry Brigade, 603 Commando Company and 1st Amphibious Commando would then be delivered to San Carlos and advance to the east. Marine Corps Major Raul Cufre, of the Tactical Divers, had devised Plan SZE-21 to install 601 and 602 Commando Companies, the 601 Border Guard Special Forces Squadron and a 1st General San Martin Cavalry Regiment squadron behind British lines to link up with the 4th Airborne Brigade. However, the Argentines did not have air superiority to ensure protection for the parachute drop and British attrition on helicopters undermined Cufre's plan. These plans, and the inability of the RAF to destroy the Stanley Airport runway to prevent Pucaras attacking British positions, led Major General Moore to ask Rear Admiral Woodward to keep aircraft on stand-by to support the attack.

Moore was forced to cancel the attack until the following night, 11/12

June, when it became apparent 5 Infantry Brigade was still not ready. Another reason was logistics, in particular a lack of artillery ammunition. The commanding officers of 4th Field and 29 Commando Regiments both wanted 1,000 rounds per gun, however, adding 700 rounds to the existing 300 shells dumped with each of the thirty light guns would mean four days of flying. Poor weather could extend this into a week. Moore decided that each gun would have 500 rounds. Throughout the 11th, the two brigades prepared for the battle. Early in the day, a Wessex 5 flying from Teal Inlet attacked Stanley Town Hall and the Police Station with an AS-12. Later, four Sea Harriers tossed twelve bombs on to Stanley Airport but still the Pucaras were able to take off. As night fell, 3 Commando Brigade stirred.

3 Para and Mount Longdon

Lieutenant Colonel Pike's plan for 3 Para was restricted by the Argentine occupation of Wireless Ridge, a large minefield to the south protecting the approaches to Stanley from the west and the narrowness of the ridge which was just wide enough for one infantry company. His aim was take advantage of every opportunity and exploit as far east as possible:

A Company to seize the ridge north-east of the western summit ('Wing Forward'). This was defended by 2nd Platoon (First Sergeant Gonzalez).

B Company to clear the northern slopes of a suspected company position, in fact 1st Platoon (Lieutenant Baldini), and capture the two summits 'Fly Half' and 'Full Back'.

C Company in reserve and available to exploit to Wireless Ridge.

On priority call was HMS *Avenger* and 79 (Kirkee) Commando Battery. The sogginess of the terrain meant that gun detachments usually had to dig their guns out after twenty rounds and readjust. Each company had a GPMG support group formed from Wombat Platoon, whose anti-tank weapons were still afloat. D (Support) Company provided two fire bases. The Manpack Group (Major Dennison) consisted of six GPMG(SF) and an LMG manned by Drums Platoon, five Milan posts and eighteen stretcher-bearers from the Army Catering Corps, REME, RAPC, RCT and mess staff doubling up as ammunition porters, each carrying the not inconsiderable weight of 600 rounds of link ammunition, and the primary battalion-manned RAP. The Vehicle Group consisted of five BVs, three requisitioned tractors and trailers and four civilian Land Rovers carrying the Mortar Platoon, one Milan post, the secondary RAMC-manned RAP, 3 Section, 9 Parachute Squadron RE, and a 32nd Guided Weapon Regiment Blowpipe section.

The Battalion left their positions in the general area of Mount Kent as night fell. The Manpack Group sliced through B Company while half of 5 and all

179

of 6 Platoons became separated from the main column for about half an hour. There was then a delay in crossing the airportable bridge over the Murrell River, which was also being used by 45 Commando for its attack on Two Sisters. B Company (Major Mike Argue) approached the start line ('Free Kick') behind time. To ensure that B Company crossed at H-Hour at 8.01 pm, he changed direction to approach Free Kick from the west, as opposed to the north-west.

On Mount Longdon, the platoons had nothing to report, which was unusual after a period of intense activity, and although Major Carrizo-Salvadores ordered extra vigilance, he told Sergeant Nista to switch off the Rasit ground radar, in case it was detected by British electronic warfare. At 8.15 pm 3 Para crossed Free Kick. Covered by the Manpack Group, by 9.15 pm B Company had advanced 500 yards and was in shadow below Baldini's position. 6 Platoon (Lieutenant Jonathan Shaw) angled to the south-east to clear the southern slopes of Fly Half of 3rd Platoon (Lieutenant Neirotti). As the Company climbed, 5 Platoon (Lieutenant Mark Cox) found room to manoeuvre among the crags, however below them 4 Platoon (Lieutenant Ian Bickerdike) was being channelled into rocks. At about 9.30 pm, the silence was shattered when Corporal Ian Milne, a 4 Platoon section commander, stepped on a mine. Surprise lost, the attack went 'noisy' as B Company, supported by 79 (Kirkee) Commando Battery shelling Argentine positions, advanced up the rocky slope.

Below Fly Half, 6 Platoon had encountered stiff resistance from Corporals Geronimo Diaz and Gustavo Pedemonte's infantry sections, and Corporal Domingo Lamas's marine machine-gunners. When Lieutenant Neirotti and his platoon sergeant were both wounded, Captain Lopez took over 3rd Platoon and gave Shaw's men a torrid time, made worse when the paras missed a bunker and had to turn back and deal with it. The deeper the Platoon penetrated the Argentine defences, the more difficult the advance became, even when they moved into open ground. 6 Platoon then strayed into the crossfire of a 0.50 Browning firing on 5 Platoon and stopped. With Full Back about 700 yards to the east, Shaw had lost twelve dead and wounded.

Squeezed into narrow rock runs, 5 Platoon was taunted by Argentines swearing American jargon and rolling grenades down the slopes into a feature that became known as Grenade Alley. The swearing and finding dead and wounded marine infantry dressed in camouflaged fatigues led 3 Para to believe that they were facing mercenaries. In fact, 7th Infantry Regiment recruited from a Buenos Aires suburb where the reservists adopted American phraseology after watching American films. The paras' tactical formation broke up as individuals and small groups slowly battled up the slopes, forcing their way between Baldini's platoon and Lama's marine machine-gunners. 4 Platoon, moving north around Fly Half, drove into Baldini's right flank and seeped into Gonzalez's platoon. A machine gun was silenced by Sergeant Ian McKay, the Platoon Sergeant, with 66mm and small-arms fire. When Carrizo-

Salvadores saw that Baldini's situation was serious and then heard that he had been killed, he launched a counter-attack at about midnight with the 45-strong 1st Platoon, 10th Engineer Company (Lieutenant Quiroga) along the spine of the ridge. Meanwhile Platoon Sergeant Rolando Spizuocco had assembled the remnants of 1st Platoon and withdrew to the company defence line near the Command Post.

As B Company battled toward the high ground, the rocky ridges began to give way to moorland. 600 metres to the east, Full Back was silhouetted against the moon. It was about 11.30 pm. Ahead were well-protected Argentine positions on reverse slopes. Every move by 4 Platoon drew withering, accurate fire from a 0.50 Browning machine gun in a bunker manned by 2nd Platoon. The Argentines taunted the paras, 'Hey! Amigo!' followed by a burst of fire. It had to be silenced. When Lieutenant Bickerdike and his signaller, Private Cullen, were both wounded as they sprinted from a shallow depression to recce the position, Bickerdike shouted, 'Sergeant McKay! It's your Platoon now!' The next natural bound was just 35 metres, but miles under fire. Shouting for covering fire from Corporal Ian Bailey's section, McKay, Bailey and Privates Burt and Jones broke cover straight into a hail of fire that killed Burt and wounded Jones. The three survivors attacked another position and then Bailey was wounded. He described McKay 'going on to the next position but there was no one else with him. The last I saw of him, he was going on running towards the remaining positions in that group.' (Middlebrook, *Operation Corporate*)

A short time later the troublesome 0.50 Browning ceased firing. McKay's lone attack weakened the Argentine defence and he was later awarded a posthumous Victoria Cross for an act of gallantry that turned the battle in favour of 3 Para.

Meanwhile, A Company (Major David Collett) had almost reached the top of the northern slopes to attack Wing Forward, but when the mine exploded, they came under fire from First Sergeant Gonzalez's platoon. At about 1.25 am, with the Company unlikely to make progress, Lieutenant Colonel Pike ordered Collett to move around to the west of Mount Longdon, pass through B Company and seize Full Back. As the Company passed close to where Corporal Milne was still being treated, three soldiers from 2 Platoon helping him into a BV were wounded by another mine.

At Brigade HQ, Brigadier Thompson was concerned that 3 Para had been brought to a virtual standstill and dispatched a guide from D (Patrol) Company to bring up 2 Para as reinforcements. Pike had reported that there was fierce resistance on the feature and it was difficult to pinpoint the exact locations of the enemy among the rocks.

Messages then arrived indicating that the Battalion was on the move again. When Major Argue, who was close behind 5 Platoon, heard that 4 Platoon had lost both its senior commanders, he sent Sergeant Des Fuller to take command. Sergeant Fuller:

I talked to Lt Bickerdike and called all the section commanders together. With covering fire from Cpl McLaughlin's section, 4 and 5 Platoons skirmished forward together. Some enemy positions were still discovered and several men were wounded moving forward. It was clear that some positions had been deserted. As we continued up the slope from position to position, enemy grenades exploded but fortunately not effectively. Cpl McLaughlin passed through us and reached a good forward position near the top of the hill. I passed the rest of 4 Platoon through to his position. Mr Cox then met up with me and I asked him to take over from Cpl McLaughlin at the top, which he did . . . Sergeant-Major Weekes appeared telling us to withdraw the casualties and evacuate this area which was about to be shelled. (3 Para Post Operation Report)

At about 2.00 am, the Manpack Group joined 6 Platoon and the stretcher-bearers evacuated some casualties from the primary RAP established by Colour Sergeant Brian Faulkner in the shelter of Grenade Alley. Within fifteen minutes of the first contact, Captain Burgess, the Regimental Medical Officer, was treating the first casualties. One stretcher-bearer recalled: 'I didn't have enough guys and because there were so many casualties it meant a number of trips. I remember taking one young lad out. I'll never forget him. He was alive when I carried him but he died in my arms. It was his eighteenth birthday.'

During the night the medics dealt with 48 British and 5 Argentines, with 20 evacuated before first light. The lack of natural protection from the shelling made life difficult, and twice, when counter-attacks threatened, Faulkner deployed men fit enough to defend the RAP. The wounded were evacuated to the RAMC-manned RAP a mile west of Murrell Bridge by BVs, which could take two stretchers or seven walking wounded. 3 Para would comment on the inadequacy of the plastic lightweight stretcher, but favourably on the high standard of first aid.

By 1.30 am, Major Carrizo-Salvadores knew that he was losing the battle. He had not heard from Gonzales for some time and the British had seized the western summit. Communications with Lieutenant Colonel Gimenez on Wireless Ridge had been lost, however he relayed messages to him through Army Group, Stanley. When he asked for reinforcements, he heard Gimenez being instructed to send snipers. At about 11.00 pm, First Lieutenant Raul Castaneda burst into his Command Post with his reservist 2nd Platoon, C Company, from Wireless Ridge, all from the same Buenos Aires suburb and most equipped with night-vision goggles. After being briefed by Carrizo-Salvadores and with three soldiers from Command Platoon as guides, Castaneda joined First Sergeant Gonzales defending Wing Forward. His men soon gained a reputation for reckless courage and helped Gonzales buy time for Carrizo-Salvadores to organize an orderly withdrawal to the company defence line on Full Back.

After its battering, Major Argue withdrew B Company into cover and reorganized. Leaving 6 Platoon to deal with Neirotti's platoon, he grouped the beaten-up 4 and 5 Platoons into a composite platoon commanded by Lieutenant Cox and then advanced again against Argentine positions he believed to be weakening. A and C Companies, behind B Company, were under increasingly accurate artillery fire. Lieutenant Colonel Pike then instructed 79 (Kirkee) Commando Battery and HMS *Avenger* to plaster Wing Forward to keep Gonzales quiet while Cox advanced behind a shifting barrage, using a sheep track as his axis. Cox had hardly advanced 40 metres before his Platoon came under heavy fire from Argentines who emerged from bunkers as the shelling shifted. A particularly troublesome sangar was destroyed by Company HQ and then, confident that the nearest Argentine positions had been overwhelmed, Cox again advanced but came under fire from both flanks, leading to three paras being wounded.

With B Company now at less than 50 per cent strength, Pike instructed A Company to take over the lead. Supported by the suppressive firepower of Manpack Group and with orders that no occupied Argentine positions were to be left in their rear, A Company's advance was methodical. Meanwhile 79 (Kirkee) Commando Battery had shifted to shelling the positions held by Corporal Lamas' marine machine-gunners and Sergeant Pedro Lopez's 120mm Mortar Platoon near Full Back. The Battalion would include in their post-operation report the widely held view that the '58 pattern fighting order was difficult to fight in, particularly when picks or shovels were attached. Second Lieutenants John Kearton, of 1 Platoon, and Ian Moore, an Australian, of 2 Platoon, told their men to remove their webbing and stuff ammunition, grenades and dressings into their pockets. Noticing that the arcs of fire of two machine guns which had held up B Company left a narrow safe gap between some rocks, A Company squeezed through the rocks. Major Collett:

> The lesson from B Company's advance was to ensure that positions were taken out systematically leaving none behind. Supporting artillery was maintained and on the whole 1 Platoon was crawling forward, the enemy was seen to be withdrawing. 1 Platoon followed 2 Platoon across the open area and both platoons, 1 on the right and 2 on the north began to clear the enemy trenches with bayonets. Once Full Back was secure, 3 Platoon moved forward to the eastern end of Mount Longdon. (3 Para Post Operation Report)

By 5.00 am, Major Carrizo-Salvadores knew that his B Company had been defeated. Ignoring instructions from Brigadier General Jofre to abandon Mount Longdon, and although he knew that more reinforcements from C Company would not be arriving, he was, nevertheless, confident that his company battle group was in sufficiently good order to counter-attack and could rescue men taken prisoner. Earlier in the battle, he had considered negotiating a truce to recover his wounded. However, as the pace of the 3

Para advance quickened, the supporting barrage was stopped and although the Argentines rigorously defended Full Back, A Company seized it at about 6.30 am. Almost the final act of the Argentines was the wounded Corporal Manuel Medina, of Castaneda's platoon, firing a recoilless rifle along the ridge, killing three of the Manpack Group. Carrizo-Salvadores abandoned his command post when a Milan missile smashed into nearby rocks, and, finally convinced by Jofre to help in the defence of Stanley, called for machine-gun and mortar fire from Sergeant Lucero's machine-gunners and Major Jaimet's infantry on Tumbledown. When he led his battered company into Stanley, they mustered seventy-eight men, many of them sappers, from the 287 with which he had begun the battle.

As 3 Para prepared to face counter-attacks from Wireless Ridge, daybreak brought a damp, heavy mist. 2 Troop, 9 Parachute Squadron RE checked the Argentine positions for booby traps and made safe several Cobra missiles. Sergeant McKay was found in the marine machine-gun bunker which had given B Company such a difficult time.

Mount Longdon had fallen after ten hours of severe fighting which cost 3 Para eighteen killed and forty-eight wounded, most of them in B Company. Captain Giles Orpen-Smellie, the Battalion Intelligence Officer, had been wounded in the right arm during the fighting:

A medic, Sergeant Sibley of D Company, patched me up at the time and put my arm in a traditional white sling. I felt more stupid than injured. Some time later, after daybreak, I led a group of Argentine PWs and their escort down to the PW collection point where the Assistant Intelligence Officer, Sergeant Pearson, took charge of them. This was close to the RAP so I went across to get someone to look at my arm. I quickly realised that the Medical Officer and his team were far too busy to deal with a malingerer like me so I turned around and went back up the mountain. Before doing so, I got rid of the sling and tucked the arm inside my smock, which was a much more practical arrangement in the circumstances. Later, I was casevaced back to the Main Dressing Station at Teal Inlet and from there back to the *Uganda*.

Eleven years after the war, claims by Corporal Carrizo that he was shot after surrendering were rejected when a photograph taken by a *Daily Express* photographer showed paras treating him. A former Parachute Regiment officer claimed that he had witnessed a British soldier shoot a wounded Argentine and others that the ears of killed Argentines had been collected by a British soldier. Interestingly, none of these allegations were aired immediately after the Argentine surrender, indeed several 7th Infantry Regiment interviewed by Daniel Kon, for his book on 10 Infantry Brigade, *Los Chicos de la Guerra*, commented upon their humane treatment after capture. A Scotland Yard investigation proved inconclusive and the Argentine authorities distanced themselves from Carrizo's allegations.

45 Commando and Two Sisters

Lieutenant Colonel Whitehead's plan for 45 Commando was a silent, two-phase, right straight jab and left hook attack on Two Sisters, which was defended by the C Company, 4th Infantry Regiment (Major Ricardo Cordon) combat team. Whitehead was restricted by being in the centre of the Brigade attack, however his patrols had found a route from Mount Kent. The three-phase plan was for:

X Company to seize the western peak ('Long Toenail') from the west and form a firebase for Phase Two.

Y and Z Company to approach from Murrell Bridge ('Pub Garden') and attack the eastern peak ('Summer Days') from the north-west.

The entire Commando then to regroup and assault Mount Tumbledown.

In direct support were 8 Commando Battery and HMS *Glamorgan*. Replacing the Milan firings posts destroyed in the air raid on 27 May was Milan Troop, 40 Commando which joined X Company. 45 Commando's Milan Troop was converted to a heavy weapons troop. During the morning, Y and Z Companies and Tac HQ moved from Mount Kent to an assembly area east of Murrell Bridge and then, setting off at about 5.00 pm, began the 7-kilometre march to the start line south-east of Murrell Bridge which was reached at 9.00 pm, having been secured by 2 Troop, 9 Parachute Squadron, which was supporting 3 Para.

At 5.00 pm, X Company (Captain Ian Gardiner) set off along the 6-kilometre track east from south of Mount Kent, however Milan Troop, carrying the firing posts and forty missiles, each weighing thirty pounds, found the going difficult. Gardiner had estimated that it would take three hours to reach his start line, but it was not until 10.30 pm that his men reached the forming-up place. Feeling there was no alternative but to inform Whitehead, he broke radio silence and admitted that he was late. Whitehead calmy replied, 'Carry on as planned. I will do nothing until I hear from you.' Greatly relieved, Gardiner told his troop commanders, 'Put the last six hours behind you, make your final preparations in your own time and, when you are completely ready, let me know and we will go.' Ten minutes later they were ready.

At 11.15 pm, X Company splashed across the chilly Murrell River. To the north, Mount Longdon was under attack and the Argentines were shelling Murrell Bridge. Reaching the base of Long Toenail, 3 Troop took over the advance and then at 12.30 am, after advancing about 600 metres, came under heavy machine-gun fire from the 3rd Platoon (Second Lieutenant Llambias-Pravaz). Llambias-Pravaz had graduated in April and commanded a platoon of Guarini Indians weakened by casualties and sickness. Supported by Corporal Mario Pacheco's 10th Engineer Company section, the Argentines taunted the

Royal Marines with war cries. With 8 Commando Battery on another fire mission and the Mortar Troop 81mm baseplates sinking into the turf every few rounds, Milan Troop fired missiles at Llambias-Pravaz's men, and then 2 Troop (Lieutenant Chris Caroe) advanced against stiff opposition from Lieutenant Martella's Support Platoon in the rocks. Clinging to a foothold using fighting-in-built-up-area techniques, the Troop was forced off by a defensive fire mission, however they regained another foothold, forced the Argentines to abandon positions and dealt with the machine-gunners covering the retreating Argentines. When it became obvious that the fighting around Long Toenail was more than a patrol, Major Cordon alerted his command.

Needing to take advantage of the darkness, at 12.16 am, Whitehead did not wait for X Company to seize Long Toenail and instructed Y (Major Davis) and Z (Captain Michael Cole) Companies to advance on Summer Days, clear in the moonlight. Shortly after Z Company had crossed its start line, an Argentine defensive fire mission pounded the ground they were about to cross. 400 metres short of the summit, Corporal David Hunt, a section commander in 8 Troop (Lieutenant Clive Dytor), reported that he could see people moving on the ridge. Dytor joined him:

> I didn't believe him but borrowed one of his riflemen's night sights, and yes, I could see them. I saw one man talking to another head – it turned out later that it was the head of one of their Browning 0.5-inch machine-gunners. From my section on the left, I could hear men saying they could see them as well. The first thing to do was to stop the marines firing. I could hear them saying 'I can see him. I can see him. Let's kill him.' (Middlebrook, *Operation Corporate*)

The Argentines were from Second Lieutenant Perez-Grandi's 2nd Platoon. In a whispered discussion on the radio, Dytor told Cole what he had seen:

> There was a bit of an argument then. The company commander must have reported to the CO and then I head an order for me 'From Nine. Move forward.' Nine was the CO. I said 'No' because I knew they would see us as soon as we stood up and we would lose a lot of blokes. The conversation went on for some time. I wasn't speaking directly to the CO; we were not on the same net. (Middlebrook, *Operation Corporate*)

When a flare fired by an Argentine fizzled along the ground, Perez-Grandi's men were startled to see the Royal Marines and a firefight developed, with most of the Argentine fire cracking overhead. Most Royal Marines later admitted that the Argentine cover was good and their own fire ineffective. Marine Steve Oyitch in 9 Troop:

> The firefight went on for about an hour. We were laughing and joking about it; we were in dead ground and their fire was passing over our

heads the whole time. I was behind a rock and I kept pushing my rifle around it and getting a few rounds off. I could see their trenches and positions through my night sight; they had them as well, much better then ours, but their cover was good and I don't think our fire was much good either. (Middlebrook, *Operation Corporate*)

However, the stalemate stopped when the 3rd Artillery Group and 6th Infantry Regiment Mortar Platoon began to shell the western fringes of Summer Days. Oyitch:

Their artillery was getting close and 7 Troop, the left hand point Troop, started taking casualties. You couldn't hear them coming but you could see the red glow of the fuze coming through the darkness – and that's when I started to get frightened. Our section was in a circle – about ten yards wide – and one mortar bomb landed right in the middle. It lifted me right up and threw me straight on my back. The man in front was wounded in the arm and chest and Corporal Burdett was badly wounded in the foot. That's when Gordon Macpherson was killed; he was just lifted and thrown into rocks and must have died instantly. That just about put an end to my section's usefulness in the battle. Wounded from other Troops were brought back to us and we, in effect, became the casualty post. (Middlebrook, *Operation Corporate*)

Three Royal Marines and a Condor Troop sapper were killed. In Y Company, the death of Marine 'Blue' Nowak is remembered by the small blue square on the Company flag. In spite of the discomfort of the shelling, Whitehead ordered both companies to stay where they were and organized artillery fire on Long Toenail. When Corporal Edward Holt's Forward Observation Officer was wounded, Holt took over his duties. His Military Medal citation reads:

When his officer was wounded, Holt took over completely the leadership of his team, continuing to produce artillery fire with coolness and skill, while he and the company he was supporting was being subjected to intense and accurate enemy machine gun fire. His outstanding leadership continued in subsequent operations right up to the cessation of hostilities. Bombardier Holt has shown qualities of leadership and courage under fire and professional skill far beyond those expected of his rank and experience. (*London Gazette*)

3rd Artillery Group was still shelling the western edge of Summer Days, however when mortar rounds fell behind Z Company, Lieutenant Dytor realized that staying still was achieving nothing and withdrawal was now out of the question. He remembered an incident during the Second World War when the Black Watch were pinned down in fighting in North Africa

187

and the Adjutant stood up, waved his stick and said, 'Is this the Black Watch?' Although he was then killed, it stimulated the Battalion into action. Dytor:

> I remember thinking about that and then, before I knew it, I suppose, I was up and running forward in the gap between my forward sections. I shouted, 'Forward everybody!' I talked to my blokes afterwards; they were amazed. One of them told me that he had shouted out to me 'Get your fucking head down, you stupid bastard.' I ran on, firing my rifle from the hip and I heard, behind me, my Troop getting up and coming forward, also firing. The voice I remember most clearly was that of Corporal Hunt. I think that what happened was that Corporal Hunt was the first man to follow me, his section followed him, the other sections followed and the Troop Sergeant came up the rear, kicking everybody's arse. So, 4, 5 and 6 Sections came up abreast, pepper potting properly. I could hear the section commanders calling 'Section up, section down!' It worked fantastically; it was all done by the section commanders and the Troop Sergeant at the rear shouting to everybody on the move and the hare-brained Troop Commander out at the front. That assault up that hill was the greatest thrill of my life. Even today, I think of it was a divine miracle that we went up, 400 metres, I think it was, and never had a bad casualty. Only one man was hurt in the Troop, with grenade splinters from a grenade thrown by a man in his own section. When we had been waiting on the start line, I prayed that the Lord would give me strength and courage to lead my men and do what you will and He did just that. (Middlebrook, *Operation Corporate*)

Charging up the hill, shouting 'Zulu! Zulu!' Z Company ran into stiff resistance, 7 Troop from Perez-Grandi's platoon and 8 Troop from Second Lieutenant Mosquera's 1st Platoon. Lieutenant Colonel Whitehead then arrived and ordered Dytor to seize the southern slopes of Summer Days. 8 Troop advanced with a captured .50 Browning, although few Royal Marines knew how to use it, and cleared the positions held by Mosquera's battered platoon, but were then pulled up by B Company, 6th Infantry Regiment pasting the crest. It was about 2.40 am.

The options of Y Company, which had lost two troop officers wounded by shelling, had been limited by Z Company until Whitehead ordered Davis to move south until Y Company was alongside Z Company. As Y Company fought across the saddle between the two peaks of Two Sisters, they came under heavy fire from Cordon's command post and from B Company, 6th Infantry Regiment, one of whose reservists, 0.50 machine-gunner Private Oscar Poltronieri was overrun several times but each time made his way back to his platoon. In order to avoid a 'blue on blue' in the darkness, Whitehead instructed Dytor to stop and Y Company to seize Summer Days. Wary of a suspected wire-controlled mine, 4 Troop captured the summit at 4.18 am. To the south, X Company had overrun Long Toenail. Major Cordon was captured in his command post. Second Lieutenant Aldo Franco, with his 3rd Platoon B Company 6th Infantry Regiment, commanded the rearguard and fell back to an alternative position on the eastern slopes, known as Cambio. Only Second Lieutenant Llambias-Pravaz's platoon escaped from Two Sisters, and joined M Company, 5th Marine Infantry Battalion on Sapper Hill.

When X Company reached Summer Days, Major Davis sent Corporal Harry Siddall and Bombardier Holt 400 metres to the eastern slopes to deal with a suspected mortar position. The citation for Siddall's Military Medal reads:

> Because of difficult terrain and lack of routes, Corporal Siddall left his section to his rear in a firm base. From his forward position, he heard enemy approaching. When the four-man patrol closed, he opened fire, killing one man and capturing the remaining three, one of whom was wounded. Corporal Siddall's sustained qualities of leadership and determination showed a complete indifference to adverse conditions and his personal safety. (*London Gazette*)

At about 4.30 am, HMS *Glamorgan* and HMS *Yarmouth* had left the gun line, leaving HMS *Avenger* to support 3 Para and were 17 miles offshore, taking a short cut across the shore-based Exocet box, when a radar operator picked up a signature similar to a 155mm shell. When HMS *Avenger*, 10 miles to the north, then reported the signature to be a land-based Exocet, HMS *Glamorgan* opened fire, however the Exocet skipped on to her Flight Deck and skidded into the hangar. Burning fuel from her Wessex flooded into the Galley and a fireball thundered into the gas turbine room. Nine men were killed and fourteen others injured, mostly chefs and helicopter maintenance crews.

The Battle for Two Sisters ended two and a half hours after 45 Commando crossed their start line and was essentially won by Dytor's charge, for which he was awarded the Military Cross. The Royal Marines were astonished at the ease with which Two Sisters had been captured. As the Commanding Officer remarked when daylight exposed the near invincibility of Two Sisters, 'If we had a Company up here, we would have died of old age before it was captured.' Three Royal Marines were killed and one Royal Engineer. Corporal Hunt, incorrectly identified as serving with 42 Commando in the *London Gazette*, was awarded the Military Medal. It was he who Dytor had identified as being wounded by the grenade splinter. Ten Argentines were killed, fifty wounded and fifty-four taken prisoner.

Mount Harriet

During the afternoon, 1st Welsh Guards advanced from Bluff Cove into a position south of Mount Harriet to protect the right flank of 42 Commando. However, communications broke down, even with the intervention of Brigade HQ, and Lieutenant Colonel Vaux was irritated when their Recce Platoon moved east across the moorland toward the forming-up place, in full view of Mount Harriet and drew Argentine artillery fire. Vaux wanted the Argentines to concentrate on watching Mount Challenger. His plan to capture Mount Harriet is widely regarded as an example of a classic night attack:

J Company to create a diversion on Mount Wall and keep 4th Infantry Regiment focused on the west.

1st Welsh Guards Recce Platoon to secure the start line.

K and L Company to make a wide march south across the Stanley–Fitzroy track and right hook Mount Harriet from the south.

K Company to seize the eastern summit.

L Company to then take the western summit, Zoya, and exploit to Goat Ridge ready to support 45 Commando's attack on Mount Tumbledown.

On call was 7 (Kirkee) Commando Battery and HMS *Yarmouth*, and in support was 2 Troop, 59 Commando Squadron RE (Captain Hicks).

At 4.15 pm, as the light faded, K Company left Mount Challenger for the 8-mile approach. Guided through the minefield by 11 Troop, it crossed the Stanley–Fitzroy track and formed up north of the road near a lake. The Milan gunners, which included a detachment from the Welsh Guards, found the going difficult. Two were deployed to cover Argentine exploitation from the east, in particular with their Panhard AML-90s. During the night, an ineffective Argentine counter-attack was driven off by the Welsh Guards Recce Platoon. At about 5.30 pm, L Company moved off and had a moment's anxiety when there was a negligent discharge. As planned, the gunners shelled Mount Harriet. At about 6.30 pm, the composite 35-strong Porter Troop, from Headquarters Company, left with the GPMG (SF) tripods and sights and 10,000 rounds of ammunition ready for immediate use once Mount Harriet had been captured.

Meanwhile, the 1st Welsh Guards Recce Platoon had secured the start line. Lieutenant Symes:

The Start Line was secured at about 22.30. I personally sent the code-word 'Wild Crags' . . . though I insisted on speaking to an officer . . . 42 Commando was due to start its assault at midnight. At 10pm, there was no sign of the Commando – it transpires they were waiting to hear from us, but, of course, communications had broken down.

Assuming that something had gone wrong, Lieutenant Symes drew his Platoon away from the apex of the fence marking the start line in order to withdraw from the area in darkness. It was while this was happening that 11 Troop arrived and when the Welsh Guards could not be found, Lieutenant Beadon gained permission for his Troop to secure the start line. No sooner had the Royal Marines began to do so when the Welsh Guards were seen and they then completed the task.

At 10.00 pm, just as HMS *Yarmouth* started bombarding Mount Harriet and K Company crossed the start line, Captain Wheen radioed that L Company had strayed off route and, although wary of minefields, was confident of reaching the forming-up place on time. On Mount Wall, the 9 Troop diversion drew machine-gun fire from Mount Harriet, Mortar Troop illuminated Zoya and Milan Troop then loosed off several Milans at the Argentine position.

K Company covered about 700 metres in about thirty minutes and, undetected in the shadows of Mount Harriet, they began to infiltrate into the 4th Infantry Regiment Command Company's position, at the eastern end of Mount Harriet. When a Mortar Platoon sentry, Corporal Mario Cortez, heard rustling in the frozen grass, he thought it was a Special Forces Group patrol until he realized his error and opened fire. Finding it difficult to pinpoint enemy positions, the Royal Marines adopted fighting-in-built-up-area tactics and stormed Argentine trenches and bunkers, however it took nearly forty-five minutes of stiff fighting before the lower eastern positions were overrun. Corporal Laurence Watts, a section commander, was killed when he attacked a tented position. 1 Troop overran the Mortar Platoon, denying Lieutenant Colonel Soria valuable support and 2 Troop dealt with the 12th Infantry Regiment Combat Team Solari platoon on the eastern slopes. Confused by the sheer momentum of the attack, the inexperienced conscripts wavered until rallied by First Lieutenant Jorge Echeverria, Soria's Intelligence officer, until he was badly wounded. Dealing with prisoners was already becoming a problem.

As K Company bit deeper into the Argentine positions, 1 and 3 Troops began to intermingle. 3 Troop then reported stiffening resistance from a machine-gun position, which was manned by a 1st Cavalry Regiment platoon, about 80 metres to their front, south-east of the summit. Corporals Mick Eccles and 'Sharkey' Ward, both in 3 Troop, were having 'a fag and a rethink' when Corporal Steve Newland, who had heard their Troop was pinned down, joined them and then went off to see what he could do:

I crawled around this boulder . . . and looked around the corner of the rock, thinking that there had to be a sniper somewhere. There was more than a sniper; it was a half-troop. About ten of them lying on a nice, flat rock, table-top rock overlooking our positions. They had a machine-gun on the left and the rest of them were lined out with rifles. Every time one of ours tried to move forward, one of them would shoot at him, so it looked as if there was only a sniper. I sat back behind this rock and whispered down my throat mike to Sharkey about what I'd found. I told him to keep the lads and I'd see what I could do . . . I picked up my SLR, changed the magazine and put a fresh one on and slipped the safety catch. I then looped the pin of one grenade onto one finger of my left hand and did the same with the other. I pulled one grenade straight into the machine gun. Pulled the other. I dodged around the back of the rock and heard two bangs. As soon as they had gone off, I went in and anything that moved got three rounds . . . I went back around the corner of the rock, changed the mag and was about to go back when Sharkey called on the net 'Get out! We are going to put two 66s in!' I ran down the hill and dived into this little hollow . . . I heard Sharkie on the radio 'It's clear. They've given up . . . make sure they don't get out the back' . . . I went up by a different route and as I rounded the rock, I saw one of the guys I had hit. I'd only got him in the shoulder but he'd gone down like the rest . . . I automatically thought he was dead. But he was far from that, because as I came back around the corner, he just squeezed off a burst from his automatic. He must have realized he was going to die unless he got me first. I felt the bullets go into both my legs . . . I was so angry I fired 15 rounds into his head.

The three corporals were awarded Military Medals. 3rd Artillery Group was accurately shelling Mount Harriet using Lieutenant Colonel Soria's command post, which had been set on fire by a phosphorous grenade, as its target indicator. K Company pressed on, captured the Argentine RAP post and reached Zoya.

Vaux released L Company at 11.00 pm. Within 150 metres of crossing the start line, they ran into a deluge of fire from the HQ 3rd Infantry Brigade Defence Platoon (Second Lieutenant Oliva) defending the central southern slopes:

About this time, Lieutenant Whitely was injured when L Company came under heavy fire from enemy located on K Company's objective. L Company retaliated with GPMG fire, which caused a heated radio broadcast from K Company. As they began their attack an hour after K Company, the element of surprise was lost and they came under heavy fire within 200 metres of crossing their Start Line, taking three casualties almost immediately. Captain Wheen called for Milan fire at the machine gun position. They cleared six machine gun positions, which involved an advance over 600 metres, and as each position could only be taken by a Troop or a section at a time, it took L Company five hours to reach their objective. The Company had to skirmish forward over rocky and sometimes open terrain, which required surgical precision fire missions to cover the advance. The Argentine defence was far more resolute than K Company had experienced as these were the main positions, and far better protected. L Company had eleven casualties in some of the most ferocious fighting before reaching the western end of Harriet. (Vaux, *March to the South Atlantic*)

The Milan fired by Lance Sergeant Bennett proved vital for the Royal Marine momentum. Shortly before his command post was overrun, Soria joined First Lieutenant Arroyo on the western summit to organize a counter-attack, however when he saw that his Regiment was cut off from Stanley, and concluding that it was folly to commit inexperienced conscripts, he ordered his men to make their way to Tumbledown. Only 2nd Platoon, A Company (Second Lieutenant Silva) on Goat Ridge and 3rd Platoon (Jimenez-Corvalan) on the northern slopes of Mount Harriet avoided capture. Soria was captured soon afterwards. 10 Troop guided Lieutenant-Colonel Vaux and Tac HQ to Mount Harriet using the southern cleared route, where Vaux modified his plan and instructed L Company to seize Goat Ridge. Coming under fire from Silva's platoon withdrawing to Tumbledown, a fire mission resolved the resistance.

The formidable fortress of Mount Harriet had been captured and over 300 Argentines surrendered at a cost of two Royal Marines killed and twenty-eight wounded. The Argentines had lost five 4th Infantry Regiment conscripts, together with one man from 1st Cavalry Regiment, three from HQ 3rd Brigade Defence Platoon, and one sapper; about fifty-three men were wounded.

3 Commando Brigade had seized the Outer Defence Zone. At 4.30 am, with only two hours of darkness remaining, Lieutenant Colonel Whitehead radioed Brigadier Thompson that 45 Commando was ready to exploit to Mount Tumbledown, but much to his frustration, he was ordered to remain where he was. The guns were low on ammunition, 8 Commando Battery had fired 1,500 rounds during the night and, critically, Mount Longdon and Mount Harriet had yet to be captured. With their equipment still at Teal Inlet, Whitehead permitted his men to scavenge the Argentine positions. Sleeping bags and boots were prized, as were the Argentine ration packs with their cigarettes and, usually, a tot of Scotch whisky. Condor Troop checked the Argentine positions for booby traps. At 7.50 am, Lieutenant Colonel Pike reported that there was an opportunity for 3 Para to advance to Wireless Ridge, but Brigadier Thompson vetoed this, knowing that it would be enfiladed from Mount Tumbledown.

As the morning mist cleared, Argentine artillery shelled the lost peaks, killing four men of 3 Para and wounding seven others, including Corporal Denzil Connick, who lost both legs. He was instrumental in forming the South Atlantic Medal Association (1982), which is open to those awarded the campaign medal, to immediate next-of-kin and to Falkland Islanders; its motto 'From The Sea, Freedom' epitomized the British aim of the campaign. 42 Commando had seven Royal Marines wounded, including Marine Steve Chubb, who had been captured at South Georgia.

Even though the night had again proven that the Argentines were prepared to fight, Brigadier General Jofre was appalled by the loss of the Outer Defence Zone and severely criticized Major Cordon for losing Two Sisters. To bolster wavering units, he threatened to shell any unit considering withdrawal. Brigadier General Menendez signalled the Joint Operations Centre: 'We need immediate support from the mainland to bombard defined targets. The National Reserve must do all that is possible to prevent the fall of Stanley.'

Later in the day, a fifty-strong 2nd Airborne Infantry Regiment platoon flew in and joined 7th Infantry Regiment on Wireless Ridge. 603 Commando Company and the Amphibious Commando Grouping remained on short notice to move to the Falklands. Of concern to the Argentine gunners was that by the end of 12 June, most of their 155mm ammunition had been used up. At about midday, the Argentine artillery came under intense counter-battery fire. First Lieutenant Jorge Cerezo, who commanded C Battery, 4th Airborne Artillery Group near Moody Brook had five 105mm M56 pack howitzers in a circle to provide 360 degree fire support. Each gun had sixty rounds and at the battery ammunition point 500 metres away was a further 2000 rounds. The British bombardment of the Argentine front line was continuous and caused numerous casualties which demoralised the troops. The attrition rate was so severe Lieutenant Colonel Balza, who was commanding the Argentine artillery, ordered the Forward Observation Officers to be relieved every two days. Every time he was given a fire mission, the British shelled the gun positions, however their inaccuracy sometimes permitted the Argentines to return fire. When the situation became untenable, everyone took cover in shelters until the bombardment ceased. Cerezo reckoned that the patron saint of gunners, Saint Barbara, protected his Battery and prevented major losses. An enemy shell destroyed a B Battery shelter but no one was hurt, just shaken up. On another occasion a detachment had loaded a gun and was forced to take cover when they saw it fire after a direct hit. Two soldiers in the command post were killed by naval gunfire and a B Battery gunner was mortally wounded by counter-battery fire. When the guns sank in the muddy waterlogged gun pits and recoil problems began to develop, Balza ordered them to be removed to firmer and drier ground.

Chapter Fourteen

The Battles of Mount Tumbledown and Wireless Ridge
12 to 14 June

The morning of 12 June dawned bright but cold. 3 Commando Brigade had destroyed 4th Infantry Regiment and severely damaged 7th Infantry Regiment. Army Group, Stanley was surrounded and had three choices – fight, swim or surrender. Even though the odds were stacked against him, Brigadier General Menendez chose to fight.

5th Marine Infantry Battalion (Lieutenant Colonel Robacio) knew that it would be attacked next. Robacio reinforced O Company with 1st Amphibious Engineer Platoon and instructed his Operations Officer, Major Antonio Pernias, to move them to block Pony Pass through which the road to Stanley passed. This left N Company defending Mount Tumbledown and Mount William.

High on Tumbledown was the composite 4th Platoon (Second Lieutenant Vasquez). He was joined in the morning by Lieutenant Silva's 4th Infantry and Lieutenant Mosterin's 12th Infantry Regiment's platoons, which had retired from Mount Harriet, bringing the defenders to ninety-two men. Vasquez had too few radios, which meant orders would have to be relayed by runner and therefore he was determined to keep his men near to him. On his right was the 5th Amphibious Engineer Platoon (Second Lieutenant Mino) and in depth on the northern slopes, overlooking Mount Longdon and Wireless Ridge, was 3rd Platoon (First Sergeant Lucero).

On the saddle to Mount William was 2nd Platoon (Second Lieutenant Oruezabala) and on Mount William was 1st Platoon (Second Lieutenant Bianchi), reinforced by Second Lieutenant Jimenez-Corvalan's platoon withdrawn from Two Sisters. On Sapper Hill was M Company and Second Lieutenant Llambias-Pravaz's 4th Infantry Platoon. B Company, 6th Infantry Regiment (Major Jaimet) was replaced in its blocking position covering the Estancia track by two troops of 181st Armoured Reconnaissance Squadron. A Company, 3rd Infantry Regiment (Major Berazay) was near Moody Brook with orders to support Tumbledown and Wireless Ridge. Its 120mm Mortar Platoon was on Sapper Hill.

Major General Moore met with his brigade commanders during the morning at HQ 3 Commando Brigade to review Phase Two. Wilson was under intense pressure to follow through – quickly. Phase One had produced hundreds of prisoners, however intelligence on Argentine intentions was unclear because the prisoner selection for interrogation at Fitzroy was slow. A surveillance drone would have provided answers but the Task Force lacked a locating battery. At about 4.00 pm, Brigadier Wilson issued orders for Phase Two. The 2nd Scots Guards and 1/7th Gurkha Rifles were to be flown to an assembly area on Goat Ridge, attack Tumbledown and Mount William that night and be in a position to support the Gurkhas break out on to Stanley Common. H-Hour was set at midnight but first a large minefield had to be breached. Wilson was not certain that this could be done in the twelve hours of darkness. The 1st Welsh Guards were assigned as Brigade reserve. Lieutenant Colonels Morgan and Scott were worried that their battalions were to be flown to assembly areas in the dark and then advance across ground about which very little was known. Without well-recognized navigation features, a clearly identifiable axis of advance was going to be difficult. No time was to be allowed for recces and rehearsals, so necessary to the preparation of an advance to contact. H-Hour was set at 8.00 pm. According to one officer at that O Group, Lieutenant Colonel Morgan asked, 'Brigadier, are you sure there is time available?' Lieutenant Colonel Scott was also not happy:

> I was horrified. We would be helicoptered into assembly areas in the dark (a potential shambles) – we would not have known even which way we were facing, no recce, no rehearsal, no shake out, no direction finding, no axis of advance. Furthermore, I knew the gun ammo had not been brought forward – confirmed by Tony Holt. The helicopters had been used to resupply 3rd Commando Brigade and had not brought up our ammo. So we would have had minimal arty support. I asked for the delay. Wilson agreed but knew he was going to get a hard time from Moore and Thompson, so credit goes to him. This then left me with a proper time for the recce.

Major Chris Davies recalls: 'It would have been madness to expect the Scots Guards and Gurkhas to go virtually from line of march into a complex night attack over completely new ground.' (Davies, 'A Memoir of 9 Parachute Squadron, Royal Engineers')

Lieutenant Colonel Holt then mentioned that since the helicopters had spent most of the day supporting 3 Commando Brigade, the artillery did not yet have enough ammunition to support Phase Two. Wilson agreed to ask for a delay in the knowledge that he would be criticized, particularly as Mount

Longdon, Two Sisters and Mount Harriet were being shelled, which was causing casualties. This irritation was further incensed the following day when HQ 3 Commando Brigade was bombed, forcing a 'crash' move just as it was preparing to attack Wireless Ridge. The Welsh Guards were also being shelled and Lance Corporal Nicholas Thomas (07) was killed when he was ferrying equipment to and from Bluff Cove on the quad-bike donated by the Prince of Wales.

That evening, when Major General Moore told Brigadier Thompson that 5 Infantry Brigade had been given a 24-hour delay, Thompson offered two Mountain and Arctic Warfare patrols to guide the two battalions to their start lines, which was accepted. At Bluff Cove, Lieutenant Colonel Scott issued orders for the four-phase night assault on Mount Tumbledown. Precious little intelligence had arrived from the prisoners being processed at Fitzroy, so he still did not really know what he was up against:

Headquarters Company to create a diversion on the expected axis of attack from the south-west.

G Company to capture the first third of Tumbledown.

Left Flank to move through G Company and assault the summit.

Right Flank to move through Left Flank and seize the remainder of the objective.

The general axis of advance was the northern end of the saddle between Tumbledown and Mount William. Since the ridge was barely wide enough for a platoon to spread out, fire support was critical:

F (Support) Company, with six 81mm mortars and the six .50-inch Browning machine guns, and twelve 81mm mortars, six each from 42 Commando and 1/7th Gurkha Rifles.

29 (Corunna) Field Battery.

HMS *Yarmouth* and HMS *Active*.

Helmets were discarded in favour of berets as an aide to recognition. The pass-words 'Hey, Jimmy' for the Scots Guards and 'Hey, Johnny' for the Gurkhas was adopted because the Argentines could not pronounce the letter J in English.

The morning of 13 June dawned bright but with a very heavy hint of snow. During the morning, in the first laser attack of the campaign, Wing Commander Squire, flying from HMS *Hermes* and guided by a Tactical Forward Air Controller, lobbed two laser-guided bombs onto a suspected Argentine headquarters on Tumbledown, the first failing to detonate and the second dramatically destroying it. These attacks were guided from Two Sisters by Majors Mike Howes, of the Royal Regiment of Wales, and Anwyl

Hughes, of the Royal Welch Fusiliers, who commanded 601 and 602 Tactical Air Control Parties respectively.

In a flying plan starting at 8.00 am and managed by the Mobile Air Operations Team, Sea Kings and the Chinook lifted the 1,300 troops to their assembly areas south of Goat Ridge throughout the day without the knowledge of the Argentines. Sangars were built and battle preparations were interrupted by speculative shelling, wounding Lance Sergeant Billy McGeorge of the Scots Guards. Corporal Campbell and Guardsman Greenshield had their webbing discarded while they were digging in, and had it set alight when shrapnel detonated a phosphorous grenade. As patrolling was out of the question, Lieutenant Colonel Scott flew key officers to observe Tumbledown from Goat Ridge and Mount Harriet. With H-Hour set for 9.00 pm, Scott issued his confirmatory orders at 2.00 pm. Recce Platoon guides and controllers from the forming-up point to the start line were to be in place by 7.00 pm. Brigadier Wilson moved his Tac HQ to Goat Ridge. During the afternoon, snow-laden clouds rushed across the valleys as 29 (Corunna) Field Battery shelled Tumbledown and Mount William. Major Jaimet:

> It was an inferno. The British artillery fire increased in intensity. It went up and down the mountain. The whole mountain quaked and shuddered under the impacts. The rounds arrived like flying kerosene tins filled with hot metal fragments. By pure luck, none hit me, but I saw them hit some soldiers next to me and they just burned through the thickest clothing, winter parka, denim jacket, wool pullover, everything, right through to the flesh. I heard the cries of the wounded. When somebody got wounded he would call out for his mates. The shelling claimed twelve men wounded by the time it was dark . . . Everyone kept themselves under control and there were no scenes of despair or terror as often happens in some conscript armies. In Bravo Company there were 168 people and everyone behaved sensibly.

Mount Tumbledown

Soon after 4.00 pm, Major Bethell briefed the diversionary party at Mount Harriet House. The Assault Group consisted of three four-man sections from Recce Platoon, commanded by Bethell, Drill Sergeant Danny Wight and Sergeant Colin Coull respectively. The Light Machine-Gun (LMG) Group was commanded by Company Sergeant Major Les Braby, from A1 Echelon. Corporal John Foran and Lance Corporal 'Pash' Pashley from 3 Troop, 9 Parachute Squadron, provided sapper support, as did a Mortar Fire Controller, Lance Sergeant Ian Miller. Providing fire support was 3 Troop, B Squadron, the Blues and Royals (Lieutenant Mark Coreth). An hour later, the men clambered onto the Scorpions and Scimitars near the 42 Commando Rear Echelon at Mount Harriet House. A nasty wind froze the dark moorland. The ground was pitted with peat banks and littered with mines, two types of which had been identified as being powerful enough to wreck light armoured vehicles. At about 6.30 pm the Platoon dismounted and the Blues and Royals found positions to give fire support. When reports reached Major Rico at HQ Army Group, Malvinas that armour had been heard, he sent 3rd Assault Section, 602 Commando Company to Pony Pass.

With the two sappers clearing the route, Major Bethell periodically swept the ground with his cumbersome rifle-mounted night sight, as the diversion slowly advanced. By about 8.45 pm, after three false alerts, Bethell knew he had to launch a noisy attack – in fifteen minutes, G Company were due to cross their start line. When trenches and a sentry were seen about 70 metres ahead, the LMG Group moved right into a fire support position while the Assault Group advanced. When sounds and shuffling were heard from a trench, with Drill Sergeant Wight on his left and Sergeant Coull on his right, Bethell attacked; the tranquillity of the night was shattered by exploding grenades. Argentine positions in depth opened fire and the 6ft 3ins Wight was killed by the occupants of a trench that he was attacking. Lance Corporal Pashley was fatally wounded and four other guardsmen wounded. The Argentine amphibious engineers in the trenches were not best pleased to find themselves in a crossfire. The LMG Group had a difficult time neutralizing Argentine fire during nearly two hours of stiff fighting as the Assault Group fought through eleven positions, often by crawling underneath the lip of peat banks and lobbing grenades over the top. Bethell halted when there was no more return fire, and with two killed and four wounded, decided to withdraw. When Lance Sergeant Miller lost communications with Battalion HQ, Bethell radioed for Coreth to come forward and then returned to the first trenches where three pipers were dealing with the casualties. Marine First Class Private Jose Luis Fazio was at Pony Pass:

At about 2230 hours our battalion had its first intensive gun battle with British companies which appeared out of nowhere. I heard Private Roberto Barboza yell 'The English are here!' . . . I remember our Operations Officer requested the artillery to assist at 23.00 with starshells. The close quarter battle was such that the Argentine artillery was unable to drop shells on to the British attackers. I was shooting, doing my work. I don't know if I killed anyone. We just fired our rifles, that's all. Contact was maintained for over an hour before battalion headquarters ordered Obra Company to fall back . . . What we did not realise at the time was that at least a wounded Marine made his way to the amphibious engineer platoon position and hurled a grenade wounding a Major. Simultaneously the Major opened fire, killing him.

With two more wounded – Piper Duffy in the chest and Bethell in the legs – as the party withdrew, the four men carrying the dead and wounded were themselves wounded by mines. The explosions prompted Major Pernias to order the 81mm marine Mortar Platoon on Mount William and infantry

120mm mortars with M Company on Sapper Hill to open fire on the mine-field. The barrage lasted about forty minutes and more casualties would have been taken had the peat not absorbed the impacts. Leaving the two dead, Major Bethell, Corporal Foran and Piper Duffy had some intense discussions on what was a mine and what was not, nevertheless they carved a path out of the minefield. Fortunately, most were either surface-laid or could be seen underneath the turf when approached from the Argentine side.

For a long time, Coreth heard little from Bethell:

> Come 20.30, I decided the time had come. I could barely hear on the radio, but the gist was they were plainly in trouble. I decided to move . . . As we reached the forward positions, a flare outlined my vehicles . . . then we were under heavy direct fire. About 300 metres on and still 1,000 metres short of my planned fire position, the road was blocked by a huge, quite impassible crater . . . so I thought it was probably a lucky shot from a 155mm . . . I decided the only option was a risk and to creep the wagon around the crater. We had barely moved off the road, when we hit the anti tank mine. Corporal of Horse Stretton, who was behind me, saw us lifted three to four feet in the air. At this stage it was vital to provide fire support for the infantry. Sadly I could only have one vehicle firing at a time . . . It became a crazy shoot from one vehicle, sitting on the outside, reverse him, climb onto another, bring him forward, fire and so on till the last. There was some excellent shooting by all vehicles. (*The Guards Magazine*)

Next day, sappers removed fifty-seven mines from the vicinity of the shattered Scorpion.

At about 12.30 am, just as Left Flank had their first contact on Mount Tumbledown, Bethell's battered diversionary party reached Coreth's troop and returned to Mount Harriet House where the 42 Commando Medical Officer, Surgeon Lieutenant Ross Adley had established the RAP in a container. Bishop and Witherow:

> They sat in silence while the doctors stripped away the blood-soaked boots and cleaned the worst of the shrapnel from the wounds. Because of the fear of attracting the attention of an Argentinian artillery observer and bringing down shells, they had to operate by torchlight. The light caught one of the feet. It looked like a joint of butcher's meat . . . One of them asked for a cigarette. 'You've got a heart of gold, mate,' he said. 'You should have been a social worker.' (Bishop and Witherow, *The Winter War*)

Within ninety minutes, the wounded were on their way to Ajax Bay with most transferred to the *Uganda*. Expensive in terms of casualties, the diversion focused the attention of 5th Marine Infantry Battalion on the track from

Darwin and allowed G Company to get a foothold on Tumbledown. Surprisingly, there were few awards. Corporal Foran received the Military Medal; however Major Bethell was only Mentioned in Dispatches, which reflected the idiosyncrasies of the awards and honours system. He at least deserved the Military Cross.

Guided by the occasional shell fired by 29 (Corunna) Field Battery to help navigation, at 9.00 pm, G Company (Major Ian Dalzell-Job) crossed the start line, a wire fence, his objective being two machine-gun bunkers 2,500 yards ahead across open ground. To the south, the diversion was underway. Snow showers were swept across the bleak mountain by a strong wind. At about 10.30 pm, G Company went firm undetected and spread out to cover the advance of Left Flank (Major Kiszely). Both objectives had been abandoned. Phase Two was complete.

13 Platoon (Second Lieutenant James Stuart) moved into rocks on the left to support 15 Platoon (Lieutenant Alastair Mitchell) advancing across the open ground below them, in a shallow right hook. 14 Platoon (Lieutenant Anthony Fraser) was in reserve. Stuart had been commissioned less than two months. On the main feature about 300 yards ahead, Mino's engineers, Vasquez's marines and the 4th Infantry Regiment conscripts gazed through their night sights, and then at about 10.45 pm, a ripple of white flashes split the darkness ahead of the advancing guardsmen. As flares soared into the snowy darkness, bullets cracked overhead and rock splinters whined into the night. 15 Platoon and Company HQ dived for cover. Guardsman Archibald Stirling was killed and Sergeant Jackson wounded. Lieutenant Mitchell recalled: 'When I gave my orders for Tumbledown, I said to my three section commanders and platoon sergeant, "In the end this is going to disintegrate into utter chaos. It is going to be a case of little groups of guardsmen having the courage to keep going forward."' (Bilton and Kominsky, *Speaking Out*)

A counter-attack led by Lance Sergeant Alan Dalgleish was defeated by heavy machine-gun fire, however he managed to shoot an Argentine, who screamed in agony. Major Kiszely shouted, 'Who did that?' No answer. 'Who did that?' Eventually, when Dalgleish replied that it had been him, Kiszely congratulated him. In amongst the rocks, 13 Platoon was suffering badly and Company Sergeant Major Bill Nicol went forward to supervise casualty evacuation. While dragging the seriously wounded Guardsman Ronald Tambini into cover, he asked Tambini to push with his feet, but the Guardsman respectfully said, 'I've been shot, sir,' and died. Nicol also found the mortally wounded Platoon Sergeant John Simeon and when he knelt beside him, his rifle across his body in the approved weapon-training fashion, a bullet ricocheted off the barrel and passed through his hand. The same rifleman may have shot all three. Second Lieutenant Vasquez:

The British soldiers crept up on the platoon position just before midnight. Before long the platoon was completely surrounded and on the verge of being overrun so I decided that the 81 millimetre mortar platoon of Ruben Galluisi should fire on our platoon. At that moment Argentine mortar bombs landed in the middle of the position, we had no other choice. The British had to withdraw and we started swearing at them. That was how the British were driven out during that first attack. I had up to then lost five of my own men.

Guardsman Shaw had a lucky escape when three rifle magazines that he had stuffed in the left breast pocket of his jacket stopped a bullet. Nicol had his revenge when he was handed a Carl Gustav by Lance Sergeant McGuinness and fired three projectiles at three sangars. The shock of the firestorm brought Left Flank to a halt. Lieutenant Mitchell:

> There were many occasions where we would be sitting behind a rock and forty metres away, just out of grenade range, an Argentine would be sitting behind a rock. One of us would poke a head round the rock and take a potshot at him and he would take a shot at us, and so it went on. They didn't sit in their holes and wait to be shot at, they came out and tried to have a go at us from the flanks. They had a great weight of firepower because their FAL rifles could go on automatic. It began to dawn on us after a few hours, when we simply couldn't move, that things were tough. We did get extremely close to them and we were pinned down. (Bilton and Kominsky, *Speaking Out*)

For the next three freezing hours, Left Flank was pinned down. Angry clouds rushing across the full moon spun eerie shadows and snow across the battlefield. The cold slowed down the body metabolism and helped the wounded to survive. A defensive fire mission from 29 (Corunna) and 97 (Lawson's Company) Field Batteries landed in front of 15 Platoon, however both sides were often a few yards apart and communications were poor. Some shells clipped rocks. The Battery Commander, Major Gwyn, was quietly compelling on the radio as he controlled the artillery. Listening to the fighting on Mount Harriet was Lieutenant Colonel Vaux: 'One impression that will never fade was the timeless Oxford English dialogue on the Scots Guards net. This was quite different from the crisp, varied tones of "Four Two" or the parachute battalions with us. But Guards officers also spoke far more than their radio operators, and always in measured, courteous terms' (Vaux, *March to the South Atlantic*).

At Main HQ near Fitzroy, Major Brendan Lambe heard Brigadier Wilson frequently 'chivvying' Lieutenant Colonel Scott not to lose the momentum, until the Scots Guards eventually switched off the rear link radio. Scott asked Lieutenant Colonel Chaundler if 2 Para, then attacking Wireless Ridge, could fire on Tumbledown, however Chaundler had his own problems, in particular the SAS raid on Cortley Ridge. Scott refused reinforcements from a 1/7th

Gurkha Rifles company because the frontage along Tumbledown was just about adequate for a platoon. Captain Spicer, the Battalion Operations Officer:

> Major Roger Gwyn, the Battery Commander, was keen to avoid him [Scott] being killed like 'H' Jones. The Commanding Officer asked my opinion and I advised him not to go up to be seen. He would only be pinned down too. I also told him that we still had confidence in the Company Commander's ability to do the job, and that we should let him get on with it. (McManners, *Scars of War*)

The combination of the noise and survival as men scuttled from one position to another led to command and control over the radio breaking down. Attempts to dislodge the Argentines with 84mm Carl Gustav and 66mm anti-tank missiles and M79 grenade launchers were only partially successful. On Mount Harriet, the Machine Gun Platoon was firing at extreme range. Major Davies and Squadron Sergeant Major Walker, were watching the battle with a Royal Marines sentry when they saw a line of soldiers approaching them. Davies shouted 'Halt!' There was a scuffle of boots on rocks and then in a Scottish accent, 'Don't shoot!' The group turned out to be a party seeking ammunition. Mortar Platoon fought to keep the 81mm mortars on a stable platform on the soft ground but every time a bomb was fired, the recoil drove the base plate deeper into the soft ground and degraded accuracy and distance. Digging the mortar from the mud, moving to firmer ground and re-adjusting fire all took precious minutes. Several parts broke while firing on maximum charge. For a time, only one mortar was operational.

Although a few Argentines taunted the guardsmen, Second Lieutenant Vasquez kept his 4th Platoon and the Army platoons as a single cohesive body. Morale was high. At about 3.00 am, O Company moved back from Pony Pass to the saddle linking Tumbledown and Mount William. The Scots Guards were now facing three companies, the Marine N and O Companies and B Company, 6th Infantry Regiment. G Company had several men wounded by artillery and mortar fire. 8 Platoon joined the Company Quartermaster Sergeant taking the wounded from the Company Aid Post for the 2,500-yard carry to the RAP on Goat Ridge. By 3.00 am, 13 Platoon had inched forward and overran the 5th Amphibious Engineer Platoon, their resolve in tatters. When Brigadier General Jofre heard that they had abandoned their positions, he radioed Robacio and Lieutenant Colonel Gimenez, then engaged with 2 Para on Wireless Ridge, and warned, 'Anyone seen to transmit an unauthorized order to fall back should have their head blown off.' By dislodging the engineers, Stuart outflanked Vasquez and weakened the defence of Tumbledown. Meanwhile, Lieutenant Colonel Scott and Major Kiszely had planned to destroy the Argentine resistance with an advance preceded by three salvoes. Mitchell:

At this stage the situation had changed slightly. The platoon on my left had managed to get into the rocks and were able to fire down into the Argentine trenches from above. We were then able to move round to the flank. Thirteen or fourteen of us lined out. I was worried that we were going to run into our own shells. I also thought: This is possibly the end of me and my platoon. But, frankly, after four or five hours of being shot at and shooting people, I couldn't give a damn any more. I wanted to go in there and get it sorted. (Bilton and Kominsky, *Speaking Out*)

Stuart and Company Sergeant Major Nicol organized 13 Platoon into a fire support group and Company HQ joined 15 Platoon. As Lieutenant Nicol brought down the third salvo, 13 Platoon opened fire, which was the signal for Left Flank to advance. 97 (Lawson's Company) Field Battery:

The Battery was directly supporting the Scots Guards as they advanced up Tumbledown Mt. However, as they pushed on they came up against machine gun posts. When the artillery finally neutralised him, the only emotion the Command Post experienced was one of relief. It took a dangerously close co-ordinated illumination over a frontage of 340 metres to finally destroy the enemy positions. ('4 Field Regiment in the Falkland Islands')

Lieutenant Mitchell: 'Sure enough the three salvoes came in and on the last one, there was almost a deathly hush in the battle. There was a plaintive cry from me of "Is that really the last one?" to John Kiszely and his radio operator said "Yes".' (Bilton and Kominsky, *Speaking Out*)

But no one moved. Displaying the same qualities of inspirational leadership as Lieutenant Dytor, Major Kiszely shouted, 'Are you with me, Jock?' Silence. Then replies began to filter in from the darkness 'Aye, sir. I'm wi' ye!' Still not certain whether his men would follow, Kiszely told them he was going whether they were with him or not. Breaking cover, the Guards advanced up the hill, bayonets fixed, systematically destroying Argentine positions. Mitchell:

We ran straight into the middle of the Argentine position, which was only 60 to 70 yards away. Once in there, we started skirmishing through. People dropped grenades, shooting at close range. Some enemy were bayoneted. In the middle of the enemy position, we suddenly felt the resistance crash. It was an intangible thing. Suddenly the Argentines who had been shouting to us a few minutes before were now streaming down the hill. (Bilton and Kominsky, *Speaking Out*)

As Major Kiszely charged up the slope, he saw a figure come out of the ground:

I swung around, pointed my rifle and pulled the trigger. I heard a click. What you are meant to do is count your rounds but, of course, it doesn't work like that. So there was only one thing to do and, without hesitation, you did it. I struck him in the chest and he fell back into his hole. Looking back on it, it is not something I am proud of at all. I knew he was going to kill me but derived no pleasure from sticking a bayonet into another person.

Left Flank bit deep into the Argentine defences. Vasquez:

It was now around three in the morning and we had been trading fire off and on for nearly three hours. The British were now amongst the rocks above us. I found out that if I started to give out orders I would draw machine-gun fire and that was the biggest shock to me. I discovered over the radio that they weren't the amphibious engineer platoon. It is a pity. In the dark the platoon came off the position too soon. Of course it was occupied by the British immediately . . . We then got fire from our own artillerymen, who put down shells all around us. That fire provided a useful breathing space, but it was evident that reinforcements would still be needed to beat the attackers off. In the fight that followed five Army personnel and two Marines died. We were alone now, with nothing around except us and the British. It was about then that Second Lieutenant Oscar Silva of the 4th Regiment was killed after he had carried a wounded Marine machine-gunner to safety through heavy fire. He then returned to the position with one of his soldiers.

4th Platoon conducted an orderly withdrawal and then, at about 4.00 pm, Major Kiszely and seven men reached the summit. Far below were the lights of Stanley, the ultimate objective. But the fighting was far from over. Lance Sergeant Clark Mitchell was shot dead when an Argentine machine-gunner opened fire on the summit, and wounded three others, including Lieutenant Mitchell:

There was a crack behind me and someone had been hit. It all seemed to be in slow motion; in fact it was my brain thinking rather faster. As I turned to run for the nearest cover myself, I suddenly felt something like enormous hammer blows to my legs. The tracer from the rounds was like scarlet rods round me. My rifle had been hit and disappeared. I found myself crawling into the nearest dip in the ground. I noticed that my legs, and especially my right leg, were very stiff already. I put my right hand down to touch my leg and two of my fingers went in up to the knuckle. (Bilton and Kominsky, *Speaking Out*)

For fifteen minutes, Kiszely and three fit men held the summit of Tumbledown until several more 15 Platoon and Company Headquarters arrived followed by 14 Platoon, which was almost at full strength. 15 Platoon had lost five killed and twelve wounded.

Lieutenant Colonel Robacio ordered Major Jaimet to reinforce Vasquez, who had taken up positions about 250 yards from the summit. Leaving his Mortar Platoon with the marines, Jaimet moved on to the saddle between Tumbledown and Mount William and, at about 4.30 am, instructed 1st Platoon (Second Lieutenant Augusto La Madrid) to reinforce Vasquez. Jaimet was aware that the summit had been captured. Had the radios and night sights of Jaimet's platoons been fully charged, and mortar and machine-gun ammunition not been wasted supporting Wireless Ridge, all B Company could have counter-attacked and time could have been gained to allow M Company to be moved from Mount William on to Mount Tumbledown for a Battalion counter-attack. This missed opportunity probably cost the Argentines the battle.

Expecting Lieutenant Mino's 5th Amphibious Engineer Platoon to join him, Second Lieutenant La Madrid issued quick orders with his customary enthusiasm – advance, allow no one to pass and conscript any withdrawing Argentines to join the Platoon. Several of his men had helmet-mounted, night-vision devices and although all were willing, none of them had seen the ground over which they were about to advance. La Madrid:

> We moved off through a gap in the rocks; I spread my men out behind the men who were still fighting. My orders were not to let anyone pass, not even Argentine soldiers. I went forward to make a reconnaissance and could see that the British had two machine guns and a missile launcher in action. I went through another gap in the rocks and was surprised by three men speaking in English behind and above me and firing over the top of me. I could see them with my night binoculars; there were about twelve of them in all. I was anxious to get back to my platoon. I took a rifle grenade and fired at where I had seen the first three men. I heard it explode and some shouts and cries of pain, and the sound of someone falling down the rocks. (Middlebrook, *The Fight for the 'Malvinas'*)

It seems likely that 1st Platoon had clashed with 14 Platoon and inflicted four casualties. So far, the battle for Tumbledown had lasted seven hours of hard fighting. At about 6.00 am, Right Flank (Major Simon Price) arrived on the summit after being in reserve behind G Company. Lance Sergeant McDermid:

> It snowed most of the night but there was no opportunity for a brew in case the Company was ordered to move. Not really aware of the fighting because the wind was in the wrong direction and Left Flank was about a mile away. Everyone was asking 'What the hell is going on up there? What are we waiting for?' I was scared but did not regard this as shameful. However, I was wearing the three chevrons of a Lance

Sergeant and must now live up to them. At 04.30, the order came, 'Move now' and Right Flank set off, passing through G Company. It was then that the Company met stretcher-bearers bringing casualties down the ridge.

Major Kiszely briefed Major Price that an enemy group, including a machine gun, was about 250 yards down the slope and efforts to dislodge them had failed. With daylight due in about an hour, time was short. Price planned a right hook with 2 Platoon (Second Lieutenant Mathewson) advancing along the southern ridge, while 3 Platoon (Lieutenant Robert Lawrence) moved along the left flank. 1 Platoon (Second Lieutenant The Viscount Dalrymple) was to provide fire support from Left Flank's position. Lance Sergeant Tom McGuiness:

> Right from the word Go when we joined the QEII, we thought in our hearts that we would get down there and there would be no fighting; they would throw their rifles down. We were too confident; I think 50% of us felt like that. There was no real sense of fear but it was a shock when they fired at us. (Middlebrook, *Operation Corporate*)

Price's Forward Observation Officer, Captain Miller, then said that he would be unable to register on the target because he had just been told that 1/7th Gurkha Rifles were advancing to Mount William below the northern slopes of Tumbledown. This was, in fact, incorrect, nevertheless without artillery and mortar fire to soften up the enemy, Price was reliant upon Carl Gustavs and 66mm for close fire support. In the saddle between the centre and eastern summits, 2 and 3 Platoons clashed with La Madrid's platoon. La Madrid:

> I ran back to my position and ordered my men to open fire. We stopped them, but they thinned out and came round our flanks; their deployment was good. They also engaged us with light mortars and missile launchers (more likely 66m light anti tank projectiles). This went on for a long time, and we suffered heavy casualties; we had eight dead and ten wounded. We started to run short of ammunition, particularly for the machine-guns. (Middlebrook, *The Fight for the 'Malvinas'*)

Corporal Marco Palomo's section took the brunt of Right Flank's advance and held up 2 Platoon. 3 Platoon, accompanied by the Company Second-in-Command, Captain Ian Bryden, employed simple fire and movement tactics and every time they came to a stubborn position, it was stormed by small groups of men with grenades, rifle and bayonet. Winning a foothold on a ledge abandoned by the Argentines and attacking in two columns, one led by Bryden and the other by Lawrence, Platoon Sergeant Robert Jackson silenced the machine gun that had wounded three Left Flank by discarding his rifle, climbing rocks and throwing a grenade. He and Lance Sergeant Baxter then cleared an Argentine position menacing 2 Platoon. Guardsman Andrew Pengelly, his GPMG slung across his back, scaled rocks to give covering fire but was later wounded. Jackson and Pengelly were both awarded the Military Medal. Corporal Graham Rennie was in 3 Platoon:

> Our assault was initiated by a Guardsman killing a sniper, which was followed by a volley of 66mm anti tank rounds. We ran forward in extended line, machine gunners and riflemen firing from the hip to keep the enemy heads down enabling us to cover the open ground in the shortest possible time. Halfway across the open ground, 2 Platoon went to ground to give covering fire support enabling us to gain a foothold on the enemy position. From then on we fought from crag to crag, rock to rock, taking out pockets of enemy and lone riflemen, all of whom resisted fiercely.

When 3 Platoon seeped around the Argentines' right flank and threatened to cut La Madrid off from Major Jaimet, covered by Palomo's section, La Madrid fell back, but the Scots Guards advanced quickly and the fighting became close quarter. Private Montoya is said to have wrestled with a Guardsman but there is nothing in Scots Guards accounts about this. La Madrid:

> I could see that we were outflanked, with the British behind us, so we were cut off from my company. Some of my men had been taken prisoner. I reorganized and found that I was down to sixteen men. I started to retire. The British above me were firing machine-guns, but we passed close to the rocks, actually under the machine-gun fire. I left six men in a line with one machine-gun to cover our retreat, but really we were fighting all the time; we could not break contact. They came on us fast, and we fell back; it was starting to get light. The whole hill had fallen by then, and we were on lower ground, just south of Moody Brook. We eventually got through to Stanley, through what I would like to say was a perfect barrage fired by the Royal Artillery. We had to wait for breaks in the firing, but I still lost a man killed there. (Middlebrook, *The Fight for the 'Malvinas'*)

The casualty was Sergeant Eusabio Aguilar, a popular drill instructor. The Argentine defence slowly crumbled. Private Jorge Sanchez, in Vasquez's 4 Platoon:

> The fighting was sporadic but at times fierce as we tried to maintain our position. By this time we had ten or twelve dead including one officer. I hadn't fired directly at a British soldier, as they had been too hard to get a clear shot at. I can remember lying there with all this firing going

208

over my head. They were everywhere. The platoon commander then called Private Ramon Rotela manning the 60 millimetre mortar and Rotela fired it straight up into the air so that they landed on ourselves. At this point I had been up and in actual combat for over six hours. It was snowing and we were tired. Some of the guys had surrendered, but I didn't want to do this. I had only twenty rounds left and I decided to continue the fight from Mount William. I popped up, fired a rifle grenade in the direction of eight to ten British soldiers to keep their heads down, then ran for 2nd Platoon. I can remember saying some type of prayer hoping the British wouldn't shoot me in the back.

2 Platoon had a tough time clearing out Argentine positions and progress was slow until Sergeant Robertson appeared with men from 1 Platoon. A quartermaster's supply dump on the eastern tip of Mount Tumbledown was overrun and then 2 Platoon linked up with Captain Bryden's group from 3 Platoon. As Lieutenant Lawrence was about to join them, he was one of four wounded. Lance Sergeant McDermid recalled that Corporal Rennie shot someone at short range and he and Corporal Richardson covered Rennie dragging Lawrence into cover where the company medic, Pipe Sergeant Jackie Oates, treated his horrendous head wound and worked hard to keep him alive. Right Flank had some trouble reorganizing because platoons and sections had become hopelessly muddled, casualties needed to be gathered, ammunition redistributed and positions taken up for the expected counter-attack, all under effective machine-gun and mortar fire from Sapper Hill. Vasquez:

As dawn approached, I spoke to 'Habana' – that was the battalion commander's call sign – to get reinforcements. Robacio said that no reserves were available, and that fighting was also taking place all around the headquarters of the battalion. At 07.15 sharp, I remember I looked out and three British soldiers were up there, pointing their weapons at me. That finished my platoon, but we had lasted more than seven hours of actual fighting, longer than any other Argentine platoon in Malvinas.

As the infantry advanced, Sergeant Strettle and 3 Troop, 9 Parachute Squadron checked enemy positions for booby traps and mines, and helped evacuate the wounded. It was not until daylight that stretcher-bearers arrived on the summit to collect the wounded. Lieutenant Mitchell:

They were very brave carrying us down. One of them was wounded in the arm . . . he plodded on regardless, carrying it with his good arm. We carried on down the hill and suddenly a mortar round landed 200 or 300 metres away. By now it was daylight and I can see no excuse for this whatsoever . . . Within a short time they walked the mortars, adjusting them on to us. Two or three bombs went off near us. Next thing I was lying a short distance from my stretcher. I never heard the blast. I turned around. The stretcher-bearers were in pieces. One of them was completely blown to pieces . . . Guardsman Findlay was relatively uninjured. He had a chunk out of his hand . . . We met a corporal and told him where the casualties were . . . Guardsman Findlay and I got ourselves back about a kilometre with me using his rifle as a crutch and him supporting me. At times we had to slide down because my legs were seizing up. (Bilton and Kominsky, *Speaking Out*)

Guardsman Reynolds was the one wounded in the arm and killed instantly, as was Guardsman Daniel Malcomson. Eight others were wounded. For his gallantry during the night, Reynolds was awarded a posthumous Distinguished Conduct Medal. It was later suggested that the Argentines deliberately attacked stretcher-bearers on Mount Tumbledown, although this is unlikely as their mortars and artillery were entitled to shell lost ground. It should also be mentioned that while Argentine medical personnel were clearly identified with the Red Cross on brassards and helmets, British medics wore no such insignia.

On Goat Ridge, 1/7th Gurkha Rifles had expected to advance to Mount William at midnight. As the night wore on, Lieutenant Colonel Morgan was increasingly anxious because in order to begin Phase Three, he needed to be on the eastern slopes of Tumbledown by dawn at the latest. His orders included entering Stanley and, if necessary, fighting in the town. Even though the Scots Guards were still fighting, Morgan reasoned that if he followed the sheep track running beneath the northern cliffs, he would be in cover. He had been advised by Captain McManners that he risked running into a minefield because the Argentines were 'bound to have planted mines right up to the rock face'. Relieved to be on the move, led by Sergeant Hugh Wrega's section of parachute engineers, the frozen 750 men in the Gurkha battle group filed south of Goat Ridge, crossed to its northern flanks and picked up the sheep track heading east. As Battalion HQ passed the Scots Guards Tac HQ, a request for help was turned down by Morgan because he needed his Battalion at full strength.

As dawn broke with snow and low cloud, 656 Squadron arrived at the Scots Guards RAP on Goat Ridge to fly out the wounded. By then, evacuation from the eastern slopes of Tumbledown necessitated a long stretcher carry under fire and therefore Captain Drennan and his observer, Lance Corporal Rigg, flew forward in a Scout to collect wounded, but it was not without risks. On at least three occasions, a sniper from Second Lieutenant Franco's platoon opened fire at the Scout from rocks above the northern cliff of Tumbledown. Locating him was difficult, particularly as he moved between shots. A captured officer was invited by Captain Campbell-Lamerton, who commanded the Anti-Tank Platoon and spoke Spanish, to persuade the rifleman to desist, but this failed. Eventually, Corporal Gary Tyler, of Left Flank, fired a 66mm round on the Argentine's position, which mortally wounded him by blowing off both legs. At the time, Tyler was helping to evacuate casualties. Drennan and Rigg rescued sixteen wounded, including a Gurkha wounded by the shelling in front of the minefield. On occasions, Rigg stood on the Scout's skids to allow a wounded soldier to take his seat. Drennan was awarded the Distinguished Flying Cross and Rigg was Mentioned in Dispatches.

The cost to the Scots Guards battle group was eight Guardsmen and one Royal Engineer killed, and forty-three wounded with HQ Company losing two killed, including the Royal Engineer, and six wounded. G Company lost ten wounded, principally to shelling, and Left Flank suffered seven killed and twenty-one wounded. Five Right Flank were wounded. One of Lieutenant La Madrid's men christened the Scots Guards 'The panthers in the dark'. Lieutenant Lawrence's recovery was miraculous and became the subject of a television drama. Fifty per cent of the dead and wounded were officers, warrant or non-commissioned officers, which reflected the quality of leadership. At Ajax Bay, Lance Corporal Pashley's identity was muddled with Sergeant Strettle, who was alive and well. When Major Davies eventually identified him he was buried at Ajax Bay in a quiet ceremony officiated by the Scots Guards padre, Major Angus Smith, the day after the Battalion buried their own men, and later his ashes were spread over Hankley Common, a well-known parachute-dropping zone near Aldershot.

The 5th Marine Infantry Battalion had performed well, considering that it was made up almost entirely of conscript soldiers led by inexperienced young officers. Vasquez had shown the same commitment that First Lieutenant Estaban had shown at Port San Carlos and Second Lieutenant Baldini on Mount Longdon. Robacio, who came in for criticism from some British officers for being too sentimental, had total command of N Company and the Army platoons involved, and deserves credit for doing all that was possible to limit British gains. He felt that Brigadier General Menendez had not reacted aggressively enough to the British landings. His positioning of heavy weapons on Sapper Hill before the Argentine surrender provided a defensive barrier that would only have been breached at heavy cost in men and equipment. In the forty-four days since 8 April, 5th Marine Infantry Battalion had suffered sixteen dead and sixty-four wounded. Vasquez's stubborn defence had cost the Argentines seven marines and five army killed, several wounded and others missing. Of the amphibious engineers, only Lieutenant Mino was wounded. Between them, the 4th and 12th Infantry Regiment platoons lost five killed. When La Madrid reorganized, he mustered just sixteen from the forty-five who had started the counter-attack; several had been captured and five killed. Lieutenant Franco's 6th Infantry Regiment platoon lost three killed. About fifty Argentines were wounded, some of whom were recovered by the Marines' Medical Officer, Captain Ferrario and a medical party; most were from Jaimet's infantry company.

Wireless Ridge

Shortly before dark on 12 June, Major Hector Gullen, Thompson's liaison officer, arrived at 2 Para with the instructions, 'It's Wireless Ridge, tonight.' As Lieutenant Colonel Chaundler began planning the operation, he then received a message from Brigade HQ that 5 Infantry Brigade had been given a 24-hour delay before Phase Two. The paras settled down to a second chilly night without sleeping bags, most sleeping fitfully as a sharp frost carpeted the moors.

Chaundler planned an all-arms, four-phase noisy night attack from the north, not the west as expected by the 7th Infantry Regiment, supported by close, direct and indirect fire support from 8 and 79 Commando Batteries, the Blues and Royals and HMS *Ambuscade*:

Phase One.

D Company to seize Rough Diamond.

Phase Two.

A and B Companies to attack Apple Pie.

Phase Three.

C Company to attack Position X, which was also the limit of eastern exploitation.

Phase Four.

D Company to seize Blueberry Pie and advance east toward Cortley Hill.

The ground was boggy, dotted with ponds and small lakes. Chaundler said that the assault would be supported by an SAS diversionary attack on Cortley Hill, although there were some misgivings about what the SAS were meant to do as opposed to what they would do.

During the afternoon of 13 June, Chaundler was given his final orders by Thompson at Brigade HQ shortly after being bombed by the Skyhawks. His communications with Thompson then became difficult and Livingstone's sapper section found itself transmitting messages and relaying reports to Brigade HQ via 59 Independent Commando Squadron RE. As night fell, 2 Para moved to about 600 metres north of Wireless Ridge. Temperatures dived with frequent snow showers shielding a bright full moon. Major Gullen had arrived with very recent intelligence suggesting that a minefield protected the northern approaches to Apple Pie, but Chaundler stuck to his plan.

C (Patrol) Company was securing the start line when they were forced to adjust it after being caught by an airburst. At 9.45 pm, Wireless Ridge was shelled to soften up the defenders and then at 10.00 pm, D Company advanced across very boggy ground, against limited opposition, and seized Rough Diamond from C Company, 7th Infantry Regiment, which folded quickly under heavy fire from Machine Gun Platoon and the Blues and Royals. The accuracy and high rate of the fire from the light tanks greatly boosted morale. The Argentine 155mms then forced the paras to shelter in the abandoned positions for the next two phases by accurately shelling Rough Diamond.

In driving sleet, A and B Companies were held up by A Company, 7th Infantry Regiment on Apple Pie. Private Mike Curtis:

> Mortar illumination rounds were erupting above the enemy positions and explosions ripped through the ridge. The tracer was criss-crossing, with patterns of red light hitting rocks and ricocheting into orbit. Milans were firing from our right, roaring towards the bunkers. The Scimitars and Scorpions were putting down an unbelievable rate of fire, hundreds and hundreds of rounds. Why the fuck couldn't we have had those beasts at Goose Green? (Curtis, CQB)

A Company pivoted and then went firm as B Company assaulted. Curtis:

> Collins shouted, 'Go right! Go right!' Suddenly, the ground disappeared from beneath me and I was up to my neck in water. I had fallen into a pond. The water was so cold that I was in instant shock. My heart seemed to stop beating. Then I came to my senses, swallowing and gagging on the filthy black bog. Flailing around, weighed down with ammunition, for a split second I thought I was going to drown. The cold felt as if I'd walked in front of a train. I couldn't breathe. (Curtis, CQB)

Curtis was unceremoniously hauled from the pond and, soaked to the skin, could hardly operate the trigger of his GPMG. Eventually, he opened fire to cover this section advancing through a minefield – the mines were so frozen that they failed to explode. After Apple Pie was captured, his friends put together a change of clothes for him. Several other members of 2 Para also fell into the ponds.

Meanwhile the Argentines abandoned Position X shortly before Patrol Company captured it at about 10.45 pm. Supported by the remainder of the Battalion and the Blues and Royals on Apple Pie, D Company advanced south toward Blueberry Pie. The CVR(T)s had already found the going rough and two vehicles were hauled out of deep 155mm craters. When Lance Corporal of Horse Dunkeley was knocked out when his cupola latch snapped, Trooper Ford guided the Scimitar to the RAP where he met Captain Roger Field, who leapt at the opportunity to command the vehicle, but not the Troop – that was Lieutenant Innes-Ker's responsibility.

Beginning Phase Four, D Company climbed onto the western crags of Wireless Ridge and, advancing east, met stiffening resistance from the airborne infantry platoon in positions covering Gimenez's command post. The Blues and Royals played a key role in suppressing enemy fire, although Innes-Ker's Scorpion broke a sprocket, which was repaired under heavy shelling. After a short delay because artillery was diverted to support the withdrawal of the Advanced Forces from Cortley Hill, D Company advanced toward Blueberry Hill. 12 Platoon – commanded by Lieutenant Jonathan Page after the death of Lieutenant Barry at Goose Green – became involved in a short and nasty firefight in an action later described by Major Neame as 'an interesting affair'.

Brigadier General Jofre had earlier instructed Major Berazay to assemble his 3rd Infantry Regiment Company, 10th Armoured Recce Squadron and B Company, 25th Infantry Regiment, who were marching from Stanley Airport, at the ruins of Moody Brook for a regimental-sized counter-attack. In support was 4th Airborne Artillery Group. When Berazay arrived at the shattered barracks there was no sign of the infantry, however there were about seventy cavalrymen who had retreated after making a stand on the western slopes of Wireless Ridge. Shattered by the weight of fire unleashed on them, they had lost six killed, had nearly fifty wounded and were in disorder after an ineffectual and unco-ordinated night counter-attack. Jofre told Berazay to wait for B Company, 25th Infantry Regiment but when it failed to appear, Berazay placed machine guns near a small building and launched a counter-attack with his 3rd Infantry Regiment Platoon and the cavalrymen. Private Patricio Perez:

> As we climbed the ridge, we came under heavy fire. The worst thing was the cries of the wounded, shouting for help. You felt a lot of pain but you also wanted to avenge them . . . At one point I took cover behind a rock. I was carrying two rifles and I noticed that there was a sniper who was pinning me down. I wanted to come out of my rock and kill but I couldn't because the firing was so intense. (Bilton and Kominsky, *Speaking Out*)

The fighting raged around a line of telegraph poles until the Argentines withdrew, losing three killed and leaving four wounded.

By about 4.30 am, 7th Infantry Regiment had been decisively defeated. However with the promise of reinforcements, Lieutenant Colonel Gimenez clung on to Wireless Ridge. Near St Mary's Church in Stanley, intent on helping Berazay, Major Carrizo-Salvadores, helped by the Army chaplain

Father Fernandez, assembled a platoon, issued each man with a fresh magazine and, with everyone singing the 'Malvinas March', led them to the centre of Wireless Ridge from Moody Brook. When 2 Para saw them it caused some alarm. D Company was still reorganizing and small arms and artillery ammunition were very short; the orders were passed to 'Fix bayonets'. Chaundler sought a fire mission and gave orders to fire anything and everything at the counter-attack. Carrizo-Salvadores's last-ditch attack won the admiration of the paras. Reluctantly withdrawing, he joined the strong point around the Felton Stream bridge. By 7.00 am, 2 Para had captured Wireless Ridge. The remnants of 7th Infantry Regiment assembled at the Racecourse where Menendez visited them. During its two battles with the British, most of the officers were either killed, wounded or captured. Of the 130 NCOs, twenty-two had been killed.

While 2 Para were preparing to attack Wireless Ridge, HQ LFFI authorized the SAS to raid Cortley Ridge. It had originally been planned that the SAS would attack the land-based Exocet, however when this proved impractical, the raid on Cortley Ridge was authorized. The problem was that 3 Commando Brigade attacking Wireless Ridge were not told. Defending the refinery was 3rd Platoon, H Company, 3rd Marine Infantry Battalion (First Lieutenant Jorge Monge) and B Battery, 101st Anti-Aircraft Regiment with eight 30mm Hispano-Suiza guns and ten .50 Browning machine guns. The unit formed the northern arc of the Stanley garrison air defence system. Largely unaffected by the bombardment of Stanley, it had stood by to reinforce Mount Longdon. During 12 June, 601 and 602 Army Commando Companies took up a blocking position several hundred yards to the west of the fuel tanks.

The original idea was for an SBS patrol to swim across the Murrell River to Wireless Ridge and then attack the refinery. When this scheme became impractical, two troops of D Squadron and one from G Squadron joined for a hurriedly planned raid. The idea was to secure a beach with a recce patrol and then land the assault group supported by machine guns and a 60mm mortar. On 12 June, Sergeant Buckle and his coxswains, Lance Corporal Gilbert and Marines Kavanagh and Nordic, of 1st Raiding Squadron, Royal Marines, were towed from HMS *Fearless* by the minesweeper-trawler HMS *Cordella*. They lay up on Cochon Island in Berkeley Sound and next night they met up with the SAS at Blanco Bay. With nine soldiers from the Boat Troop to each Rigid Raider, the force raced across Port William Bay but was heard by a Border Guard commando on board the *Almirante Irizar*, now lit up as a hospital ship. He was part of a Special Forces Group operation en route to Beagle Ridge to direct air support and 155mm artillery onto the British rear, and was collecting supplies. Not unnaturally, he switched on a searchlight and caught the boats full in the beam. Cortley Ridge was immediately alerted and the Argentines opened fire. 'David' was with fire support group:

As they hit the beach, the whole world opened up on them and us. It was horrific. Far from being lightly defended, there was the minimum of a full battalion. This is a lot of firepower. Our position had obviously been communicated to the defensive force from the observation post above, which we had not known about. Then I heard the crack of high velocity weapons being fired at us from above and behind. So we were getting it from both sides. Just to add to the fun and games, the Argies then turned ground-mounted Roland anti aircraft guns in our positions. I took a patrol to find them but they were well hidden and we could not locate their positions. As a result, the whole Squadron was rendered ineffective. The fire was so accurate, we were all pinned down, and anyone who had shown his head clearly would have had it taken off. This left Boat Troop very exposed. They had to fight their way out and back to the boats. (Bilton and Kominsky, *Speaking Out*)

An SBS NCO and two SAS were wounded. Captain Hugh McManners, on Beagle Ridge, heard a report from the SAS wanting artillery support to cover their withdrawal and spent a frustrating forty minutes attempting to organize naval gunfire support, but without luck. He then asked Captain John Keeling, Adjutant, 29 Commando Regiment, then supporting 2 Para, a request that was greeted with 'Bloody Special Forces; the whole world has to stop for them, I suppose'. Nevertheless, Keeling arranged thirty-six rounds for effect. Offshore, the Royal Marine coxswains worked frantically to keep the temperamental outboard engines running, and then, as shells bracketed Cortley Hill, nudged their boats forward to collect the raiding party. 'David':

The bravery of those guys in the Rigid Raiders was amazing. They risked their lives to get the blokes out. If they hadn't gone in when they did, the Troop would have been wiped out. The ground fire was so intense, the only way they could evade being blown out of the water was by using the Argentinean hospital ship as cover. They went underneath the bow of the ship and the enemy stopped firing. The Rigid Raiders were literally riddled with holes. We had two blokes hit. One had a chest wound which I patched up. The other was hit in the upper part of the leg and testicles. Two Gazelles helicopters came in to casevac them. That was brave flying too. (Bilton and Kominsky, *Speaking Out*)

Three Rigid Raiders beached near Watts Bay and were set on fire. The fourth sank a few metres offshore and the occupants had to swim ashore. The Argentines on Cortley Hill were jubilant. According to John Parker in his book *SBS*, Special Forces admitted that they had broken a cardinal rule by

216

carrying out a 'Boys' Own' comic book raid, because they did not want to miss the fun. Far from diverting Argentine pressure on 2 Para, urgently needed artillery had to be redirected. However, according to Ruiz-Moreno in his book *Commandos in Action,* the raid shattered Argentine plans to insert Special Forces in the British rear areas.

Chapter Fifteen

Phase Three – Mount William and Sapper Hill
14 June

As the battle for Tumbledown was ending, 1/7th Gurkha Rifles were moving along a path below the northern cliffs of Tumbledown with Sergeant Hugh Wrega's 9 Parachute Squadron section leading. About halfway along the track, when he reported a minefield covering the north-western slopes of Tumbledown, Morgan instructed him to find a way around. Fortunately, the Argentines had not laid mines right up to the cliff face and the Battalion edged through a gap. By the time the Gurkhas reached the eastern slopes and formed up to assault Mount William, the Scots Guards were masters of Tumbledown. In the gloomy dawn, Captain Villarraza's Forward Observation Officer on Sapper Hill, Second Lieutenant Marcelo De Marco, radioed 3rd Artillery Group for airburst, which wounded eight Gurkhas. Sergeant Wrega's section then breached a minefield on the saddle through which D Company advanced to Mount William to find it abandoned. Major Kefford prepared a firebase for the advance to Stanley Common. For his night's work, Wrega was awarded the Military Medal.

On Tumbledown, everyone dived for cover when a sniper opened fire, a bullet cracking overhead between Lieutenant Colonel Morgan and his radio operator when Tac HQ were sheltering behind a rock. The Forward Observation Officer, Captain Keith Swinton, then announced to his bombardier that he believed he had been shot. The Bombardier replied, 'So you have, sir.' Swinton was evacuated to the RAP on Goat Ridge where the doctors put him to one side to be treated later. When Swinton protested that he had a serious chest wound, the medics told him he would undoubtedly live since the bullet had entered his chest, passed within an inch of his heart and exited without causing serous damage. The sniper turned out to be a member of the Scots Guard Recce Platoon who, seeing soldiers in the open, assumed them to be Argentines assembling for a counter-attack. When Lieutenant Colonel Morgan reported to Brigade HQ that Mount William was captured, he was told by Brigadier Wilson, 'Stanley is yours.' Morgan was slightly shocked by the order because he was opposed by an infantry brigade, two armoured car squadrons, seven 105mm batteries, one 155mm battery and several anti-aircraft batteries that could be used in the ground role. In his favour, Argentine morale was crumbling. As Morgan was preparing his orders, he was told by Wilson to go no further forward.

By the morning of 14 June, the Argentine forces were penned around Stanley and were under ceaseless bombardment, shelling and Harrier attacks. Fortunately, civilian casualties were low with three women killed when a British artillery shell hit a house. Sapper Hill was the last feature.

After supporting the attack on Mount Harriet, 1st Welsh Guards withdrew to the lake south of the feature under intermittent 155mm fire. On 12 June, Lieutenant Colonel Rickett warned the Battalion for the attack on Sapper Hill, as part of Phase Three. Next day, since Mount Harriet was a better vantage point for spotting, Major Jordan and a fire direction team from 97 Field Battery were flown to a position about 500 metres south of the feature and began the weary climb. However, shortly after setting off, 155mm shells shelled the slopes, forcing the group into cover for the next forty-five minutes. On the summit, it was evident that the registration of targets for the attack on Tumbledown was not yet complete and since the Scots Guards were a higher priority, adjustments for the Welsh Guards were discontinued. Jordan arrived back at Battalion HQ just as Rickett's final orders were confirmed – be ready to exploit the attack on Mount Tumbledown by seizing Sapper Hill. Shortly after dark on 13 June, at about the same time as the Scots Guards started attacking Tumbledown, the Welsh Guards advanced towards a suspected enemy position about 2,000 metres south-west of Mount William. Since Brigade Intelligence believed there were three company positions on its axis of advance, Lieutenant Symes was instructed to send three patrols, one to each position, and report on the strength and disposition of the enemy. Lieutenant Hendicott listened to the 59 Independent Commando Squadron radio net and briefed Ricketts on likely minefields. At 6.45 pm, the Battalion set off in a long single file south of the road to Stanley with Symes's Recce Platoon protecting the right flank. Rickett: 'This was one of the most unpleasant nights that I can remember in my life, being shelled while virtually trapped in a horribly difficult stone run. Eventually we extricated ourselves from this and continued our advance with the Recce Platoon now in contact with Argentine minefields on the edge of Mount William.'

By 10.00 pm, the Battalion had advanced only about a mile from their lay-up position. Lieutenant Hendicott was surprised to find himself posted to the rear of the column with Battalion HQ as opposed to with the Commanding Officer. Hendicott:

We had only moved about three kilometers and it was then that both Staff Sergeant Smith and I commented on the fact that we were close to the area that I had briefed as being a minefield. The land also suggested a possibly mined area – a route between a lake and an area of very boggy ground south of the main road into Port Stanley. There were also some pieces of white tape at intervals on the ground (I later found that this was 2 Troop's safe route marked for them to lead 42 Commando to their start line). No more than five minutes later we heard a small explosion – an anti personnel mine. The column stopped moving and we heard a light helicopter nearby and soon we were shelled accurately. (MacDonald, 'Operation Corporate 59 Independent Commando Squadron RE')

The helicopter was probably a 656 Squadron Scout collecting Tumbledown casualties. Lance Corporal Chris Pretty was a section commander in 9 Troop, C Company, 40 Commando (Lieutenant Carl Bushby) at the front of the column:

We passed around a small hillock and started moving alongside a small re-entrant. In the light of the moon we could see a stationary armoured vehicle across the valley pointing in the same direction as us. Using our infrared sites, it was one of the Scorpions. Going on a bit further and we were heads down with weight of equipment and supplies but keeping alert as we are not far from the Argentine positions. There was then a quiet 'Whump'. And then about three seconds later, this terrible high-pitched screaming. Somewhere down the back of the column there had been an explosion and we thought it might have been a grenade going off in someone's pouches. Word then came down the line that Lance Corporal 'Mac' Macgregor, in 7 Troop, had trod on an anti-personnel mine, which had blown his foot over the heads of those following him to hit one of the blokes in the face. As soon as we heard the word 'mine', we froze literally from the cold and also from not moving. The Troop officer, Lieutenant Paul Allen, then walked back down the column to see how things were going with Mac when he also trod on a mine, which also blew a foot off. Apparently he was pretty calm about it.

The Scorpion was supporting the Scots Guards diversionary attack on Pony Pass. Unwilling to move forward or, indeed into cover, off the track, the troops gingerly gathered in small groups in areas judged to be safe. The Welsh Guards were trapped in a minefield of unknown size and liable to be late for the 5 Infantry Brigade operation. Rickett sent his Adjutant, Captain Julian Sayers, to halt any movement until the minefield had been breached. Hendicott:

By now most men knew what had happened and they were reluctant to move to let me pass. It was with more than trepidation that I edged my way forward, past almost two hundred guardsmen and marines. I have never seen so many men remain so still for so long and it was then that I realized the faith they all had in me and my Troop; we were their main hope of getting out of their predicament – an entire battalion group in a minefield. I finally reached the scene of the casualties and was surprised that I was not at the head of the column and that both casualties had taken place within a couple of metres of one another . . . I was pleased to see that Corporal Smith had already started his section breaching the gap which had developed ahead. (MacDonald, 'Operation Corporate 59 Independent Commando Squadron RE')

A sapper or assault engineer crawls forward and prods the ground with a 6-inch spike. If he strikes something, he carefully clears away the earth to find out what it is. If it is a mine, it is defused and set to one side for eventual disposal. It seems likely that the pressure pad of the mines had frozen but were gradually pushed down as about thirty Royal Marines walked over them and then exploded. Rickett was anxious to advance and decided to press on. When 9 Troop came to the end of the tape, they saw some Royal Engineers sat down and, assuming that the minefield had been breached, the Royal Marines passed them, each man saying 'Cheers, lads', unaware that the sappers were actually taking a rest. Lance Corporal Pretty estimated the Welsh Guards were caught in the minefield for about four hours. A helicopter sent to evacuate the casualties drew artillery and mortar fire. The Battalion found a position about 800 metres to the south of Mount Harriet and watched the fighting on Tumbledown. The halt allowed Hendicott to debrief the sappers who had accompanied the Recce Platoon patrols. It turned out they had all entered the same minefield that had given Major Bethell such trouble. One patrol had captured four Argentines, who had been made to carry the bodies of Drill Sergeant Wight and Lance Corporal Pashley.

Learning that La Madrid's counter-attack on Tumbledown was in trouble, Brigadier General Jofre was infuriated when Mino's amphibious engineers again withdrew without any authority. When he ordered 5th Marine Infantry Battalion to regroup on Sapper Hill, Lieutenant Colonel Robacio and Major Jaimet were furious because they believed they were in a position to counterattack. Six years later, they openly criticized the decision. Robacio:

On the last day of the war, 14 June, at about 6.30am I thought that we were still winning. My unit hadn't suffered any real losses. We hadn't given up any of our positions. All we had lost was a very, very small part of Mount Tumbledown. I knew that we were running out of ammunition, so I asked my headquarters for more. We were concentrating our efforts on Mount Tumbledown because that was the battle that would seal the fate of Port Stanley. Unfortunately we never received the ammunition we needed. At about 7am, I received the order to withdraw prior to surrender. Our military code states that for an

221

Argentine military unit to surrender it must have spent all its ammunition or lost at least two-thirds of its men. It was awful to have to ask
the units that were still fighting to withdraw. It was a very bitter
moment. We really felt defeated. You could see the battle coming to
an end. (Villarno, *Battalion 5*)

Jaimet appointed Second Lieutenant Franco to cover the withdrawal of the
Marine Infantry; he had already covered the Argentine withdrawal from Two
Sisters. Jofre, in an interview with the mass-circulation *Gent* news magazine,
stated:

Sometime during the morning, Robacio came on the air to advise me that
his command post, near Felton Stream, was under direct attack. There
are varying accounts of the report time, but I am sure, it was around 7am.
'We are encircled', Robacio told me in a hurried call. 'All around us are
British forces firing at us; at least 150 troops and more than a dozen
tanks. We are not in a good position.' This came as a shock to me. To
us it was apparent at the time that Special Air Service personnel dressed
in Argentine Army uniforms had mixed in with the 7th Regiment soldiers
and under their cover infiltrated to the rear of the 5th Marine Infantry
Battalion. Now we did have something to worry about.

The British troops and tanks referred to by Robacio were 2 Para and 4 Troop,
the Blues and Royals, who had been released by 3 Commando Brigade to
pursue the Argentines. There is absolutely no truth in the assertion that the
SAS were mingling with Argentine soldiers, nevertheless their psychological
value as 'super soldiers' was helpful. Brigadier General Jofre:

When I got back to Robacio I made it clear that he should regroup on
Sapper Hill. Apart from re-opened communications in the rear and an
abundance of ammunition, there would be a dozen Army radar-guided
anti-aircraft guns and C Company, 3rd Regiment to support him. In
his earlier reports he had reported a shortage of belt-fed ammunition
for the machine guns and pressing requirements for casualty evacuation.
It would be very loathsome to somehow suggest that I was a quitter,
that somehow I misled and that we did something wrong. That is
nonsense. To stay would have necessitated re-organising our deployment in broad daylight. There was no immediate response to this.
Obviously he had more confidence in the situation than I did. I patiently
chewed at my fingernails for as long as I could tolerate it. I then got on
to battalion headquarters for an explanation. I was told that O
Company was planning a counter-attack. From my point of view we
had already lost too much time and I was anxious to get the companies
off Tumbledown and the withdrawal under way while we still had darkness. It was still dark outside. I asked Jaimet if his company could hold

out for another hour as we were planning to pull the 5th Marine Infantry Battalion back and up on and around Sapper Hill. Jaimet agreed. Villarraza waited for artillery to open up to signal that he could get away. At 9.45 Jaimet was ordered to withdraw and although hindered by British fire his company was able to break clear. All 5th Marine Infantry Battalion elements had reached Sapper Hill by 10am.

Jofre, believing that British heliborne troops would assault Sapper Hill, had selected it as a strongpoint for C Company, 3rd Infantry Regiment and M Company, 5th Marine Infantry Battalion. 25th Infantry Regiment was creating another strongpoint on the outskirts of Stanley.

At about 7.30 am, Lieutenant Colonel Rickett learnt the Scots Guards no longer required reinforcement and withdrew to the lake. At about 9.30 am, Rickett received orders from Brigadier Wilson to attack Sapper Hill; a flight of Sea Kings would be with him soon. Not too happy about attacking in broad daylight, Rickett was assured that he would be supported by shelling, bombing by Harriers and by 3 Troop, the Blues and Royals. Within fifteen minutes the Welsh Guards were ready to move and when the helicopters arrived, Rickett briefed the pilots to drop the Battalion on the track south of Tumbledown and about 3 miles from Sapper Hill. Recce Platoon had reported that there were mines but not on the track itself. After a very short flight, the Welsh Guards were landed on the track, however it turned out to be an extension of 'Bethell's' minefield. Two helicopters carrying 9 Troop missed the rendezvous and approached Sapper Hill. The Argentines watched with incredulity. 'I was so mad; I wanted to shoot both helicopters out of the sky,' recalled Second Lieutenant Llambias-Pravaz. Lance Corporal Pretty remembers that it was broad daylight and his helicopter hurtled along almost at ground level. He thought the duration of the flight over the expected distance was a little long and then the nose of the Sea King lifted sharply for a battle landing. The Royal Marines braced themselves for a heavy landing and rapid debussing. Pretty:

No problem, we would be out and start our work in the normal fashion under the watchful eye of the Gurkhas. Before we had the chance to land properly, the whole of the left side of the helicopter came blasting in with bits and pieces flying everywhere. The nose was deafening. The helicopter thudded on to the deck and the guys started spilling out immediately, trying to find cover and identify where they were. We had landed on a small light coloured track in the middle of nowhere and the helicopters were still being shot up. Someone suggested it was the Gurkhas on Mount William. The helicopters then revved up and banked over to the south, leaving 9 Troop under heavy fire. Someone said that the road might be mined on both sides but it seemed better to be in the middle of a minefield than in the open without any cover. The Argentines were only a short distance away on a small hill. With the

17-year old Marine Vince Coombes giving covering fire by spraying the hill with his machine gun from the hip, I stood in the middle of the road and pushed guys off the road into cover afforded by a tiny bank about 8-feet high.

The firefight rolled backwards and forwards. Lieutenant Bushby radioed for help, but he was using a trailing antenna, as opposed to a whip aerial, and was unsuccessful. Marine Coombes was badly wounded in the arm and a second man, who was not wearing a helmet, suffered a head wound; when another thought that he had been hit in the backside, it turned that his rear pouches had been shot off. An Argentine attack on the Royal Marines right flank was driven back. Lieutenant Bushby then gingerly raised the trailing wire, fully expecting his arm to be shot off, and learnt from Captain Pillar that the Argentines were surrendering. The firing gradually slowed down and the Argentines simply evacuated Sapper Hill, as the Royal Marines very slowly got to their feet. The whole action had taken no more than ten minutes and was the last of the war. Rickett was anxious to link up with C Company:

Just as we crossed our Start Line, my Battery Commander held his radio to my ear as Tony Holt, the Gunner CO, wanted to speak urgently to me. Suffice to say that we were out of communications with 5 Brigade but the Gunners always seem to get through! I was told that white flags were up in Stanley, that we were only to fire if we were fired upon first and that the Brigade Commander wished me to hasten with all speed for Sapper Hill. By this time we could hear firing from the area of the forward troop, which had been dropped too far forward. Captain Pillar duly reported that they were under fire from the Argentine positions on Sapper Hill. He appeared rather reluctant to move his company forward. He wasn't totally in the picture on my last radio transmission with 5 Brigade, so together we all moved at best possible speed down the track, firstly to link up with his Troop and secondly, to get to Sapper Hill fast. I had already summoned the Blues and Royals Troop but it seemed to take an awful long time to catch up with us! Undaunted we linked up with 9 Troop, where one Royal Marine had been shot. We hurried past them and, at last, the Blues and Royals arrived. Jumping on the lead vehicle with my command group and telling Andy's company to follow on at best speed, we occupied Sapper Hill from the rear i.e. from the Stanley side and occupied it. There was no resistance as Argentine soldiers had been withdrawn to Stanley leaving their dead behind them. The remainder of the Battalion soon joined us and I gave out positions for the companies to man.

While the Welsh Guards were reorganizing on Sapper Hill, 45 Commando appeared from the west and the two commanding officers divided the hill between them. The iconic photograph, 'Yomping into Stanley', which appeared on the cover of many publications in 1982, features the back view of Corporal Peter Robinson and was taken by Petty Officer Peter Holdgate as 45 Commando were advancing toward Stanley just after the ceasefire. Robinson had put the Union Flag on his aerial, however it blew off in a gust of wind and fluttered into a minefield just as they approaching Sapper Hill. Delicately retrieved and 're-masted', it produced a picture that sums up the Falklands campaign. When Lieutenant Hendicott's Troop left for Sapper Hill, they were at war, and when they arrived, not only were they the first Royal Engineers on Sapper Hill, the Argentines had also surrendered. The Blues and Royals arrived soon afterwards.

As early as 5 June, Lieutenant Colonel Rose, working with Captain Bell translating, had been trying to persuade the Argentines to seek terms. Messages after Phases One and Two had not convinced Menendez to surrender; however by the time Sapper Hill had been captured, they were reminded that nowhere was not covered by artillery fire. The accidental heliborne assault on Sapper Hill convinced Brigadier General Jofre that further resistance was pointless. He recalls:

As predicted, British helicopter-borne infantry, 40th Commando Battalion, lost no time in following up until checked with a bloody nose at Sapper Hill. After that things went from bad to worse. No sooner had Jaimet reached Sapper Hill, Colonel Dalton, the Brigade Operations Officer, told me 'Many soldiers are in a strange state and the kelpers are bound to get hurt. One 3rd Regiment platoon has been told to go into the houses by a fanatical lieutenant, who has also ordered the men to kill the kelpers – something awful is happening.' I'll never forget that moment. It was like a lightning bolt had hit me. It was becoming evident to me that I was no longer at the control. 'We've had it. The lives of the kelpers are being risked.' I told General Menendez and he realized that there was no question of fighting any further. Menendez told me that he wished to talk to Galtieri to arrange a ceasefire. I agreed. It was all over. Fighting on Sapper Hill was out of the question.

At 9.00 am, Dr Alison Bleaney persuaded Naval Captain Melbourne Hussey, Menendez's chief administration officer, to urge Menendez to agree to talks. At first, President Galtieri insisted on no surrender, but when he realized the futility of further fighting, he authorized Menendez to begin negotiations. At 3.30 pm, Rose and Bell flew into Stanley to open negotiations at the Secretariat and then at 6.30 pm, Rose signalled Major General Moore that Menendez had agreed to a ceasefire.

An eerie silence drifted across the battlefield as the news spread that the Argentines were falling back. A television crew persuaded Major Dawson, at 1/7th Gurkha Rifles Battalion HQ, to shout, 'There is a white flag flying over Stanley. Bloody marvellous. Tee Hee!' It took several takes before the crew were happy. In fact, there was only one white flag and it was flying from a house, however it sounded good, particularly outside No. 10 Downing Street. 5 Infantry Brigade, in a dominant position to protect 3 Commando Brigade, was ordered by Major General Moore to go firm while 3 Commando Brigade advanced along the road into Stanley, with 2 Para leading, most radios switched off to avoid being told to halt. Eventually, Brigadier Thompson, following behind, personally ordered them to stop, which they did near the racecourse. Although the ceasefire and surrender negotiations were at a sensitive stage, the only person to continue was the ubiquitous *Evening Standard* journalist, Max Hastings, still under military discipline:

> We sat on the racecourse until, after about twenty minutes I was looking at the road and there seemed to be no movement. I thought, well I'm a civilian so why shouldn't I go ahead and see what's going on because there didn't seem to be much resistance. So I stripped off all my combat clothes and I began to walk up the road with my hands in the air and my handkerchief in my hand. (*Evening Standard*)

Hastings, setting a standard that other journalists have since followed, and risking protection under the Geneva Conventions by removing his uniform, reached the Secretariat where he met some Falkland Islanders who had just been told about the ceasefire. Then, obtaining permission to enter Stanley from an Argentine colonel, he passed bewildered Argentine soldiers withdrawing into Stanley until he reached the Upland Goose Hotel. In obtaining the scoop of his life, he could have been arrested as a spy, which could have jeopardized the negotiations.

> In Stanley, no one was sure what was happening. Defeated units were streaming into Stanley and consequently the Argentine military authorities had advised residents to stay indoors, for their own safety. Then, after a delay because of a heavy snow storm, Moore flew into Stanley at 7.30 pm and within half an hour witnessed Menendez signing the Instrument of Surrender in the building that now houses Stanley Museum. John Smith was having a cup of tea in West Store when Moore walked in and with masterly aplomb said, 'Hello, I'm Jeremy Moore. Sorry it's taken rather a long time to get here.' Seventy-four days of occupation were over. (*Evening Standard*)

Hastings summed up the war: 'I imagine when everyone has seen what little there is of this little provincial town to be seen, we shall all be asking ourselves why so many brave men had to die because a whimsical dictator, in a land of which we knew little, had at all costs to possess it.' (*Evening Standard*)

British forces took the surrender of Argentine garrisons on West Falkland and Pebble Island. On 20 June, the Argentines on South Thule surrendered to the

Recce Troop detachment, commanded by Sergeant Napier, with M Company, 42 Commando on South Georgia. Meanwhile, the 11,484 prisoners were being processed with 593 senior officers, intelligence officers and specialists retained as special category prisoners for further interrogation until 14 July. Within the week, 10,250 had been repatriated where their welcome was less than warm. A small number of Argentine engineers gave their parole to help British sappers clear mines and dismantle booby traps. A huge amount of equipment was captured including armoured cars, guns, arms and ammunition, rations and stores. When Flight Lieutenant Glover was released on 6 July, this essentially signalled the end of Argentina's expedition to recover the Falklands. The lonely Falklands soon became a fortress.

Chapter Sixteen

Postscript

The Falklands War placed the islands on the international scene and consequently they have benefited not only from the tours to view the wildlife and spectacular coastlines, but also the battlefields.

The Falkland Islands international airport is Mount Pleasant and is serviced by direct Ministry of Defence flights from RAF Brize Norton with a flight time of sixteen hours and refuelling at Ascension Island. Mount Pleasant is also the main British base and overlooks the inlet where the two LSLs were attacked that sunny day. Commercial flights are available from Santiago, Chile. Both services are accessible to civilians of any nationality, provided current immigration requirements are met. On arrival, there is much to do. The Falkland Islands are a bird-watcher's, photographer's and naturalist's dream and sometimes favourably compared to the Galapagos Islands before tourists arrived. Over fifty species of birds breed on the islands, including five types of penguins. Magnificent albatrosses ride the airwaves, just as they did following the ships of the Task Force. Along the coast, there are colonies of seals, sea lions, dolphins and killer whales. Fly-fishing on the West Falklands is found at Port Howard Lodge. For the adventurous, there are opportunities to sail, sea-kayak, mountain-bike, climb, hike and camp. Cruise ships calling in to Stanley are regular, particularly during the summer. Several veterans have given presentations on board.

In Great Britain, the South Atlantic Medal Association (82) provides a network for veterans and their families and organizes reunions not only in UK but also 'down south'. Reconciliation with their former enemies has figured strong in the strategy, although some bitterness is clearly evident among Argentine veterans, not so much at losing the war, but at their cold reception once they had been repatriated. This has not stopped formal and informal contacts, many by e-mail with www.britains-smallwars.com as the interface.

The Falklands War was probably the last war in which there were no atrocities, civilians were not deliberately targeted and was fought between two sides that generally had good commercial, sporting and historical links, and respected the Laws of Armed Conflict. Every year, SAMA (82) meets at their AGM. Commanders of units that landed on D-Day at San Carlos meet annually on 21 May at the Officers' Mess, Stonehouse Royal Marine Barracks, which houses HQ 3 Commando Brigade. At H-Hour, they toast the campaign and absent colleagues. At Pangbourne School Chapel, there is a visual memorial to the 255 Royal Navy, Royal Marines, Army, Royal Air Force, Royal Fleet Auxiliary, Merchant Navy and three civilians killed during hostilities. On the islands themselves, the British dead are buried at San Carlos, not far from where HQ 3 Commando Brigade was dug in gorse bushes; the Argentine dead are buried near Goose Green. There are several memorials: the Liberation Monument in Stanley; 2 Para on Darwin Hill; 3 Para on Mount Longdon; the Welsh Guards overlooking Port Pleasant; and the Scots Guards on Tumbledown. The Welsh Branch of SAMA (82) plan to erect a 5-ton rock transported from Mount Harriet, the scene of 42 Commando's classic night attack, as the National Monument in Wales to the Falklands Conflict. Outside RAF Waddington is Flight Lieutenant Withers's Vulcan XM-607. In true naval tradition, wreaths have marked the spot where ships sank. In Buenos Aeries, the estimated 660 Argentine dead are commemorated on a wall of names at the Monument to the Fallen.

Since the war, the Argentines had been through a painful period of international embarrassment and economic uncertainty, and the inevitable continued threats by successive governments that one day the Falklands will be part of Argentina. Certainly many prisoners were repatriated with 'Hasta la vista' – 'Until the next time'. So long as the Falkland Islanders themselves reject this and the strong British force remains, this is unlikely. However, it did not stop the French novelist, Jean Raspail, acting in the name of King Orelie-Antione, the self-styled King of Patagonia in 1860, from bizarrely seizing the Channel Island islet, Les Minquiers, in the summer of 1998. He had previously claimed the islet in 1984 in response to Britain's 'prolonged occupation of the Malvinas, a territory of Patagonia'. He was gently persuaded to leave.

Appendix

Author's Kit List

HMS *FEARLESS* RIG (worn on voyage south)

Jungle green vest; underpants; Other Ranks No. 2 Dress shirt; heavy duty sweater; lightweight trousers; socks; desert boots; beret and badge (parades only).

CAMPAIGN RIG (worn ashore)

- Jungle green vest; underpants; blue Haly Hansen long-sleeved thermal underwear; Norwegian Army shirt; heavy duty sweater; green civilian roll-necked woollen sweater; lightweight trousers; camouflaged windproof jacket with wire hood; headover; inner cotton socks; outer white Arctic woollen socks; German parachute boots; beret and badge; watch and Northern Ireland patrol gloves.
- Phial of morphine and two 'dog tags' around the neck.
- Personal weapon – 9mm Sterling sub-machine gun and sling. Captured 9mm Browning pistol in holster.

WINDPROOF JACKET

UPPER RIGHT POCKET
Issue clasp knife and pink plastic whistle; purchased woollen balaclava; part of 24-hour ration pack, lighter; and waterproof first aid pack in tobacco tin (syringe needle, Puriton tablets, Paracetamol tablets, plasters, small bandage).

UPPER LEFT POCKET (SURVIVAL POCKET)
Issue extreme cold over-mittens; Hexamine cooker and block; three metres of green twine. Waterproof survival pack in tobacco tin (waterproof matches; cotton wool; silver paper; small survival compass, scalpel blade and inoculation needle; small mirror and two Oxo cubes).

Right Lower Pocket (Intelligence materials)
MoD Police notebook; map-marking template and blue, red, black, yellow and green chinagraphs; pencils, rubber and 6-inch ruler; Intelligence aide memoir notebook; order of battle sheets; ten air mail 'bluey' envelopes; and a green smoke grenade.

Left Lower Pocket
Magazine of ten mini-flares; cold weather wristlets and goggles; and survival kit in tobacco tin – magnifying glass, waterproof matches, bandage, antisceptic cream and scalpel blade; and a red smoke grenade.

Rear internal pocket
Large face veil and white winter trousers.

Sleeve pocket
First Field Dressing, spoon and tube of camouflage cream.

LIGHTWEIGHT TROUSERS

In map pocket – Fabloned 1:250,000 map of the Falklands; two handkerchiefs.

WEBBING ORDER ('58 pattern)

Belt supported by yoke
2 x issue water bottles in pouches; black mug; butcher's knife in sheath; bayonet in sheath; and prismatic compass in its pouch.

Left Ammo Pouch
Four SMG magazines, each with thirty 9mm rounds.

Right Ammo Pouch
150 spare 9mm rounds in boxes; weapon cleaning box; and spare First Field Dressing.

Respirator Satchel
24-hour ration pack jammed into '44 pattern metal mug also for cooking; private Praktika 35mm camera; five films and lens case; candle and emergency light from lifejacket; white silk Arctic jacket; candle; boot cleaning material and dubbin; and *By The Rivers of Babylon* by Nelson de Mille.

BERGEN (Arctic Warfare on frame version)

Lightweight windproof trousers; spare Haly Hansen thermal underwear; Norwegian shirt; three pairs of Arctic woollen socks; cold weather combat hat; white and green reversible waterproof jacket and trousers; issue 'Mao Tse Tung' quilted jacket, trousers; steel helmet; tent sheet, poles, pegs and six elastic bungees; two mess tins containing 24-hour ration pack and extra dehydrated vegetables, hexamine cooker and tablets; bottle of Navy Rum; Arctic sleeping bag, sleeping mat, small airline pillow; foot powder; washing material – soap, toothbrush and toothpaste, towel, razor, two toilet rolls and 'housewife' (needle, thread, buttons and darning wool).

INTELLIGENCE OFFICE

(Royal Hong Kong Regiment (V) lightweight jungle pack attached to the Bergen. Taken everywhere and gradually filled up with captured material and documents)

- 100 x envelopes; pencils; signals pad; order of battle sheets and log sheets; prisoner handling and interrogation documentation; fabloned maps of Argentina and 1:100,000 map of the Falklands; Argentine Marine handbook (captured at South Georgia); uniform and vehicle recognition files; Technical Intelligence file classified SECRET.
- Spare 24-hour ration pack; Hexamine cooker and tablets; pair of Arctic socks; poncho; candle and torch and two spare U2 batteries (used when separated from Bergen).

NOTES
- Total weight about 100lbs
- **For landing at San Carlos** - PRC 351 radio battery and 150-round belt of GPMG 7.62mm ammunition.
- Entered Stanley with:
  - 30 rounds of ammo (Remainder given away when requested after loss of *Atlantic Conveyor*)
  - Half a ration pack.
  - 'Intelligence Office' pack filled with captured documents, photos and film.

SEAMAN'S BAG (LEFT ON HMS *FEARLESS*)

Temperate sleeping bag; DMS boots; ski-march boots; PT kit and trainers; temperate combat uniform; temperate sleeping bag; pyjamas and towel; skis, bindings and poles.

BIBLIOGRAPHY

Adkin, Mark, *Goose Green: A Battle Fought to be Won*, Leo Cooper, Barnsley, 1992. (By permission of Pen & Sword Books Ltd)

Bilton, Michael and Kominsky, Michael, *Speaking Out: Untold Stories from the Falklands War*, Grafton Books, London, 1990.

Bishop, Patrick and Witherow, John, *The Winter War: The Falklands*, Quartet Books, London, 1982.

Burden, Rodney, Draper, Michael, Rough, Douglas, Smith, Colin and Wilton, David, *Falklands: The Air War*, Arms and Armour Press, Poole, 1986. (By permission of Arms and Armour Press, a division of the Orion Publishing Group, London)

Clapp, Michael and Southby-Tailyour, Ewen, *Amphibious Assault Falklands*, Leo Cooper, Barnsley, 1996. (By permission of Pen & Sword Books Ltd)

Curtis, Mike, *CQB: Close Quarter Battle*, Corgi, London, 1998.

De La Billiere, General Sir Peter, *Looking for Trouble*, HarperCollins, London, 1994. (By permission of HarperCollins Publishers Ltd)

Denmark, Edward, *Not for Queen and Country*, Pharaoh Press, 1998.

Freedman, Sir Lawrence, *The Official History of the Falklands Campaign*, Routledge, Abingdon, 2005. (By permission of Routledge)
Volume 1 – Origins of the War
Volume II – War and Diplomacy

Frost, Major General John, *2 Para in the Falklands: The Battalion at War*, Buchan & Enright, London, 1983.

Hastings, Max, *Evening Standard*, Tuesday, 15 June 1982.

Jofre, Oscar and Aguiar, Felix, *La X Brigade de Infanteria Mecinazada 'General Nicholas Levalle' en accion en Malvinas*, Circulo Militar, Buenos Aires, 1992.

Lockett, Andrew, *HMS Endurance 1981–1982*, Gosport, 1983.

McManners, Captain Hugh, *Falklands Commando*, William Kimber, 1984, London.

——, *Scars of War*, HarperCollins, London, 1993.

McQueen, Captain Robert, *Naval Review*, Vol. 70, Number 9, October 1982. (By permission of Martin Middlebrook)

Middlebrook, Martin, *Operation Corporate: The Story of the Falklands War*, 1982. (By permission of Martin Middlebrook)

——, *The Fight for the 'Malvinas': The Argentine Forces in the Falkland Islands*, Viking, London, 1989.

Parker, John, *Commando*, Headline, London, 2000.

Ramsey, Jack, *SAS: The Soldier's Story*, McMillan, London, 1996.

Ratcliffe, Peter, *Eye of the Storm*, Michael O'Mara Books, London, 2000. (By permission of Michael O'Meara Books Ltd, Copyright © Peter Radcliffe)

Smith, John, *74 Days*, Century Publishing, London, 1984.

Southby-Tailyour, Ewen, *Reasons in Writing: A Commando's View of the Falklands War*, Leo Cooper, Barnsley, 1993. (By permission of Pen & Sword Books Ltd)

Thompson, Julian, *No Picnic: 3 Commando Brigade in the South Atlantic 1982*, Leo Cooper, Barnsley, 1985. (By permission of Pen & Sword Books Ltd)

Van der Bijl, Nick, *Nine Battles to Stanley*, Leo Cooper, Barnsley, 1999.

——, *5th Infantry Brigade in the Falklands*, Leo Cooper, Barnsley; 2003 (with David Aldea)

Vaux, Nick, *March to the South Atlantic*, Buchan and Enright, London, 1986.

Villarno, Amilio, *Battalion 5*, Alert Atucha y Asociados.

Wilsey, John, *H Jones VC: The Life and Death of an Unusual Hero*, Hutchinson, London, 2000. (By permission of The Random House Group Ltd)

Winton, John, *Signals from the Falklands*, Leo Cooper, London, 1995. (By permission of Pen & Sword Books Ltd)

OTHER SOURCES

'A Memoir of 9 Parachute Squadron, Royal Engineers in the Falkland Islands Campaign 1982', Major Chris Davies RE.

'4 Field Regiment in the Falkland Islands April–July 1982'.

'Operation Corporate 59 Independent Commando Squadron RE', Major R. MacDonald, 1982.

'Post Operational Report – Op Corporate 29th Commando Regiment RA'.

'Post Operational Report – Op Corporate 2nd Battalion, The Parachute Regiment'.

'Post Operational Report – Op Corporate 3rd Battalion, The Parachute Regiment'.

'The Corps in the Falklands, HQ 1 Signal Group, Tidworth'.

Index

238